D1168043

FRANCE:
CÔTE D'AZUR

Cadogan Books plc
London House, Parkgate Road, London SW11 4NQ, UK
e-mail: guides@cadogan.demon.co.uk

Distributed in North America by The Globe Pequot Press
6 Business Park Road, PO Box 833, Old Saybrook,
Connecticut 06475–0833

Copyright © Dana Facaros and Michael Pauls 1992, 1994, 1996
Updated by Nicky O'Hara 1996
Illustrations © Pauline Pears 1992, 1994, 1996

Design by Animage
Cover illustration by Povl Webb
Maps © Cadogan Guides, drawn by Map Creation Ltd

Editor: Linda McQueen
Series Editors: Rachel Fielding and Vicki Ingle

Proofreading: Linda McQueen and Jacqueline Chnéour
Indexing: Dorothy Frame
Production: Book Production Services

A catalogue record for this book is available from the British Library

ISBN 1–86011–061–4

Promenade des Anglais.

About the Authors

Dana Facaros and Michael Pauls have written over 20 books for Cadogan Guides, including four on France. They live in a farmhouse in southwest France with their two children and assorted animals.

Acknowledgements

The updater, Nicky O'Hara, would like to acknowledge the Magentas at Château de Sully (especially worth a visit). The publishers would like to thank Simon Brockbank for extra research and editorial work, Map Creation for the maps, Animage for the design, Dorothy Frame for indexing, and Andrew Gordon, sales director of Corney & Barrow, Wine Merchants since 1780, for updating the wine sections.

Please help us to keep this guide up to date

We have done our best to ensure that the information in this guide is correct at the time of going to press. But places and facilities are constantly changing, and standards and prices in hotels and restaurants fluctuate. We would be delighted to receive any comments concerning existing entries or omissions. Authors of the best letters will receive a copy of the Cadogan Guide of their choice.

Attention!

On 18 October 1996 France is changing its telephone numbers from 8 digits to 10 digits. All the phone numbers in the Provence and Côte d'Azur areas should be preceded by 04 from this date. Similarly, any Paris phone numbers should be preceded by 01 instead of 1.

Contents

The Côte d'Azur is grey old Europe's favourite fantasy escape, its dream of a generous sun on a blue sea drenched in the hot luxurious colours of Matisse and soft lights flickering in warm perfumed nights. From Victorian times, when the casino at Monte-Carlo was known as the 'cathedral of hell', to the carefree era of Brigitte Bardot wiggling on the sands of St-Tropez, this escape has always conjured up a *frisson* of illicit pleasure—temporary freedom not only from rain and sleet and the daily grind but also from the constraints of good behaviour.

The 'sunny place for shady people', as long-time resident Somerset Maugham put it, packs a lot into a small area, a mere 125 miles of irregular coastline from Menton on the Italian border to Bandol, safely beyond the orbit of Marseille. The land may be poor, but it's fragrant, producing mostly flowers,

Introduction

wine and herbs, and the scenery is filled with drama. The Côte d'Azur encompasses three mountain ranges tumbling down to the sea: the Maritime Alps, the porphyry-red Esterel, the dark, ancient chestnut-wooded Massif des Maures. Stunning capes clothed with sub-tropical gardens project into the sea, coves and beaches tucked in their side pockets; wooded islets float temptingly close to the shore; and on a clear day, from the mountain-tops, you can even make out Corsica piercing the horizon.

The ancient Romans, whose Via Aurelia first penetrated the mountain fastness of the coast, were also the first to see it as a playground. Picture, briefly, Flavia and Gaius sunning by their heated pool, before a millennium and a half of trouble intrudes, bringing intermittent third-division battles, with cut-throats in the mountains and pirate raids on the coast, forcing survivors to take refuge high up in *villages perchés*, safe from coastal danger.

The French Riviera began to rediscover its Roman vocation for pleasure some 200 years ago, when the first trickle of chilly English and Russian aristocrats moved down for the winter. This trickle turned into an international flood after 1860, when railways were built and the impoverished Grimaldis opened their casino at Monte-Carlo. By 1887, the phenomenon was packaged once and for all when poet Stephen Liégeard gave it a name: the

Côte d'Azur. Although the First World War put an end to its Belle Epoque follies, the Roaring Twenties brought the coast back into fashion as never before, as writers, artists and rich Americans in Paris for the cheap prices and booze came down and set the trend for spending summers on the coast.

After the Second World War the Côte d'Azur metamorphosed again. Paid holidays democratized the once exclusive Riviera fantasy and inaugurated an orgy of building and property speculation. Corruption, kickbacks and illegal building were rife; everyone from Aristotle Onassis on down wanted a piece of the action.'The South of France, as far as I am concerned, has had it,' Noel Coward declared in 1960. Or, as the great Sam Goldwyn put it, 'Nobody goes there anymore. It's too crowded.'

In the late 1970s the Côte d'Azur began to shift gear again, recreating itself as an international business paradise; Nice in the last thirty years has grown to become the fifth largest city in France. New convention halls and business hotels were built, new companies were drawn to the likes of Sophia-Antipolis, the Riviera's answer to Silicon Valley. Monaco, where courtesans once tickled diamonds from dukes, has become a huge tax-free haven full of trusts and banks. The Cannes film festival, for all its glitz, has become an overgrown trade fair. The *villages perchés* within easy access of the coast have turned into artsy-craftsy bazaars that reek of Disneyland. New people keep pouring in, while long-time residents have been forced to sell out, either expropriated or unable to afford the prices. The glamour and lustre of flaunted wealth that made the coast sparkle in the past is now concentrated on security and seclusion in private yachts and hideyhole villas. California has long been the Côte d'Azur's role model, and in the summer it seems to have as many cars but a lot fewer roads.

And yet, and yet, the tantalizing, hedonistic vision of a fantasy escape under the palms and mimosas remains as seductive as ever. Fashion and fame are still served by enough celebrities to support a battalion of paparazzi, and for every sin committed on the Côte d'Azur you can easily find forgiveness: in a radiant morning in Antibes' market or wandering the higgeldy-piggeldy lanes of old Nice, or by taking a lazy drive up to Peillon or Gorbio or Tourrettes-sur-Loup, or making an escape from the traffic bottlenecks on the islets off Hyères or along the wild beaches of Cap Sicié, or visiting the dazzling Fauves in the Annonciade museum in St-Tropez or Matisse's Chapelle de la Rosaire in Vence, or spending all afternoon over a portside drink at St-Jean-Cap-Ferrat. Most of all, take the time to linger and remember what Sara Murphy, one of the summer pioneers on the Côte d'Azur back in the 1920s, wrote when she reflected on her many years in Antibes: 'We ourselves did nothing notable except enjoy ourselves.' Amen.

Travel

CAFÉ DU COMMERCE

Menu

Before You Go

A little preparation will help you get much more out of your holiday in the south of France. Check the list of festivals (*see* pp.12–13) to help you decide where you want to be and when, and book accommodation early: if you plan to base yourself in one area, write ahead to the local tourist offices listed in the text for complete lists of self-catering accommodation, hotels, and campsites in their areas, or else contact one of the many companies in the UK or USA (*see* pp.25–6). For more general information and a complete list of tour operators, get in touch with a French Government Tourist Office:

UK: 178 Piccadilly, London W1V 0AL, ✆ (0171) 629 2869, ✉ (0171) 493 6594.

Ireland: 35 Lower Abbey St, Dublin 1, ✆ (1) 703 4046, ✉ (1) 874 7324.

Australia: BWP House, 12 Castlereagh St, Sydney NSW 2000, ✆ (612) 231 5244.

USA: 444 Madison Avenue, NY 10022, ✆ (212) 838 7800, ✉ (212) 838 7855; 676 N. Michigan Ave, Chicago, IL 60611, ✆ (312) 751 7800, ✉ (312) 357 6339; 9454 Wilshire Blvd, Suite 715, Beverly Hills, CA 90212, ✆ (310) 271 2358, ✉ (310) 276 2835. Nationwide information ✆ freephone (1900) 990 0040.

Canada: 1981 Av. McGill College, No. 490, Montreal, Quebec H3A 2W9, ✆ (514) 288 4264, ✉ (514) 845 4868; 30 St Patrick St, Suite 700, Toronto MST 3A3, ✆ (416) 593 4723, ✉ (416) 979 7587.

Getting There

By Air

The main **international airports** in the south are at Nice, Marseille and Toulon. Unfortunately, with the exception of Nice (the second busiest airport in France after Charles de Gaulle in Paris), they serve mainly business travellers and don't get enough holiday volume to make international fares competitive. Prices are highest in the summer and during the Easter holidays, but those who book several months in advance can usually save money. Check with your travel agent or your major Sunday newspaper for bargains or packages. There are a number of charters from London to Nice, but from most other points of departure—the rest of the UK, Ireland, North America, Australia, etc.—it's usually cheaper to fly to Paris and from there catch a cheap Air Inter flight or TGV train to the south. Check out Air France's Air and Rail scheme, which may save you money.

From Orly Airport in Paris, there are **Air Inter** flights to Nice, Cannes, Toulon and Marseille; discounts exist if you fly in low 'blue' periods (in the UK, Nouvelles Frontières, 2/3 Woodstock St, London, W1R 1HE, ✆ (0171) 629 7772 have all the Air Inter details). Students who equip themselves with the relevant ID cards are eligible for considerable reductions, not only on flights, but on trains and admission fees to museums, concerts, and more. Agencies specializing in student and youth travel can help in applying for the cards, as well as filling you in on the best deals. Try STA, ✆ (0171) 937 9921, and Campus Travel, ✆ (0171) 730 3402, in London or branches throughout the UK; STA, ✆ (03) 347 4711, in Australia; STA, ✆ (800) 777 0112, in the US; CUTS, ✆ (416) 979 2406 in Canada.

Eurostar runs a regular and frequent Channel Tunnel train service from London Waterloo to Paris Gare du Nord. It takes 3 hours and return fares are from £69 return; for information and booking, call ✆ (0345) 881 881.

Air prices and airport hassles make France's high-speed **TGVs** (*trains à grande vitesse*) a very attractive alternative. TGVs shoot along at the average of 170 mph when they're not breaking world records, and the journey from Paris's Gare de Lyon to Nice takes only 7 hours. Costs are only minimally higher on a TGV. Some weekday departures require a supplement (30–40F) and seat reservations (20F), which you can make when you buy your ticket or before departure. Another way of getting there is by overnight sleeper after dinner in Paris, although a recent spate of robberies in the compartments at night suggests that you should take extra precautions. People under 26 are eligible for a 30 per cent discount on fares (*see* the travel agencies above) and there are other discounts if you're over 65 available from major travel agents. For the TGV, reservations are compulsory.

If you plan some long train journeys, look into the variety of **rail passes**: France's national railway, the SNCF, offers a *France Railpass* that gives you either four days (they don't have to be consecutive) of unlimited travel in a 15-day period, or nine days of travel within 30 days. It includes extras like a day's free travel in Paris (from the airport, the Métro, etc.), TGV supplements (except the seat reservation), and discounts on car rentals and Channel crossings. Get it before you leave from travel agents or SNCF offices: at 179 Piccadilly, London W1, 'The Rail Shop' ✆ (0990) 30 00 03 for bookings. For simple information SNCF has created a new number whereby you pay for the pleasure of asking for train times: the 0891 number costs 48p a minute peak time, ✆ (0891) 515 477. In the USA contact 610 Fifth Ave., New York, NY 10020, ✆ (212) 582 2816 (or ✆ (800) 848 7245). Other alternatives include the well-known InterRail pass for European residents under the age of 26, which offers a month's unlimited travel in Europe and 50 per cent reductions on Channel ferries, and various Eurail passes for non-Europeans, valid for 15 days to three months.

By Coach

The cheapest way to get from London to the south of France is by National Express Eurolines coach ✆ (0990) 80 80 80; tickets available from any National Express office. There are two journeys a week: to Aix and Marseille (19 hours); and to Avignon (19 hours approximately). The Nice route has recently been cancelled.

By Car

A car entering France must have its registration and insurance papers. If you're coming from the UK or Ireland, the dip of the headlights must be adjusted to the right. Carrying a warning triangle is mandatory, and this should be placed 50m behind the car if you have a breakdown. Drivers with a valid licence from an EC country, Canada, the USA or Australia don't need an international licence. If you're driving down from the UK, going through or around Paris is almost inevitable, a task best tackled on either side of rush hour. The various *autoroutes* will get you south the fastest but be prepared to pay some 500F in tolls; the N7 south of Paris takes much longer, but costs nothing and has great scenery.

A fairly comfortable but costly option is to put your car on the train. Motorail accommodation is compulsory, in a 4-berth (1st class) or 6-berth (2nd class) carriage. Linen is provided, along with washing facilities. Compartments are not segregated by sex. Services run from both Boulogne and Dieppe to Avignon and Fréjus/St-Raphaël, and from Boulogne to Nice.

Taking Le Shuttle is the most convenient way to travel by car to France. It takes only half an hour from Folkestone to Calais on the train while remaining in your car, although you can get up to stretch your legs. Crossings in midsummer cost around £260 return; for information and bookings call ✆ (0990) 35 35 35.

If you plan to hire a car, look into air and holiday package deals as well as combination 'Train and Auto' rates to save money, or consider leasing a car if you mean to stay three weeks or more. Prices vary widely from firm to firm, and beware the small print about service charges and taxes: three firms to try in the US are France Auto Vacances, ✆ (800) 234 1426 and Europe by Car Inc, ✆ (800) 223 1516 or Renault, ✆ (800) 221 1052.

Entry Formalities

Passports and Visas

Holders of EC, US and Canadian passports do not need a visa to enter France for stays of up to three months, but everyone else still does. Apply at your nearest French consulate: the most convenient visa is the *visa de circulation*, allowing for multiple stays of three months over a three-year period. If you intend **staying longer**, the law says you need a *carte de séjour*, a requirement EC citizens can easily get around as passports are rarely stamped. On the other hand, non-EC citizens had best apply for an extended visa at home, a procedure requiring proof of income, etc. You can't get a *carte de séjour* without this visa, and obtaining this is a trial run in the *ennuis* you'll undergo in applying for a *carte de séjour* at your local *mairie*.

Health and Travel Insurance

Citizens of the EC who bring along their E111 forms are entitled to the same health services as French citizens. This means paying up front for medical care and prescriptions, of which costs 75–80 per cent are reimbursed later—a complex procedure for the non-French. As an alternative, consider a travel insurance policy, covering theft and losses and offering 100 per cent medical refund; check to see if it covers your extra expenses in case you get bogged down in airport or train strikes. Beware that accidents resulting from sports are rarely covered by ordinary insurance. Canadians are usually covered in France by their provincial health coverage; Americans and others should check their individual policies.

Getting Around

By Train

The **SNCF** runs a decent and efficient network of trains through the major cities of the south, with an added service called the *Métrazur* that links all the resorts of the Côte d'Azur from Menton to St-Raphaël as often as every half-hour in the peak summer season.

Prices have recently gone up but are still reasonable. If you plan on making only a few long hauls the France Railpass (*see* above) will save you money. Other possible discounts hinge on the day of your departure. The SNCF has divided the year into blue, white, and red days, based on demand. If you depart in a *Période Bleue* (off-peak) with a return ticket and travel over 1000km you'll get a 25 per cent discount (*Billet Séjour*). Married couples are eligible for a free *Carte Couple* which entitles one to pay half-fare when travelling together on blue days. People over 65 can purchase a *Carte Vermeille*, valid for a year of half-price blue period travel; under 26-year-olds can buy a *Carte Jeune* for half-price blue-day travel from June to September. The more children you have, the more economical an expensive *Carte Kiwi* becomes: the card is in the name of one child, and family members each purchase complimentary cards. The child then pays full fare, and everyone else half.

Tickets must be **stamped** in the little orange machines by the entrance to the lines that say *Compostez votre billet* (this puts the date on the ticket, to keep you from using the same one over and over again). Any time you interrupt a journey until another day, you have to re-compost your ticket. Long-distance trains (*Trains Corails*) have snack trolleys and bar/cafeteria cars; some have play areas for small children. Nearly every station has large computerized lockers (*consigne automatique*) which take about half an hour to puzzle out the first time you use them, so plan accordingly.

By Bus

Buses are essential for seeing small towns and villages that are not accessible on the rail network, but inland they can be tied to school and market schedules. Along the coast, and from towns like Nice up to Vence and Grasse, the services are quite efficient for travellers. Buses are run either by the SNCF (replacing discontinued rail routes) or private firms. Rail passes are valid on SNCF lines and they generally coincide with trains. Private bus firms, especially when they have a monopoly, tend to be a bit more expensive than trains; some towns have a *gare routière* (coach station), usually near the train stations, though many lines start from any place that catches their fancy.

By Car

Unless you plan to stick to the major resorts or the coast, a car is unfortunately the only way to see the best of the Côte d'Azur. This has its drawbacks: high rental car rates and petrol, and an accident rate double that of the UK (and much higher than the US). The vaunted French logic and clarity breaks down completely on the asphalt. Go slow and be careful, although in cities such as Nice you're a danger to everyone if you do not adopt the local policy—put your foot down and go with the flow.

Roads are generally excellently maintained (and well marked on Michelin maps 115 and 84), but anything of less status than a departmental route (D-road) may be uncomfortably narrow. Mountain roads are reasonable except in the vertical department of Alpes-Maritimes, where they inevitably follow old mule tracks. Shrines to St Eloi, patron of muleteers, are common here, and a quick prayer is a wise precaution. Conditions vary widely; traffic in the Côte d'Azur, the 'California of Europe', can be diabolically Californian—hectic enough on a winter Sunday, and a guaranteed holiday-spoiler in July and August. Throughout the summer, try to avoid using your car after 9am or before late evening because everyone else will want to go where you do. Petrol stations are rare in rural areas, so consider your fuel supply while planning any forays into the mountains. If you come across a garage with petrol-pump attendants, they will expect a tip for oil, windscreen-cleaning or air. The French have one delightfully civilized custom of the road: if oncoming drivers unaccountably flash their headlights at you, it means the *gendarmes* are lurking just up the way.

Always give **priority to the right** (*priorité à droite*) at any intersection—anywhere, unless you're on a motorway or on a road with a yellow diamond 'priority route' sign.

Parking on the Côte d'Azur is a permanent nightmare to which there is no solution. Everywhere else, the blue 'P' signs will infallibly direct you to a village or town's already full car park. Watch out, though, for the tiny signs that indicate which streets are meant for pedestrians only (with complicated schedules in even tinier print); and for Byzantine street parking rules (which would take pages to explain—do as the natives do, and especially be careful about village centres on market days). Many towns now have pricey guarded car parks underneath their very heart, spectacularly so in Nice, and even in smaller towns such as Vence.

Unless sweetened in an air or holiday package deal, car hire in France is an expensive proposition (350–400F a day, without mileage for the cheapest cars; *see* p.4 for hiring a car). Petrol (*essence*) at the time of writing is 5.84/5.91F a litre for unleaded, 6.09F a litre leaded. Speed limits are 130km/80mph on the *autoroutes* (toll motorways); 110km/69mph on dual carriageways (divided highways); 90km/55mph on other roads; 50km/30mph in an 'urbanized area'—as soon as you pass a white sign with a town's name on it and until you pass another sign with the town's name barred. Fines for speeding, payable on the spot, begin at 1300F and can be astronomical if you fail the breathalyser. If you wind up in an accident, the procedure is to fill out and sign a *constat aimable*. If your French isn't sufficient to deal with this, hold off until you find someone to translate for you so you don't accidentally incriminate yourself. If you have a breakdown and are a member of a motoring club affiliated with the Touring Club de France, ring the latter; if not, ring the police.

By Boat

The major towns, as well as the islands, along the Côte d'Azur are linked by regular boat services. These come in handy especially in the summer when travelling by road is hot purgatory. Most are included in the text; just look for signs near the port for the Gare Maritime.

Yacht, motorboat and sailing boat charters are big business, especially along the Riviera. Companies and individual owners hire them out by the hour or day, or in the case of yachts, by the week or fortnight. Average cost per week for a 16m yacht that sleeps six, including food, drink, and all expenses is 90,000F—about what six people would pay for a week in a luxury hotel. If things are slow you may dicker the price down. Contact individual tourist offices for lists of firms. Books on sailing in the area include *Imray's Mediterranean Almanac* by Rod Heikell and *South France Pilot* by Robin Brandon (both published by Imray Laurie); these and other nautical books and maps in English may be found at Le Silmar, 10 Rue Jean Braco, 06310 Beaulieu-sur-Mer, © 93 01 36 71.

By Bicycle

Cycling spells more pain than pleasure in most French minds; if you mean to cycle in the summer, start early and stop early to avoid heatstroke. French drivers, not always courteous to fellow motorists, usually give cyclists a wide berth; and yet on any given summer day half the patients in a French hospital are from accidents on two-wheeled transport. Consider a helmet. Also beware that bike thefts are fairly common, especially along the Côte d'Azur, so make sure your insurance covers your bike—or the one you hire.

Getting your own bike to France is fairly easy: Air France and British Airways carry them free from Britain. From the US or Australia most airlines will carry them as long as they're boxed and are included in your total baggage weight. In all cases, telephone ahead. Certain French trains (called *Autotrains*, with a bicycle symbol in the timetable) carry bikes for free; otherwise you have to send it as registered luggage, and pay a 40F fee, with delivery guaranteed within 5 days. The best maps, based on ordnance surveys, are put out by the Institut Géographique National (1:50,000 or 1:100,000), available in most French bookshops.

You can hire bikes (most of them 10-speed) at most SNCF stations and in major towns. The advantage of hiring from a station means that you can drop it off at another, as long as you specify where when you hire it. Rates run at around 50F a day, with a deposit of 300–400F or credit card number. Private firms hire mountain-bikes (VTTs in French) and racing bikes.

On Foot

A network of long-distance paths or *Grandes Randonnées*, GR for short (marked by distinctive red and white signs), take in some of the most beautiful scenery in the south of France. Each GR is described in a *Topoguide*, with maps and details about camping-sites, *refuges*, and so on, available in area bookshops or from the Comité National des Sentiers de Grande Randonnée, 8 Av. Marceau, 75008 Paris, ✆ (1 16) 47 23 62 32. An English translation covering several GRs in the region, *Walks in Provence,* is available from Robertson McCarta, 122 King's Cross Rd, London WC1.

There are 5000km of marked paths in the Alpes Maritimes alone. Of special interest are: **GR 5** from Nice to Aspremont, **GR 52** from Menton up to Sospel, **GR 52a** and **GR 5** through Mercantour National Park, both of which are open only from the end of June to the beginning of October. **GR 51**, nicknamed 'the balcony of the Côte d'Azur', from Castellar (near Menton) takes in the Esterel and Maures before ending at Bormes-les-Mimosas.

In Provence, **GR 9** begins in St-Tropez and crosses over the region's most famous mountains: Ste-Baume, Ste-Victoire, the Lubéron and Ventoux. **GR 4** crosses the Dentelles de Montmirail and Mont Ventoux en route to Grasse.

Special Interest Holidays

There are a number of ways to combine a holiday with study or a special interest. For information, contact the French Centre on ✆ (0171) 792 0337 or the Cultural Services of the French Embassy: 22 Wilton Crescent, London SW1, ✆ (0171) 235 8080, or at 972 Fifth Ave., New York, NY 10021, ✆ (212) 439 1400. French universities are easy to enter if you're already enrolled in a similar institution at home; tuition fees are nominal but room and board are up to you. The Cultural Services can send a prospectus and tell you what paperwork is required.

in France

Alliance Française, 2 Rue Paris, 06000 Nice, ✆ 93 62 67 66, ✎ 93 85 28 06: French classes on all levels. Courses last a month but they can and will tailor to your needs.

Association Neige et Merveilles, La Minière de Vallauria, 06430 St-Dalmas-de-Tende, ✆ 93 04 62 40: offers photography and film courses for beginner and advanced from the end of March to mid-November.

Atelier du Safranier, 2 bis Rue du Cannet, 06600 Vieil Antibes, ✆ 93 34 53 72: year-round courses in painting, engraving, lithography, etc.

L'Ecole du Moulin, Restaurant L'Amandier, Mougins 06250, ✆ 93 75 35 70, and Hôtel Beau Rivage, Rue Bréa, 06300 Nice, ✆ 93 75 35 70: year-round *Cuisine du Soleil* cookery courses lasting a week under the auspices of Roger Vergé Inc.

Institut de Paléontologie Humaine, 1 Rue René Panhard, 75013 Paris, ✆ (16 1) 43 32 62 91: has places for palaeontology students or fans who can spend a minimum of 15 or 30 days excavating caves in southeast France (address your letter to M. Henry de Lumley).

from the UK

Abercrombie & Kent, Sloane Square House, Holbein Place, London SW1W 8NS, ✆ (0171) 730 9600. Hotel accommodation and tailor-made holidays to the Var and Côte d'Azur.

Allez France, 27 West St, Storrington, West Sussex, RH20 4DZ, ✆ (01903) 742 345: city breaks in Nice, wine tours, gastronomic holidays, short breaks in Antibes, Juan-les-Pins and Gorges du Verdon.

Andante, Grange Cottage, Winterbourne Dauntsey, Salisbury, Wiltshire SP4 6ER, ✆ (01980) 610 555, ✉ (01980) 610 002. Archaeological and historical study tours, including artists on the Côte d'Azur.

CV Travel, 43 Cadogan Street, London SW3 2PR, ✆ (0171) 581 0851, ✉ (0171) 584 5229. Country-house accommodation and tailor-made holidays.

DB Jazz Tours, 4 Cotswold Court, Broadway, WR12 7AA, ✆ (01386) 852194: visits to jazz festivals in Nice And Antibes.

Euro Academy, 77a George Street, Croydon CR0 1LD, ✆ (0181) 686 2363. French language courses with activities or sports options in Nice.

LSG Theme Holidays, 201 Main Street, Thornton LE67 1AH, ✆ (01509) 231 713 or (01509) 239 857 (24 hrs): a French-run company offering language classes at all levels; painting courses; cookery courses; photography; horseriding, cycling, rambling and nature-watch and regional discovery.

Martin Randall, 10 Barley Mow Passage, London W4 4PH, ✆ (0181) 742 3355, ✉ (0181) 742 1066. Lecturer-accompanied cultural tours of Provence.

from the USA

Abercrombie & Kent, 1520 Kensington Road, Oakbrook, IL 60521, ✆ (708) 954 2944, ✉ (708) 954 3324: rail tours on the Côte d'Azur.

Baumeler Tours, 10 Grand Avenue, Rockville Centre, NY 11570, ✆ (516) 766 6160: cycling in Provence.

Dailey-Thorp Travel, 330 West 58th Street, New York, NY 10019, ✆ (212) 307 1555: music and opera tours.

Int'l Curtain Call, 3313 Patricia Avenue, Los Angeles, CA 90064, ✆ (310) 204 4934: opera and music tours, e.g. Paris–Avignon–Aix-en-Provence–Cannes.

Le Boat Inc., 215 Union Street, Hackensack, NJ 07601, ✆ (201) 342 1838, ✉ (201) 342 7498: crewed motor or sailing yacht and bareboats from Côte d'Azur ports.

Progressive Travels Inc., 224 West Galer, Suite C, Seattle, WA 98119, ✆ (206) 285 1987, ✉ (206) 285 1988: luxury and standard cycling and walking tours in Provence. Ballooning available.

Practical A–Z

Climate

The Cote d'Azur has a Mediterranean climate, one wafted by winds that give it a special character. The most notorious is the **mistral** (from the Provençal *mistrau*, or master) supposedly sent by northerners jealous of the south's climate—rushing down the Rhône and gusting east as far as Toulon and west to Narbonne, sparing the hot-house of the Côte d'Azur. Although the coast began its career as a winter resort, this doesn't mean it's always warm by any means—it could be brilliant in December and January or you can get thoroughly wet and chilled.

In the average year, it rains as much in Nice (750mm per year) as Brest. Recent years have been drier than average, turning the forests of the south into tinder-boxes.

If you have the luxury of choosing when to visit, May and June are the best months on the Riviera—nearly always bright and sunny and not intolerably hot and crowded as in July and August. The flowers add a blaze of colour wherever you look; the flower markets in Nice and Antibes are stunning. But each season has its pros and cons. In January all the tourists are in the Alps; in February the mimosas and almonds bloom on the Côte d'Azur. In April and May you can sit outside at restaurants and it's often warm enough for the first swim of the year. July and August are bad months, when everything is crowded, temperatures and prices soar and tempers flare, but it's also the season of the great festivals in Juan-les-Pins and Nice. Things quieten down considerably once French school holidays end in mid-September. In October the weather is traditionally mild on the coast, although torrential downpours have been known to happen; the first snows fall in the Alps. November is another bad month; it rains and many museums, hotels, and restaurants close down. December brings Christmas holiday tourists and the first skiers.

average temperature chart in °C (°F)

Jan	Feb	Mar	Apr	May	June	July	Aug	Sept	Oct	Nov	Dec
11(52)	12(54)	14(56)	17(62)	20(69)	22(72)	24(75)	26(79)	25(77)	20(69)	16(61)	13(55)

Consulates

UK: Nice: 12 Rue de France, ✆ 93 82 32 04.

USA: Nice: Rue Maréchal-Joffre, ✆ 93 88 89 55.

Canada : Marseille: 24 Av. du Prado, 6ᵉ, ✆ 91 37 19 37.

Ireland: Antibes: Villa les Chênes Verts, 152 Bd. Kennedy, Antibes, ✆ 93 61 50 63.

Crime and the Police

There is a fair chance that you will be had in the south of France; thieves and pickpockets are drawn like magnets to the flashy fish on the Côte d'Azur. Road pirates prey on motorists blocked in traffic, train pirates prowl the overnight compartments looking for handbags and cameras, car bandits just love the ripe pickings in cars parked in isolated scenic areas or tourist car parks; bicycles left in public view present an irresistible challenge to a surprising number of seedy prestidigitators. Although violence is rare, the moral of the story is basic common sense: leave anything you'd really miss at home, carry travellers' cheques and insure your property, especially if you're driving. Report thefts to the nearest *gendarmerie*, not a pleasant task but the reward is the bit of paper you need for an insurance claim. If your passport is stolen, contact the police and your nearest consulate for emergency travel documents. Carry photocopies of your passport, driver's licence, etc. By law, the police in France can stop anyone anywhere and demand an ID; in practice, they only tend to do it to harass minorities, the homeless, and scruffy hippy types. If they really don't like the look of you they can salt you away for a long time without any reason.

The drug situation is the same in France as anywhere in the west: soft and hard drugs are widely available, and the police only make an issue of victimless crime when it suits them (your being a foreigner just may rouse them to action). Smuggling any amount of marijuana into the country can mean prison, and there's not much your consulate can or will do about it.

Disabled Travellers

When it comes to providing access for all, France is not exactly in the vanguard of nations; many Americans who come over are appalled. But things are beginning to change, especially in newer buildings. Access and facilities in 90 towns in France are covered in *Touristes quand même! Promenades en France pour les voyageurs handicapés*, a booklet usually available in the tourist offices of large cities, or write ahead to the Comité National Français de Liaison pour la Réadaptation des Handicapés, 30–32 Quai de la Loire, 75019 Paris. Hotels with facilities for the handicapped are listed in Michelin's *Red Guide to France*.

RADAR (The Royal Association for Disability and Rehabilitation), 25 Mortimer Street, London, W1N 8AB, ✆ (0171) 637 5400, Minicom ✆ (0171) 637 5315: all aspects of travel information covered.

Mobility International USA, PO Box 3551, Eugene, OR 97403, USA, ✆ (503) 343 1248: all aspects of travel information covered.

Environment

'Come to the Côte d'Azur for a change of pollution,' they say. Constantly threatened by frequent oil spills, a suffocating algae mistakenly released into the sea at the Oceanographic Institute of Monte-Carlo, too many cars and too many people, the 'California (read Florida) of Europe', from Marseille to Menton, may be the first place in southern Europe to achieve total ecological breakdown. When you consider that a quarter of the coast is under concrete, it's no surprise.

As elsewhere in the Mediterranean, a sad litany of forest fires heads the television news in summer. Most forests are pine—Aleppo pines in limestone, maritime pines in the Maures and Esterel. Here they often close roads in summer to decrease the chance of fires. Most are caused by twits with matches (you'll be more careful, won't you?), though many fires are deliberately instigated by speculators who burn off protected forests to build more holiday villas and golf courses. Fires often lead to erosion and flooding, though the local governments now do a good job of reforestation.

The most spectacular environmental non-issue continues to be the overbuilding of the Côte d'Azur. The damage is done; one of the most exceptional parts of the Mediterranean coast has been thoroughly, thoughtlessly, irreparably ruined. Since the war there has simply been too much money involved for governments to act responsibly; most of the buildings you'll see were put up illegally—but there they are. Though this is changing—a politically connected developer near St-Tropez was recently forced to demolish an illegal, half-built project—local governments continue to promote industrial and tourist growth in areas where there is absolutely no room to grow. Paris bureaucrats are as responsible as local politicians; in public transport, for example, they insist on pushing a new TGV route around the coast, bringing down even more people instead of improving local transport that might cut down on the ferocious traffic they already have. The new route is a monster, cutting across scores of scenic areas and wine regions.

Other enemies of the Côte d'Azur include: the army, which has commandeered enormous sections of wilderness, including Ile du Levant; and regularly blows them to smithereens in manoeuvres and target practice; and the lack of water, a direct result of overbuilding, choking the few surviving herb and flower farms.

In August, ecological dysfunction reaches its apogee on the sands of St-Tropez's crowded beaches, laced with trash, condoms, syringes and human excrement. People—ususasly innocent bystanders—are killed each year in power-boat and jet-ski accidents.

Festivals

The Côte d'Azur offers everything from the Cannes Film Festival to the village fête, with a pilgrimage or religious procession, bumper cars, a *pétanque* tournament, a feast (anything from sardines to paella) and an all-night dance, sometimes to a local band but often a travelling troupe playing 'Hot Music' or some other electrified cacophony. A *bravade* entails some pistol- or musket-shots; a *corso* is a parade with carts or floats. St John's Day (24 June) is a big favourite and often features bonfires and fireworks.

Note: Dates change every year. For complete listings and precise dates of events in Provence, pick up a copy of the annual lists, available in most tourist offices.

calendar of events

January

27	*Fête de Ste-Dévote*, **Monaco**
End of month	**Monte-Carlo** rally

February

3	Festival of olives and late golden Servan grapes, **Valbonne**
First week	International Circus Festival, **Monaco**
10 days at Carnival	*Fête du Citron*, **Menton**
Carnival	**Nice** has the most famous festivities in France
Ash Wednesday	*Les Pailhasses* at **Cournonterral**, a 14th-century parade of boys in straw and turkey feathers, who try to squirt wine on passers-by
10	*Corso du Mimosa*, **Bormes-les-Mimosas**

March

25	*Festin es Courgourdons*, folklore and dried sculpted gourds, **Nice**

April

Throughout month	International Tennis Tournaments, **Monaco** and **Nice**
Maundy Thursday/ Good Friday	Procession of the Dead Christ, **Roquebrune-Cap-Martin**

May

Third week after Easter	*Bravade St-François*, **Fréjus**
Second week	**Cannes** Film Festival
Second weekend	*Fête de la Rose*, **Grasse**
16–17	*Bravade de St-Torpes*, **St-Tropez**
Ascension weekend	**Monaco** International Grand Prix
Late May-mid July	International music festival, **Toulon**

June

Throughout month	*Festival de la Danse et de l'Image*, **Toulon**
15	*Bravade des Espagnols*, **St-Tropez**
Corpus Christi	*Procession dai limaça*, **Gorbio**

July

July–August	International Fireworks Festival, **Monaco**; modern music festival, **St-Paul-de-Vence**
Throughout month	International Music Festival, **Vence**
4–14	*Festival Américain*, **Cannes**
Second Sunday	*Fête de St-Pierre*, with water jousts, etc., **Cap d'Antibes**
Mid-July	Jazz festivals in **Nice** and **Toulon**; film festival, **La Ciotat**
Last two weeks	International Jazz Festival, **Juan-les-Pins**
Last Sunday	Donkey races and village fête, **Lacoste**
End July	Folklore festival and *Bataille des Fleurs*, **Nice**
July–Aug	Châteauvallon Dance Festival, **Ollioules**
July–Sept	Provence Festival, with classical music concerts, **Sanary**

August

All month	Chamber Music festival, **Menton**
First Sunday	Jasmine festival, **Grasse**
5	Passion procession, **Roquebrune**

September

First Sunday	*Festin des baguettes*, **Peille**
last week–first week Oct	*Nioulargue*, yacht race in **St-Tropez**

December

All month	Festival of Italian Cinema, **Nice**

> *... and south of Valence, Provincia Romana, the Roman Provence, lies beneath the sun. There there is no more any evil, for there the apple will not flourish and the Brussels sprout will not grow at all.*
>
> Ford Madox Ford, *Provence*

Eating is a pleasure in the south, where seafood, herbs, fruit and vegetables are often within plucking distance of the kitchen and table. The high quality of these fresh native ingredients demands minimal preparation—Provençal cooking is perhaps the least fussy of any regional French cuisine, and as an added plus neatly fits the modern definition of a healthy diet. For not only is the south a Brussels sprout-free zone, but the artery-hardening delights of the north—the rich creamy sauces, butter, cheese and egg dishes, mega-calorie desserts—are rare birds in the land of olives, apricots, and almonds.

Some of the most celebrated restaurants in the world grace the Côte d'Azur, but there are plenty of stinkers, too. The most tolerable are humble in their mediocrity while others are oily with pretensions, staffed by folks posing as Grand Dukes and Duchesses fallen on hard times, whose exalted airs are somehow supposed to make their clients feel better about paying an obscene amount of money for the eight *petits pois à la graisse de yak* that the chef has so beautifully arranged on a plate. These places never last more than a year or two, but may just be in business as you happen by.

Restaurant Basics

Restaurants generally serve food between 12 noon and 2pm and in the evening from 7 to 10pm, with later summer hours; *brasseries* in the cities generally stay open continuously. All post menus outside the door so you know what to expect; if prices aren't listed, you can bet it's not because they're a bargain. If you have the appetite to eat the biggest meal of the day at noon, you'll spend a lot less money. Almost all restaurants have a choice of set-price menus; many offer a cheaper lunch special—the best way to experience some of the finer gourmet temples. Eating *à la carte* will always be much more expensive, in many cases twice as much; in most average spots no one ever does it. A few expensive restaurants on the Côte d'Azur have no set-price menus at all.

Menus in inexpensive places sometimes include the house wine (*vin compris*); if you choose a better wine anywhere, expect a scandalous mark-up. Don't be dismayed, it's a long-established custom (as in many other lands); the French wouldn't dream of a meal without wine, and the arrangement is a simple device to make food prices seem lower. If service is included it will say *service compris* or *s.c.*, if not *service non compris* or *s.n.c.* Some restaurants offer a set-price gourmet *menu dégustation*—a selection of chef's specialities, which can be a great treat. At the other end of the scale, in the bars and brasseries, is the *plat du jour* (daily special) and the no-choice *formule*, which is more often than not steak and *frites*.

A full French meal may begin with an apéritif, hors-d'œuvre, a starter or two, followed by the *entrée*, cheese, dessert, coffee and chocolates, and perhaps a *digestif* to finish things off. If you order a salad it may come before or after, but never with your main course. In everyday eating, most people condense this feast to a starter, main course, and cheese or dessert. Vegetarians who don't eat fish will have a hard time in France, but most establishments will try to accommodate them.

When looking for a restaurant, homing in on the one place crowded with locals is as sound a policy in France as anywhere. Don't overlook hotel restaurants, some of which are absolutely top notch even if a certain red book refuses on some obscure principle to give them more than two stars. To avoid disappointment, call ahead in the morning to reserve a table, especially at smarter restaurants, and especially in the summer. One thing you'll soon notice is that there's a wide choice of ethnic restaurants, mostly North African (a favourite for their economical *couscous*—spicy meat and vegetables served on a bed of steamed semolina with a side dish of *harisa*, a hot red pepper sauce); Asian (usually Vietnamese, sometimes Chinese, Cambodian, or Thai); and Italian, the latter sometimes combined with a pizzeria, although beware, quality very much depends on proximity to Italy, i.e. the pasta and pizza are superb in Nice and tolerably good in Toulon. Don't expect to find many of these outside the Côte and the big cities; country cooking is French only (though often very inventive). But in the cosmopolitan centres, you'll find not only foreign cuisine, but specialities from all over France. There are Breton *crêperies* or *galetteries* (with wholewheat pancakes), restaurants from Alsace serving *choucroute* (sauerkraut and sausage), Périgord restaurants featuring *foie gras* and truffles and *les fast foods* offering *basse cuisine* of chips, hot dogs, and cheese sandwiches.

There are still a scattering of traditional French restaurants that would meet the approval of Auguste Escoffier, the legendary chef (and Riviera native); quite a few serve regional specialities (*see* below) and many feature *nouvelle cuisine*, which isn't so *nouvelle* any more, and has come under attack by devoted foodies for its untoward expense (only the finest, freshest and rarest ingredients are used), portions (minute compared to usual restaurant helpings, because the object is to feel good, not full), and especially because many *nouvelle cuisine* practitioners have been quacks. For it is a subtle art, to emphasize the natural flavour and goodness of a carrot by contrasting or complementing it with other flavours and scents; disappointments are inevitable when a chef is more concerned with appearance than taste, or takes a walk on the wild side, combining oysters, kiwis and cashews or some other abomination. But *nouvelle cuisine* has had a strong influence on attitudes towards food in France, and it's hard to imagine anyone going back full-time to smothering everything in a *béchamel* sauce.

The Cuisine of the Côte d'Azur

The cuisine of the Côte d'Azur is pure Mediterranean—a mix of Provençal and Italian, with garlic in most dishes and a seafood tradition that goes back to the days when fishing smacks bobbed in what are now million-dollar berths for mega-yachts. Many traditional dishes are forerunners of *nouvelle cuisine*, and their success hinges on the quality of the ingredients and fragrant olive oil, like the well-known *ratatouille*—aubergines (eggplant), tomatoes, garlic and courgettes (zucchini) cooked separately to preserve their individual flavour, before being mixed together in olive oil.

Among the starters, a refreshing summertime favourite is *salade Niçoise*, interpreted in a hundred different ways even in Nice. Most versions contain most of the following: tomatoes, cucumbers, hard-boiled eggs, black olives, onions, anchovies, radishes, artichokes, green peppers, croûtons, green beans, and sometimes tuna and even boiled potatoes. In Nice pasta dishes come in all sorts of shapes, but the favourites are *ravioli* and *gnocchi* (potato dumplings), two forms served throughout Italy and invented here when Nice was still *Nizza* (the city has many other special dishes: *see* p.86). Another dish that tastes best in the summer, *soupe au pistou* is a thick minestrone served with a fresh basil, garlic, and pine-nut sauce similar to Italian *pesto*. *Tian* is a casserole of rice, spring vegetables and grated cheese baked in the oven; *tourta de blea* is a sweet-savoury Swiss chard pie. *Mesclun* is a salad of dandelion leaves, lamb's lettuce, lettuce, endive, fennel, chicory and herbs, and a favourite hors-d'œuvre is *tapenade*, a purée of olives, olive oil and capers.

Aïoli, a kind of mayonnaise made from garlic, olive oil and egg yolks, served with cod, snails, potatoes or soup, is for many the essence of the region. The world-famous *bouillabaisse* is a thick soup of five to twelve kinds of Mediterranean fish, flavoured with saffron; the fish is removed and served with *rouille*, a sauce of fresh red chilli peppers crushed with garlic, olive oil, and the soup broth. Because good saffron costs a bomb and the fish, especially the gruesome *racasse* (scorpion fish) are rare, a proper *bouillabaisse* will run to at least 200F. A slightly less expensive but delicious alternative is *bourride*, a soup made from white-fleshed fish served with *aïoli*, or down a gastronomical notch or two, *baudroie*, a fish soup with vegetables and garlic. *Bouillabaisse* is a Marseille dish, and in Nice you should ask for *soupe de poisson*, the city's own fish soup speciality. A very different kettle of fish is the indigestible Niçoise favourite, *estocaficada*, stockfish (and stockfish guts) stewed with tomatoes, olives, garlic, and eau-de-vie. Less adventurous, and absolutely delicious, is *loup au fenouil*, sea bass grilled over fennel stalks and flambéd in Pernod.

Lamb is the most common meat dish; real Provençal lamb (becoming increasingly rare) grazes on herbs and on special salt-marsh grasses from the Camargue and Crau. Beef is quite tough but usually comes in the form of a *daube*, slowly stewed in red wine and often served with ravioli. A Provençal cook's prize possession is the *daube* pan, which is never washed, but wiped clean and baked to form a crust that flavours all subsequent stews. Rabbit, or *lapin à la Provençale*, is simmered in white wine with garlic, mustard, tomatoes and herbs. A more daunting dish, *pieds et paquets* is tripe stuffed with garlic, onions and salt pork, traditionally (although rarely in practice) served with calf's trotters. Stuffed courgette (zucchini) flowers, tarts of Swiss chard, and grilled tomatoes with garlic and breadcrumbs are popular vegetable dishes. Local cheeses are invariably goat—*chèvre*—little roundlets flavoured with thyme, bay, and other herbs. *Lou Pevre*, *Banon* and *Poivre d'Ain* are among the best.

Markets, Picnic Food and Snacks

The food markets are justly celebrated for the colour and perfumes of their produce and flowers. They are fun to visit, and become even more interesting if you're cooking for yourself or are just gathering the ingredients for a picnic. In the larger cities they take place every day, while smaller towns and villages have markets on one day a week, which double as a social occasion for the locals. Most markets finish around noon.

Other good sources for picnic food are the *charcuteries* or *traiteurs*, both of which sell prepared dishes sold by weight in cartons or tubs. You can also find counters at larger supermarkets. Cities are snack-food wonderlands, with outdoor counters selling pastries, crêpes, pizza slices, *frites*, *croque-monsieurs* (toasted ham and cheese sandwiches) and a wide variety of sandwiches made from *baguettes* (long thin loaves of bread).

Nice is a happy hunting ground for nibblers, with a wide variety of snacks that can easily be combined for a light, inexpensive meal. Put the ingredients of a *salade Niçoise* in between bread and you have a delicious, messy *pan-bagnat*. If you're dressed up, there are less gooey treats like *socca*, a kind of thin cake popular throughout the Ligurian coast, made of ground chick peas and water, baked, and sold by the slice in the old town (in 1908 the city council tried to ban this peasant food for lowering the tone, until the protests of the people saved it); and *fougasse*, another Ligurian speciality, a flat bread baked with bits of bacon, or in a sweet version with sugar. Nice is also the home of a pungent kind of pizza called *pissaladière*, baked with onions, olives and anchovies (from *pissala*, a condiment made of anchovies and spices); and of sandwiches made from the delicious *porquetta*, roast suckling pig filled with herbs and spices, more commonly wolfed down in Umbria.

Drink

You can order any kind of drink at any bar or café—except cocktails, unless it has a certain cosmopolitan savoir-faire or stays open into the night. Cafés are also a home from home, places to read the papers, play cards, meet friends, and just unwind, sit back, and watch the world go by. You can sit hours over one coffee and no one will try to hurry you along. Prices are listed on the *Tarif des Consommations*: note they are progressively more expensive depending on whether you're served at the bar (*comptoir*), at a table (*la salle*) or outside (*la terrasse*).

French coffee is strong and black, but can be lacklustre next to the aromatic brews of Italy or Spain (you'll notice an improvement in the coffee near their respective frontiers). If you order *un café* you'll get a small black *express*; if you want milk, order *un crème*. If you want more than a few drops of caffeine, ask them to make it *grand*. For decaffeinated, the word is *déca*. Some bars offer *cappuccinos*, but again they're best near the Italian border; in the summer try a *frappé* (iced coffee). The French only order *café au lait* (a small coffee topped off with lots of hot milk) when they stop in for **breakfast**, and if what your hotel offers is expensive or boring, consider joining them. There are baskets of *croissants* and pastries, and some bars will make you a *baguette* with butter, jam or honey. If you want to go native, try the Frenchman's Breakfast of Champions: a *pastis* or two, and five non-filter *Gauloises*. *Chocolat chaud* (hot chocolate) is usually good; if you order *thé* (tea), you'll get an ordinary bag. An *infusion* is a herbal tea—*camomille*, *menthe* (mint), *tilleul* (lime or linden blossom), or *verveine* (verbena). These are kind to the all-precious *foie*, or liver, after you've over-indulged.

Mineral water (*eau minérale*) can be addictive, and comes either sparkling (*gazeuse* or *pétil-lante*) or still (*non-gazeuse* or *plate*). If you feel run-down, Badoit has lots of peppy magnesium in it—it's the current trendy favourite. The usual international corporate soft drinks are available, and all kinds of bottled fruit juices (*jus de fruits*). Some bars also do fresh lemon and orange juices (*citron pressé* or *orange pressée*). French children are also fond of fruit syrups— red *grenadine* and ghastly green *diabolo menthe*.

Beer (*bière*) in most bars and cafés is run-of-the-mill big brands from Alsace, Germany, and Belgium. Draft (*à la pression*) is cheaper than bottled beer. Nearly all resorts have bars or pubs offering wider selections of drafts, lagers, and bottles.

The strong spirit of the Midi comes in a liquid form called *pastis*, first made popular in Marseille as a plague remedy; its name comes from the Latin *passe-sitis*, or thirst quencher. A pale yellow 90 per cent nectar flavoured with anis, vanilla and cinnamon, pastis is drunk as an apéritif before lunch and in rounds after work. The three major brands, *Ricard*, *Pernod*, and *Pastis 51* all taste slightly different; most people drink their '*pastaga*' with lots of water and ice (*glaçons*), which help make the taste more tolerable. A thimble-sized *pastis* is a *momie*, and you may want to try it mixed: a *tomate* is with grenadine, a *mauresque* with orgeat (almond and orange flower syrup), and a *perroquet* is with mint.

wine

One of the pleasures of travelling in France is drinking great wines for a fraction of what you pay at home, and discovering excellent labels you've never seen in your local shop. The south holds a special place in the saga of French wines, with a tradition dating back to the Greeks, who are said to have introduced an essential Côtes-du-Rhône grape variety called *syrah*, originally grown in Shiraz, Persia. Nurtured in the Dark and Middle Ages by popes and kings, the vineyards of Provence still produce most of France's wine—certainly most of it plonk, graded only by its alcohol content. Some of Provence's best-known wines grow in the ancient places near the coast, especially its quartet of tiny AOC districts *Bellet, Bandol, Cassis* and *Palette*. But the best-known wines of the region come from the Rhône valley, under the general heading of *Côtes-du-Rhône*, including *Châteauneuf-du-Pape*, *Gigondas*, the famous rosé *Tavel*, and the sweet muscat apéritif wine, *Beaumes-de-Venise*. Elsewhere, winemakers have made great strides in boosting quality in the past 30 years, recognized in new AOC districts.

If a wine is labelled AOC (*Appellation d'Origine Contrôlée*) it means that the wine comes from a certain defined area and is made from certain varieties of grapes, guaranteeing a standard of quality. *Cru* on the label means vintage; a *grand cru* is a great, noble vintage. Down the list in the vinous hierarchy are those labelled VDQS (*Vin de Qualité Supérieure*), followed by *Vin de Pays* (guaranteed at least to originate in a certain region), with *Vin Ordinaire* (or *Vin de Table*) at the bottom, which may not send you to seventh heaven but is usually drinkable and cheap. In a restaurant if you order a *rouge* (red) or *blanc* (white) or *rosé* (pink), this is what you'll get, either by the glass (*un verre*), by the quarter-litre (*un pichet*) or bottle (*une bouteille*). *Brut* is very dry, *sec* dry, *demi-sec* and *moelleux* are sweetish, *doux* sweet, and *méthode champenoise* sparkling. If you're buying direct from the producer (or a wine co-operative, or *syndicat*, a group of producers), you'll be offered glasses to taste, each wine older than the previous one until you are feeling quite jolly and ready to buy the oldest (and most expensive) vintage. On the other hand, some sell loose wine *à la* petrol pump, *en vrac* ; many *caves* even sell the little plastic barrels to put it in.

Health and Emergencies

Local hospitals are the place to go in an emergency (*urgence*). If you need an ambulance (SAMU) dial 15; police and ambulance, ☎ 17; fire, ☎ 18. Doctors take turns going on duty at night and on holidays even in rural areas: *pharmacies* will know who to contact or telephone *SOS Médecins*—if you don't have access to a phone book or Minitel, dial directory enquiries, ☎ 12. To be on the safe side, always carry a phone card (*see* telephones, below). If it's not an emergency, the *pharmacies* have addresses of local doctors, or visit the clinic at a *Centre Hospitalier*. Pharmacists are also trained to administer first aid, and dispense free advice for minor problems. *Pharmacies* themselves open on a rotating basis. Addresses are posted in their windows and in the local newspaper.

Doctors will give you a brown and white *feuille de soins* with your prescription; take both to the pharmacy and keep the *feuille* for insurance purposes at home. British subjects who are hospitalized and can produce their E111 forms will be billed later at home for 20 per cent of the costs that French social insurance doesn't cover.

Money and Banks

The **franc** (abbreviated with an F) consists of 100 centimes. Banknotes come in deno[...] tions of 500, 200, 100, 50 and 20F; coins in 20, 10, 5, 2 and 1F, and 50, 20, 10, an[...] centimes. You can bring in as much currency as you like, but by law are only allowed to take out 5000F in cash. Traveller's cheques or Eurocheques are the safest way of carrying money; the most widely recognized credit card is VISA (*Carte Bleue* in French) which is accepted almost everywhere; with it or any major bank card with a PIN number you can draw up to 2000F a go from most automatic cash dispensers. If you plan to spend a lot of time in rural areas, where banks are few and far between, you may want to opt for International Giro Cheques, exchangeable at any post office.

Banks are generally open from 8.30am–12.30pm and 1.30–4pm; they close on Sunday, and most close either on Saturday or Monday as well. Exchange rates vary, and nearly all take a commission of varying proportions. *Bureaux de change* that do nothing but exchange money (and exchanges in hotels and train stations) usually have the worst rates or take out the heftiest commissions, so be careful. It's always a good bet to purchase some francs before you go, especially if you arrive during the weekend.

Opening Hours, Museums and National Holidays

While many **shops** and supermarkets in Nice and Cannes are now open continuously Tuesday–Saturday from 9 or 10am to 7 or 7.30pm, businesses in smaller towns still close down for lunch from 12 or 12.30pm to 2 or 3pm, or in the summer 4pm in the afternoon. There are local exceptions, but nearly everything closes down on Mondays, except for grocers and *supermarchés* that open in the afternoon. In many towns Sunday morning is a big shopping period. Markets (daily in the cities, weekly in villages) are usually open mornings only, although clothes, flea and antique markets run into the afternoon. On the coast, it is common for tourist attractions and shops to be open daily on weekdays, but always check.

Most **museums** close for lunch as well, and often on Mondays or Tuesdays, and sometimes for all of November or the entire winter. Hours change with the season: longer summer hours begin in May or June and last until the end of September—usually. Some change their hours every darn month. We've done our best to include them in the text, but don't sue us if they're not exactly right. Most close on national holidays and give discounts if you have a student ID card, or are an EC citizen under 18 or over 65 years old; most charge admissions ranging from 10 upwards. Churches are usually open all day, or closed all day and only open for mass. Sometimes notes on the door direct you to the *mairie* or priest's house (*presbytère*) where you can pick up the key. There are often admission fees for cloisters, crypts, and special chapels.

On French **national holidays**, banks, shops and businesses close; some museums do, but most restaurants stay open. They are: January 1, Easter Sunday, Easter Monday, May 1, May 8 (VE Day), Ascension Day (40 days after Easter), Pentecost (7th Sunday after Easter) and the following Monday, July 14 (Bastille Day), August 15 (Assumption of the BVM), November 1 (All Saints'), November 11 (First World War Armistice), and Christmas Day.

In addition to the aforementioned holidays, Monaco takes the day off on January 27th (*Fête de Ste-Dévote*) and November 19th (*Fête Nationale Monégasque*).

'or *Bureau de Poste*, easily discernible by a blue bird on a yellow back-
offices are open in the cities Mon–Fri 8am–7pm, and Saturdays 8am until
ffices may not open until 9am, break for lunch, and close at 4.30 or 5pm.
poste restante at any of them; the postal codes in this book should help
your mail get there in a timely fashion. To collect it, bring some ID. You can purchase stamps
in some tobacconists as well as post offices.

Post offices offer free use of a Minitel electronic directory, and usually have at least one telephone booth with a meter—the easiest way to phone overseas. Most other public telephones
have switched over from coins to *télécartes*, which you can purchase at any post office for 40F
for 50 *unités* or 96F for 120 *unités*. The French have eliminated area codes, giving everyone
an eight-digit telephone number, which is all you have to dial within France (though *see*
below for further changes). For international calls, first dial 19, wait for the change in the dial
tone, then dial the country code (UK 44; US and Canada 1; Ireland 353; Australia 61; New
Zealand 64), and then the local code (minus the 0 for UK numbers) and number. The easiest
way to reverse the charges is to spend a few francs ringing the number you want to call and
giving them your number in France, which is always posted in the box; alternatively ring your
national operator and tell him or her that you want to call reverse charges (for the UK dial 19
00 44; for the US 19 00 11). France's international dialling code is 33. For directory enquiries,
dial ✆ 12; international directory enquiries is ✆ 19 33 12 followed by the country code, but
note that you'll have to wait around the telephone for them to ring you back with your
requested number.

change of telephone numbers

On 18 October 1996 France is changing its telephone numbers from 8 digits to 10 digits. All
the phone numbers in the Provence and Côte d'Azur areas should be preceded by 04 from this
date. Similarly, any Paris phone numbers should be preceded by 01 instead of 1. When calling
abroad from France, dial 00 instead of 19.

Racism

Unfortunately in some parts of the Côte d'Azur the forces of bigotry and reaction are strong
enough to make racism a serious concern. We've heard some horror stories, especially about
Nice, where campsites and restaurants suddenly have no places if the colour of your skin
doesn't suit the proprietor; the bouncers at clubs will inevitably say it's really the cut of your
hair or trousers they find offensive. If any place recommended in this book is guilty of such
behaviour, please write and let us know; we will not only remove it in the next edition, but
forward your letter to the regional tourist office and relevant authorities in Paris.

Shopping

All in all, this is not a brilliant region for the holiday shopper. Traditional handicrafts have died
out rather, though attempts are being made to revive them—inevitably in the tourist areas.
Typical items are the *santons*, terracotta Christmas crib figures dressed in 18th-century
Provençal costumes, usually as artful as the concrete studies of the Seven Dwarfs sold at your
neighbourhood garden centre.

Every town east of the Rhône has at least one boutique specializing in Provençal skirts, bags, pillows and scarves, printed in intense colours (madder red, sunflower yellow, pine green) with floral, paisley or geometric designs. Block-print fabrics were first made in Provence after Louis XIV, wanting to protect the French silk industry, banned the import of popular Indian prints. Clever entrepreneurs in the papal-owned Comtat Venaissin responded by producing cheap imitations still known in French today as *indiennes*. The same shops usually sell the other essential bric-à-brac of the south—dried lavender pot-pourris, sachets of *herbes de Provence* (nothing but thyme and bay leaves), orange and lemon perfumed soaps.

Big-name French and Italian designers and purveyors of luxury goods have boutiques at Cannes, Monaco, St-Tropez and Nice. Moustiers, Vallauris and Biot have hand-made ceramics and glassware, Salernes makes world-famous tiles, and at least a million artists wait to sell you their productions. Cogolin specializes in pipes and saxophone-reeds; Grasse sells perfumes and essential oils. The sweet of tooth will find western Provence heaven. Nearly every town has its own speciality: candied fruits in Apt, the chocolates and *calissons* (almond biscuits) of Aix, *berlingots* (mint-flavoured caramels) in Carpentras, *nougats* in Vence, *marrons glacés* in Collobrières, and orange-flavoured chocolates called *papalines* in Avignon. Most will be available in shops in the larger towns of the Côte.

Sport and Leisure Activities

bicycling

See 'Getting Around', p.6.

fishing

You can fish in the sea without a permit as long as your catch is for local consumption; along the Riviera captains offer expeditions for tuna and other denizens of the deep. Freshwater fishing requires an easily obtained permit from a local club; tourist offices can tell you where to find them.

football

Professional football in the south is dominated by the three Ms: Marseille Olympique, 1993 winners of the European Cup now stripped of their crown following match-rigging allegations, followed by Monaco (who replaced them as the French entry in the 1994 European Cup), which is almost as wealthy, and Montpellier, the bright star in Languedoc—other first-division teams are in Toulon and Nîmes, and Cannes, who have seen a spectacular resurgence in 1994.

gambling

If you're over 21, every big resort along the coast comes equipped with a **casino** ready to take your hard-earned money. Scandals have plagued a few—Nice, especially (*see* p.82). Even if you aren't a gambler, a few are worth a visit: Monte Carlo, for its cynical mix of the voluptuous and the crass; or Cannes, for high-fashion vice. Or you can do as the locals do and play for a side of beef, a lamb, or a VCR in a **Loto**, in a local café or municipal *salle de fête*. Loto is just like bingo, although some of the numbers have names: 11 is *las cambas de ma grand* (my grandmother's legs) and 75, the number of the *département* of Paris, is *los envaïsseurs* (the invaders). Everybody plays the horses, at the local bar with the *PMU* (off-track betting) outlet.

golf

Increasingly popular in France, there are courses near most of the major resorts on the Côte d'Azur, and literally a hundred more planned or under construction. Cannes offers golfers the most choice, with three courses in Mandelieu and three in Le Cannet. The most spectacular course is Monaco's, which was laid out around the turn of the century.

pétanque

Like pastis and olive oil, *pétanque* is one of the essential ingredients of the Midi, and even the smallest village has a rough, hard court under the plane trees for its practitioners—nearly all male, although women are welcome to join in. Similar to *boules*, the special rules of *pétanque* were according to tradition developed in La Ciotat. The object is to get your metal ball closest to the marker (*bouchon* or *cochonnet*). Tournaments are frequent and well attended.

sailing

Most of the resorts have sailing schools and boats to hire. Get a complete list from the Fédération Française de Voile, 55 Av. Kléber, 75084 Paris Cedex 16, ✆ (16 1) 45 53 68 00.

skiing

If the weather ever decides to settle down to what's expected of it (in 1990–91 Nice had as much snow as some of the Alps) you can do as in California: ski in the morning and bake on the beach in the afternoon. The biggest resorts in the Alpes-Maritimes are Isola 2000, Auron and Valberg, and, closest to Nice, Gréolières-les-Neiges. For the Alpes-Maritimes, contact the Comité Régional de Tourisme Provence Alpes Côte d'Azur, Immeuble C.M.C.I., 2 rue Henri Barbusse, 13241 Marseille, ✆ 91 39 38 00, fax 91 56 66 61.

water sports and beaches

For a selection of the coast's best beaches for sports, swimming and sunbathing, *see* pp.49, 92 and 126 in the gazetteer chapters.

Tourist Information

Every city and town, and most villages, have a tourist information office, usually called a *Syndicat d'Initiative* or an *Office de Tourisme*. In smaller villages this service is provided by the town hall (*mairie*). They distribute free maps and town-plans, hotel, camping, and self-catering accommodation lists for their area, and can inform you on sporting events, leisure activities, wine estates open for visits, and festivals. Addresses and telephones are listed in the text, and if you write to them, they'll post you their booklets to help you plan your holiday before you leave.

Where to Stay

Hotels

The Côte d'Azur has some of the most splendid hotels in Europe and some genuine scruffy fleabags of dubious clientele, with the majority of establishments falling somewhere between. Like most countries in Europe, the tourist authorities grade them by their facilities (not by charm or location) with stars from four (or four with an L for luxury—a bit confusing, so in the text luxury places are given five stars) to one, and there are even some cheap but adequate places undignified by any stars at all.

We would have liked to put the exact prices in the text, but in France this is not possible. Almost every establishment has a wide range of rooms and prices—a very useful and logical way of doing things, once you're used to it; in some hotels, every single room has its own personality and the difference in quality and price can be enormous; a large room with antique furniture, a television or a balcony over the sea and a complete bathroom will cost much more than a poky back room in the same hotel, with a window overlooking a car park, no antiques, and the WC down the hall. Some proprietors will drag out a sort of menu for you to choose the level of price and facilities. Most two-star hotel rooms have their own showers and WCs; most one stars offer rooms with or without. The following guide will give you an idea of what prices to expect.

Note: all prices listed here and elsewhere in this book are for a double room.

★★★★	400–2300F
★★★	240–700F
★★	150–500F
★	130–300F

Hotels with *no stars* are not necessarily dives; their owners probably never bothered filling out a form for the tourist authorities. Their prices are usually the same as one-star places.

Alas, although it's impossible to be more precise, we can add a few more generalizations. **Single rooms** are relatively rare, and usually two-thirds the price of a double, and rarely will a hotelier give you a discount if only doubles are available (again, because each room has its own price); on the other hand, if there are three or four of you, **triples or quads** or adding extra beds to a double room is usually cheaper than staying in two rooms. Prices are posted at the reception desk and in the rooms to keep the management honest. Flowered wallpaper, usually beige, comes in all rooms with no extra charge—it's an essential part of the French experience. **Breakfast** (usually coffee, a croissant, bread and jam for 30F–50F) is nearly always optional: you'll do as well for less in a bar. As usual rates rise in the busy season (holidays and summer, and in the winter around ski resorts), when many hotels with restaurants will require that you take **half-board** (*demi-pension*—breakfast and a set lunch or dinner). Many hotel restaurants are superb and described in the text; non-residents are welcome. At worst the food will be boring, and it can be monotonous eating in the same place every night when there are so many tempting restaurants around. Don't be put off by obligatory dining. It's traditional; French hoteliers think of themselves as innkeepers, in the old-fashioned way. In the off-season board requirements vanish into thin air.

Your holiday will be much sweeter if you **book ahead**, especially anywhere near the Côte d'Azur from May to October. The few reasonably priced rooms are snapped up very early across the board. Phoning a day or two ahead is always a good policy, although beware that hotels will only confirm a room with the receipt of a cheque covering the first night (not a credit card number). Tourist offices have complete lists of accommodation in their given areas or even *département*, which come in handy during the peak season; many will even call around and book a room for you on the spot for free or a nominal fee.

Chain hotels (Sofitel, Formula One, etc.) are in most cities, but always dreary and geared to the business traveller more than the tourist, so you won't find them in this book. Don't confuse chains with the various **umbrella organizations** like *Logis et Auberges de France*, *Relais de Silence*, or the prestigious *Relais et Châteaux* which promote and guarantee the quality of independently owned hotels and their restaurants. Many are recommended in the text. Larger tourist offices usually stock their booklets, or you can pick them up before you leave from the French National Tourist Office.

Bed and breakfast: In rural areas, there are plenty of opportunities for a stay in a private home or farm. *Chambres d'hôtes*, in the tourist office brochures, are listed separately from hotels with the various *gîtes* (*see* below). Some are connected to restaurants, others to wine estates or a château; prices tend to be moderate to inexpensive. *Friendly Home* (Les Amaryllis, 6 Rue du Marc, 06600 Antibes, ✆ 93 34 93 01, ✉ 93 34 66 31) is a bed and breakfast society offering rooms, villas, and apartments along the Côte d'Azur from Nice to Mandelieu, all within 10km of the coast. Prices range from 200F to 400F for two people with breakfast.

Youth Hostels, Gîtes d'Etape*, and* Refuges

Most cities and resort areas have youth hostels (*auberges de jeunesse*) which offer simple dormitory accommodation and breakfast to people of any age for around 40–70F a night. Most offer kitchen facilities as well, or inexpensive meals. They are the best deal going for people travelling on their own; for people travelling together a one-star hotel can be just as cheap. Another down-side is that many are in the most ungodly locations—in the suburbs where the last bus goes by at 7pm, or miles from any transport at all in the country. In the summer the only way to be sure of a room is to arrive early in the day. Most require a Youth Hostels Association membership card, which you can usually purchase on the spot, although regulations say you should buy them in your home country (UK: from YHA, 14 Southampton Street, London WC2; USA: from AYH, P.O. Box 37613, Washington DC 20013; Canada: from CHA, 1600 James Maysmyth Dr, 6th floor, Gloucester, Ottawa, Ontario K1B 5N4; Australia: from AYHA, 60 Mary St, Surrey Hills, Sydney, New South Wales 2010.) Another option in cities are the single-sex dormitories for young workers (*Foyers de Jeunes Travailleurs et de Jeunes Travailleuses*) which will rent out individual rooms if any are available, for slightly more than a youth hostel.

A *gîte d'étape* is a simple shelter with bunk beds and a rudimentary kitchen set up by a village along GR walking paths or a scenic bike route. Again, lists are available for each *département*; the detailed maps listed on p.7 mark them as well. In the mountains similar rough shelters along the GR paths are called *refuges*, most of them open summer only. Both charge around 40F or 50F a night.

Camping

Camping is a very popular way to travel, especially among the French themselves, and there's at least one campsite in every town, often an inexpensive, no-frills place run by the town itself (*camping municipal*). Other campsites are graded with stars like hotels from four to one: at the top of the line you can expect lots of trees and grass, hot showers, a pool or beach, sports facilities, and a grocer's, bar and/or restaurant, and on the coast, prices rather similar to one-star hotels (although these, of course, never have all the extras). But beware that July and

August are terrible months to camp on the Côte d'Azur, when sites become so overcrowded (St-Tropez is notorious) that the authorities have begun to worry about health problems. You'll find more living space off the coast. If you want to camp outside official sites, it's imperative to ask permission from the landowner first, or risk a furious farmer and perhaps even the police.

Tourist offices have complete lists of campsites in their regions, or if you plan to move around a lot pick up a *Guide Officiel Camping/Caravanning*, available in French bookshops. A number of UK holiday firms book camping holidays and offer discounts on Channel ferries: Canvas Holidays, ✆ (0383) 621 000; Eurocamp Travel, ✆ (0565) 62 62 62; Keycamp Holidays, ✆ (081) 395 4000. The French National Tourist Office has lists.

Gîtes de France and Other Self-catering Accommodation

The south of France offers a vast range of self-catering: inexpensive farm cottages, history-laden châteaux with gourmet frills, sprawling villas on the Riviera, flats in modern beach resorts or even on board canal boats. The *Fédération Nationale des Gîtes de France* is a French government service offering inexpensive accommodation by the week in rural areas. Lists with photos arranged by *département* are available from the French National Tourist office, or in the UK from the official rep: **Gîtes de France**, 178 Piccadilly, London W1V 9DB, ✆ (071) 493 3480. Prices range from 1000F to 2000F a week. Other options are advertised in the Sunday papers or contact one of the firms listed below. The accommodation they offer will nearly always be more comfortable and costly than a *gîte*, but the discounts holiday firms can offer on the ferries, plane tickets, or car rental can make up for the price difference.

in the UK

Air France Holidays, Gable House, 18–24 Turnham Green Terrace, London W4 1RF, ✆ (0181) 742 3377. Apartments.

Allez France, 27 West Street, Storrington, West Sussex RH20 4DZ, ✆ (01903) 742 345: wide variety of accommodation from cottages to châteaux.

Angel Travel, 34 High Street, Borough Green, Sevenoaks TN15 8BJ, ✆ (01732) 884 109: villas, *gîtes* and flats.

The Apartment Service, 5–6 Francis Grove, London SW19 4DT, ✆ (0181) 944 1444, ✆ 944 6744. Selected apartment accommodation in cities for short or extended stays.

Beach Villas, 8 Market Passage, Cambridge CB2 3QR, ✆ (01223) 311 113: self-catering by the sea, especially for families.

Belvedere Holiday Apartments, 5 Bartholomews, Brighton BN1 1HG, ✆ (01273) 323 404: studio flats and apartments along the coast.

Camper & Nicholsons, 31 Berkeley Street, London W1X 5FA, ✆ (0171) 491 2950. Charter yachts.

Crystal Holidays, Crystal House, Arlington Road, Surbiton KT6 6BW, ✆ (0181) 390 3335: villas in Languedoc-Roussillon and the Côte.

Dominique's Villas, 13 Park House, 140 Battersea Park Road, London SW11 4NB, ✆ (0171) 738 8772: large villas and châteaux with pools etc. in Provence and on the Côte.

French Life Holidays, 26 Church Street, Horsforth, Leeds LS18 5LG, ✆ (01532) 390 077: apartments and *gîtes* in the south of France.

French Villa Centre, 175 Selsdon Park Road, South Croydon CR2 8JJ, ✆ (0181) 651 1231: *gîtes*, *villages de vacances*, and villas near the coast and in the Var and Vaucluse.

International Chapters, 102 St. John's Wood Terrace, London NW8 6PL, ✆ (0171) 722 9560: farmhouses, *châteaux*, and villas in Provence and the Côte.

Owners Abroad, Second Floor, Astral Towers, Betts Way, Crawley RH10 2GX, ✆ (01293) 560777.

Palmer and Parker Villa Holidays, The Beacon, Penn HP10 8ND, ✆ (01494) 815 411: upmarket villas with pool.

Westbury Travel, 1 Belmont, Lansdown Road, Bath, BA1 5DZ, ✆ (01225) 44516: apartments, villas, and *gîtes* inland and by the sea.

in the USA

At Home Abroad, 405 East 56th St, New York, NY 10022, ✆ (212) 421 9165: châteaux and farmhouses, Provence and the Côte.

Hideaways International, P.O. Box 1464, Littleton, MA 01460, ✆ (508) 486 8955: farmhouses and châteaux.

Overseas Connections, 70 West 71st St, Suite 1C, New York, NY 10023, ✆ (516) 725 9303.

RAVE (Rent-a-Vacation-Everywhere), 328 East Main St, Suite 526, Rochester, NY 14604, ✆ (716) 965 0260.

Historical Outline

Fréjns

The Côte d'Azur, a part of Provence since Roman times, does not have much of a history of its own. The difficult, rocky coastline has kept big cities and dense populations away since antiquity, when this coast was little more than an rocky obstacle to mariners between Italy and the heartland of Provence. Nevertheless, tools and traces of habitation around Monaco go back as far as 1,000,000 BC, and someone was in the neighbourhood for most of the millennia that followed—southern France is one of the most ancient stamping grounds of mankind.

Milestone Events

c. **60,000** BC   Neanderthal Man turns up in the region.

c. **40,000** BC   That quarrelsome and unlovable species *Homo sapiens* appears and chases the poor Neanderthals away or kills them off.

c. **3,500** BC   Neolithic civilization arrives, with settled agriculture, stock-raising, dolmens and astronomy.

c. **1000** BC   Native Ligurian peoples of the coast begin to build fortified villages, including Nice.

c **600** BC   Arrival of the Celts and Greeks in Provence.

The Greeks were interested mainly in founding trading colonies, of which the first was Massalia (Marseille). Soon Massalia was founding colonies of its own: Nice and Hyères were among the most important. Greek influence over the indigenous peoples was strong from the start; as with everywhere else they went, they brought the vine (wild stocks were already present, but no one had worked out what to do with them) and the olive, and also their art. The Greeks on the coast and the Celts in the hinterlands sometimes fought each other, and sometimes got on well enough.

218 BC   Hannibal's army and the elephants march through Liguria on their way to Italy. Caught in the middle of the Punic Wars, Ligurians, Greeks and Celts alike discover that there are much bigger fish in the pond waiting to gobble them up.

125 BC   The Romans save Marseille from a Celtic attack.

It rapidly became clear that the aggressive republic wanted to keep Liguria and the Rhone valley for itself. The Romans reorganized the terrritory into their first 'provence' (the origin of Provence), their first conquest outside Italy. Over the next century, Provence became thoroughly integrated into the Roman world.

121 BC   First Roman road in the region, the Via Domitia, built by Domitius Ahenobarbus, the vanquisher of the Celts. The Celts were not through yet, though. Resistance continued intermittently until 14 BC; the great monument

at La Turbie, on the border of Gaul, commemorates the defeat of the last hold-outs in the Alps.

49 BC   Massalia punished by Caesar for supporting Pompey in the Roman civil wars. Thereafter, the influence of the Greek city gives way to newer, more Romanized towns, including Fréjus on the Côte.

476 AD   With the end of the Roman Empire, Provence and the Côte become part of the Visigothic Kingdom of Italy. In 535 the Franks snatch them away from the Visigoths, though they are never able to assert much control; the region drifts into *de facto* independence.

c. **700**   The Arabs begin their invasions of southern Gaul from Spain. After the Franks defeat them at Poitiers (732), Charles Martel comes down south to wreak havoc in Provence. In this dark age, the Côte d'Azur remains one of the most backward and inaccessible parts of the Mediterranean—a perfect place for pirates. Arab corsairs hold parts of the coast, including St-Tropez and the Montagne des Maures, until the 970s.

879   The Kingdom of Provence is proclaimed by a great-grandson of Charlemagne, though this is little more than a façade for feudal anarchy. Though the Kingdom was united with the Kingdom of Burgundy in 949, and formally passed to the Holy Roman Empire in 1032, the tapestry of battling barons and shifting local alliances continued without effective interference from the overlords.

1002   The first written document in the Provençal language appears.

1095   Beginning of the Crusades.

1125   The Counts of Barcelona control most of Provence south of the Durance.

1297   Francesco Grimaldi seizes Monaco for Genoa; in 1308, the Grimaldis purchase Monaco outright from Genoa (they've held on to it ever since).

1309   The 'Babylonian Captivity' begins when the Papacy installs itself in Avignon.

1388   Nice throws out its Angevin rulers and pledges allegiance to the County of Savoy.

c. 1450   The Côte attains its first artistic distinction with the Nice school of painters, creating fine altarpieces in the Renaissance manner in many of the region's churches.

1481   Upon the death of Good King René, Provence is annexed by France.

From the start, the French pursued a policy of eradicating Provence's rights and institutions, along with its language and culture. Royal guarantees of the Provençal laws and parliament were soon exposed as lies, and the region gradually came under stricter control from Paris. The 1539 Edict of Villars-Cotterets decreed French as the official language throughout the kingdom, and the work of replacing Provençal—Europe's first literary language, the language of the troubadours—was only completed by the Paris-controlled public schools in the 19th and 20th centuries.

1542   First massacres of Protestants in Provence, beginnings of the Wars of Religion.

1598   Henri IV decrees religious tolerance with the Edict of Nantes.

1696   The French briefly occupy Nice (and do it again in 1705, during the War of the Spanish Succession). The Niçois fear them: they think the French are cannibals.

1766   Cranky old Tobias Smollett's *Travels through France and Italy* puts the Côte on the map for British tourists.

1789   French Revolution begins.

Provence and the south played only a small role in what was essentially a Parisian drama. In 1792 volunteers from Marseille had brought the Marseillaise to Paris, while local mobs wrecked and looted hundreds of southern churches and châteaux. Soon, however, the betrayed south became violently counter-revolutionary. The royalists and the English occupied Toulon after a popular revolt, and were only dislodged by the brilliant tactics of a young commander named Bonaparte in 1793.

1815   Napoleon lands at Golfe-Juan from Elba to start the Hundred Days. Today the tourist offices promote the 'Route Napoléon', where Napoleon passed through —but at the time he had to sneak along those roads in an Austrian uniform, to protect himself from the Provençaux. The south never managed much enthusiasm for Napoleon or his wars. The Emperor called the Provençaux cowards, and said theirs was the only part of France that never gave him a decent regiment.

Menton

1834	Ex-Chancellor Lord Brougham 'discovers' Cannes.
1848	In Europe's year of revolutions, Menton and Roquebrune successfully revolt against the rule of the Grimaldis of Monaco.
1860	Nice and its hinterlands (now the *département* of Alpes-Maritimes) join France after a Stalin-style plebiscite. This was the price exacted by Napoleon III in 1860 for French aid to Vittorio Emanuele II in Italy's War of Independence.
1887	Minor poet and journalist Stephen Liégeard gives the Côte d'Azur its name.
1902	First Monte Carlo Rally held.

GRAND PRIX, MONACO.

After 1910, economic factors conspired against all of southern France: rural depopulation, caused by the breakup of the pre-industrial agricultural society, drained the life out of the villages—and out of the dying Provençal culture. The First World War decimated a generation—go into any village church in the south and look at the war memorial plaques; from a total population of a few hundred, you'll see maybe 30 names of villagers who died for the 'Glory of France'. By 1950, most inland villages had lost at least half their population; some died out altogether. While all this was happening, the towns and villages along the coast found new life as tourist preserves, beginning when the Côte became the centre of the international high life in the 20s .

1920	Moyenne Corniche road built.
1931	The first year the hotels on the Côte d'Azur stay open in summer.
1942	French fleet scuttled at Toulon.
1943–4	*Les Enfants du Paradis* filmed in Nice, in the midst of the German occupation.
1944	In August, American and French troops hit the beaches around St Tropez, and in a remarkably successful (and little-noticed) operation they have most of Provence liberated in two weeks. In the rugged mountains behind Nice, some bypassed German outposts hold out until the end of the war.
1946	Cannes Film Festival gets under way in earnest.
1982	Graham Greene publishes a pamphlet on organized crime on the Côte d'Azur called *J'Accuse: The Dark Side of Nice.*
1990	Under indictment for misuse of public funds, Nice mayor Jacques Médecin flees to Uruguay, advising his constituents to vote for the National Front.

The post-war era was all sweetness and ice-cream and reinforced concrete, a series of increasingly passionless snapshots: the Côte d'Azur become a myth of the masses—Grace Kelly with Cary Grant in *To Catch a Thief,* later with Rainier the Third in *Monaco,* and Brigitte Bardot showing her knickers to the paparazzi. The arrival of mass tourism put plenty of dosh in everyone's pockets while coating the fabled coast with a thick layer of villas and mimosa. The changes have in fact been momentous. The overdeveloped, often corrupt and ever more schizophrenic Côte d'Azur has become the heart of Provence—the tail that wags the dog. Besides its resorts it has the likes of IBM and the techno-paradise of Sophia-Antipolis (*see* p.108). Above all, the self-proclaimed 'California of Europe' has money, and will acquire more; in two or three decades it will be the first province in centuries to start telling Paris where to get off. Waves of Parisians and foreigners, mostly British, still come looking for the good life and a stone house to fix up (though there are no longer any of these left). They have brought life to many areas, though the traditional rural atmosphere suffers a bit. Many of the big villas that go on the market these days are purchased by wealthy Arabs.

The greatest political event has been the election of the Socialist Mitterrand government in 1981, followed by the creation of regional governments across France. Though their powers and budgets are extremely limited, this represents a major turning point, the first reversal of a thousand years of increasing Parisian centralism. Its lasting effects will not be known for decades, perhaps centuries; already the revival of the Provençal language and culture is resuming in the hinterland—English threatens to become the *lingua franca* on the coast. Politics, quietly socialist in most of the south, can still be primeval on the Med. Nice's ex-Mayor Jacques Médecin, tripped the string of his inevitable downfall with anti-semitic remarks in 1990; Jean-Marie Le Pen and his tawdry pack of adolescent bigots find their biggest following here, riding a wave of resentment against immigrants (200,000 North Africans since 1945—but this is a Provençal tradition; there were anti-Italian pogroms in Marseille and other towns in the 1870s).

Art on the Côte d'Azur

A lady once came to look at Matisse's paintings and was horrified to see a woman with a green face. 'Wouldn't it be horrible to see a woman walking down the street with a green face?' she asked him. 'It certainly would!' Matisse agreed. 'Thank God it's only a painting!'

The Côte d'Azur, thanks to its clear Mediterranean light, vibrant colour and sheer popularity as a place to live and paint in the 20th century, has played a key role in the evolution of modern art. Renoir, Picasso, Matisse and a score of other major figures were inspired to create some of their most important works here, and a fair selection of paintings, sculpture and ceramics remain in the outstanding museums and foundations which grace the coast. There's also something magical about seeing art in situ, especially art so overwhelmingly sundrenched and sensuous and full of joy—the 'realer than real' French Riviera of our collective dreams and desires.

The first blows for modern art, however, were struck back in Paris, precisely when three large canvases of everyday, contemporary scenes by Gustave Courbet got past the judges into the 1850 Paris Salon to hang among rooms of stilted, academic historical, religious and mythological subjects. Today it's hard to imagine how audacious his contemporaries found Courbet's new style, which came to be called Realism—almost as if it took the invention of photography by Louis Daguerre (1837) to make the eye see what was 'really' there. 'Do what you see, what you want, what you feel,' was Courbet's advice to his pupils. One thing Courbet felt like doing in 1854 was painting in the south, a pioneering move. The canvases he brought back to Paris startled with their bright colour and light; he anticipated all the Moderns by his emphasis on the artist's methods and techniques over subject matter.

If photography played midwife to Realism, optics had an equal part in the invention of Impressionism. In the 1860s, the revolutionary discovery that colour derives from light, not form, fired the spirits of Pissarro, Monet and company, who made it their goal to strip Courbet's new-found visual reality of all subjectivity and simply record on canvas the atmosphere, light, and colour the eye saw, all according to the latest scientific theories. Although many of the great Impressionists spent time in the south, only Renoir was to permanently relocate (to Cagnes-sur-Mer, in 1895) and then only on doctor's orders for his rheumatic arthritis.

Meanwhile, elsewhere in Provence, a Dutch admirer of the Impressionists named Vincent Van Gogh had arrived in Arles seeking the landscapes he saw in Japanese prints (one wonders a bit about his sanity from the start). The big sun of Arles in 1888 had the effect of a mystic revelation on his art, and he responded to the heightened colour and light on such an intense, personal level that colour came less and less to represent form in his art (as it did for the Impressionists), but instead took on a symbolic, emotional value, as the only medium Van Gogh found powerful enough to express his extraordinary moods and visions, as he wrote to his brother Theo: 'Instead of attempting to reproduce exactly what I have in front of my eyes, I use colour in a more arbitrary way, to express myself more forcibly.'

Van Gogh's liberation of colour from form was taken to an extreme by a group of painters that the critic Louis Vauxcelles nicknamed the Fauves ('wild beasts') for the violence of their colours. The Fauves used colour to express moods and rhythms to the detriment of detail and recognizable subject matter. As art movements go, the Fauves were a red-hot flash in the pan, lasting only from 1904 until 1908, but in those few years they revolutionized centuries of European art. 'Fauve painting is not everything,' Matisse explained. 'But it is the foundation of everything.' Nearly all the Fauves—André Derain, Matisse, Maurice Vlaminck, Raoul Dufy, Kees Van Dongen—painted in St-Tropez as guests of the hospitable painter Paul Signac. Their efforts paved the way for Expressionism, Cubism and Abstraction— avenues few of the Fauvists themselves ever explored. For after 1908 the new vision these young men had shared in the south of France vanished as if they had awoken from a mass hypnosis; all went their separate ways, leaving others to carry their ideas on to their logical conclusions. The Musée de l'Annonciade in St-Tropez has the best collection of Fauvist painting on the Côte d'Azur, although anyone lucky enough to have attended the Royal Academy's Fauve exhibition in London in 1991 will know that two-thirds of the greatest Fauves are hidden in private collections.

After the Fauves everyone went their own way. One of the leaders of the movement, Henri Matisse, settled on the Côte d'Azur after 1917, where he was generally proclaimed, with Picasso, as the greatest painter of his age. Although he was never again associated with a school, he took Fauvism to the limit, expressing himself in pure abstract colour and patterns, brimful of the luxuriant sensuality of the south. His acquaintance with Picasso dated back to 1906 (both shared a fascination with African art and masks) and when Picasso moved permanently to the Côte d'Azur in 1946 the two kept up a friendly rivalry; the Spaniard, to whom modesty was a stranger, graciously acknowledged Matisse as his equal, and in many ways his master.

The reputation of Van Gogh, Cézanne and the Fauves, and the presence of the two giants of modern art, drew scores of artists and would-be artists to the Côte d'Azur, among them Bonnard, Léger, Chagall, and de Staël. Beginning in the late 1950s, the Neo-Realist reaction to both abstract expressionism and the precious, humourless art world was reflected in the 'second' School of Nice (the first was in the Renaissance) led by multi-media iconoclasts such as Arman, César and Ben, whose works are the highlights of the Musée d'Art Contemporain in Nice. Since then, the torch of contemporary art on the Riviera has been kept alight by the Fondation Maeght in St-Paul-de-Vence, with its excellent, ever-changing exhibits of contemporary art in an idyllic setting—a place to return to, again and again.

Arman (1928–): sculptor best known for his witty combinations of junk and musical instruments, who snubbed the major exhibition of his works that inaugurated the new contemporary art museum in **Nice** to protest against anti-semitic remarks by mayor Jacques Médecin.

Bonnard, Pierre (1867–1947): although his early career is closely associated with the Nabis (a group of painters who, following Gauguin, rejected naturalism and natural colour), Bonnard changed gear in 1900 to become one of the 20th century's purest Impressionists, painting luscious, radiant colour-saturated landscapes and domestic scenes, especially after 1925 when he moved to Le Cannet, near Cannes. Always experimenting with colour and form but completely uninterested in the avant-garde, Bonnard was always popular among collectors and was one of very few foreigners admitted to the British Royal Academy (1940) (Musée de l'Annonciade, **St-Tropez**).

Bréa, Ludovico (active 1475–1544): leader of the International Gothic Nice School, influenced by the Renaissance in his later career; although commissioned to do hieratic medieval-style subjects, his precise line and beautiful sense of light and shadow stand out— still, to call him the 'Fra Angelico of Provence' like some French critics is going too far. He invented a shade of wine-red that French artists still call *rouge bréa* (Franciscan church in Cimiez, **Nice**; Palais Carnolès, **Menton**; and **Monaco** cathedral).

Chagall, Marc (1887–1985): highly individualistic Russian-Jewish painter and illustrator who drew his main themes from Jewish-Russian folklore and the Old Testament; influenced by Cubism and Orphism (the pre-First World War movement that gave intellectual Cubism a lyrical quality with colour), his art is imbued with a distinctive fairytale, imaginative quality. After spending the war years in the USA, he moved permanently to St-Paul-de-Vence in 1950, where he became interested in stained glass (Musée National Message Biblique Marc Chagall, **Nice**; Fondation Maeght, **St-Paul-de-Vence**).

Cocteau, Jean (1889–1963): poet, surrealist film director, illustrator and leader of the gay 'Villefranche band' between the wars, Cocteau was long Riviera society's arbiter of avant-garde taste. A frequent collaborator with Diaghilev, Stravinsky and Satie, his flowing draughtsmanship was inspired by his friend Picasso; when the Côte d'Azur was down on its luck in the early 1950s, he decorated the walls of the Mairie and Museum in **Menton** and the Chapelle de St-Pierre, **Villefranche-sur-Mer**, to re-create an interest in the arts and lend a new tone to the resorts.

Derain, André (1880–1954): along with Vlaminck, key Fauvist painter of extraordinary innovation and originality, who took Fauvism and Expressionism to the limit before the First World War then lapsed into more conventional academism. He designed sets and costumes for the Ballets Russes in Monaco, and is credited as the first artist in the west to take a keen interest in primitive art (Musée de l'Annonciade, **St-Tropez**).

Dufy, Raoul (1877–1953): Dufy's most original and energetic painting was as a Fauve. After flirting with Cubism with Georges Braque in L'Estaque, his style took on its characteristic graphic quality, and he spent much of his remaining life in Nice, painting pleasing lightweight decorative interiors (Musée Dufy, **Nice**).

Fragonard, Jean Honoré (1732–1806): native of Grasse and student of Boucher, Fragonard painted frivolous rococo scenes in anaemic pastels but with a verve and erotic wit that found favour with France's spiritually bankrupt nobility, who longed to escape into his canvases (Villa-Musée Fragonard, **Grasse**).

Granet, François Marius (1775–1849): native of Aix and a pupil of David; although his canvases are run-of-the-mill academic, his watercolours and sketches reveal a poetic observation of nature that became the hallmark of the Provençal school (Musée d'Art et d'Histoire, **Grasse**).

Kisling, Moïse (1891–1953): always known as Kiki, a Polish-born Jew whose painting caused a sensation in Montparnasse in 1910. Influenced by Cubism and his friends Modigliani and Chagall, he fought in the Foreign Legion in the First World War and was severely wounded, and sent to the south to die in peace. Instead he married and thrived in Villa La Baie over Bandol, becoming a feature of the Côte d'Azur, where he was famous for his good high spirits. Admired by Picasso and Braque, Kisling probably would be better known if he hadn't accepted so many commissions to paint portraits of society women, which he did with a highly personal flair, elegance and polish (Musée d'Art Moderne Méditerranéen, **Haut-de-Cagnes**).

Léger, Fernand (1881–1955): went from an early figurative manner to Cubism. Wounded in the First World War, Léger attempted to create an art that interpreted the experiences of ordinary people in war, work and play, culminating in his colourful, geometric, highly stylized figures of workers and factories. He worked in many media, especially mosaics and ceramics (Musée National Fernand Léger, **Biot**; Fondation Maeght, **St-Paul-de-Vence**).

Matisse, Henri (1869–1954): a trip to the south in the 1890s converted Matisse to luminous colours, while his first major painting and Fauve masterpiece, *Luxe, calme et volupté*, painted in St-Tropez in 1904–05, set out the main themes of his life's work: luxury, calmness and voluptuousness. After 1917 he settled in Nice, where the hot colours of the south continued to saturate his ever-sensuous, serene and boldly drawn works, qualities apparent even in the joyous paper cut-outs of dancing figures he made in his last bedridden years—his doctor, worried that the vivid intensity of the colours he chose would harm his vision, tried to make him wear dark glasses. Many art historians rate his Chapel of the Rosary in **Vence** as one of the most moving religious buildings of the 20th century (also see the Musée Matisse, **Nice** and the Musée de l'Annonciade, **St-Tropez**).

Picasso, Pablo (1881–1973): born in Málaga, Spain, the 20th century's most endlessly inventive artist is especially celebrated for his mastery of line and his great expressive power. In 1948, his blue, rose and Cubist days behind him, Picasso abandoned Paris and moved to the south of France, settling first in Vallauris, then Cannes, and finally at Mougins, where he died. 'Painting is not done to decorate apartments; it is an instrument of war against brutality and darkness.' Living on the Côte d'Azur heightened the sensuous Mediterranean and mythological aspects of his extraordinarily wide-ranging work, and, although he never stopped drawing and painting, the greatest innovations of the latter half of his career were three-dimensional, in ceramics and sculpture (Musée Picasso, **Antibes**; castle chapel at **Vallauris**).

Renoir, Pierre-Auguste (1841–1919): as serene as Van Gogh was tormented. Renoir combined Impressionism with the traditional 'gallant' themes of Fragonard, updated to the 19th century: pretty girls, dances, fêtes, children, nudes, bathers, pastorals. Racked by rheumatism, he spent his last years in Cagnes, where his career was given a new lease of life, painting warm voluptuous nudes and landscapes (Musée Renoir, **Cagnes-sur-Mer**).

Seurat, Georges (1859–91): theorist and founder of neo-Impressionism, with his technique of *pointillisme* (juxtaposing dots of pure colour to achieve a greater luminosity); although he was highly influential, none of his disciples could match his precision and vision (Musée de l'Annonciade, **St-Tropez**).

Signac, Paul (1863–1935): Georges Seurat's most faithful follower down the path of *pointillisme*. When Seurat died, Signac left Paris and discovered St-Tropez in 1892, where, influenced by the Fauves, he gradually abandoned his scientific dot theory for a freer, more attractive style that charmed and influenced the young Matisse (Musée de l'Annonciade, **St-Tropez**).

Staël, Nicolas de (1914–55): highly influential abstract painter born in St-Petersburg of noble Russian parents. He attended Fernand Léger's academy in Paris but later destroyed all his pre-war paintings in favour of his new style, a visual and sensual rather than emotive abstraction based on nature that made him on of the more appealing young leaders of the post-war movement. He moved to the Côte d'Azur in 1953 where he complained that the light was 'as nerve-racking as a pingpong ball' and committed suicide two years later (Musée Picasso, **Antibes**).

Van Dongen, Kees (1877–1968): a Fauve painter of verve and elegance, who after Fauvism became the chief chronicler of Riviera society and mores of the 1920s and 30s (Musée Chervet, **Nice**; Musée de l'Annonciade, **St-Tropez**).

Van Loo, Carle (1705–65): native of Nice and younger brother of the less successful Jean-Baptiste Van Loo, Carle was a Rococo painter in the 'grand style' and a keen rival of Boucher, painting hunting scenes, religious paintings, and designing Gobelin tapestries for the kings of France and Savoy (Musée Jules-Chéret, **Nice**).

Vuillard, Edouard (1868–1940): like his good friend Bonnard, Vuillard began as a Nabi and later became better known for his Impressionistic, intimate, domestic scenes (Musée de l'Annonciade, **St-Tropez**).

Ziem, Félix (1821–1911): started off illuminating canvases with a sense of light audacious for the period. Having found a successful formula, he repeated himself from then on. Much admired by Van Gogh, Ziem's favourite subjects were Venice and Martigues, near Marseille (Musée Jules-Chéret, **Nice**).

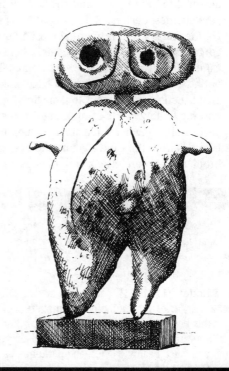

Creating the Côte d'Azur

*There was no one at Antibes this summer except me,
Zelda, the Valentinos, the Murphys, Mistinguett, Rex
Ingram, Dos Passos, Alice Terry, the Mackleishes,
Charlie Brackett, Maude Kahn, Esther Murphy,
Maquerite Namara, E. Philips Oppenheim, Mannes the
violinist, Floyd Dell, May and Crystal Eastman, ex-
Premier Orlando, Etienne de Beaumont—just a real
place to rough it, and escape from all the world.*

F. Scott Fitzgerald, in a letter to a friend

Even though in retrospect it seems inevitable that the Côte d'Azur was destined to become a hedonistic fantasyland, it owes a good deal to the personalities, desires, and imagination of its colonizers. Even from the word go, the climate, the primordial reason for its popularity, wasn't always as gorgeous as its propagandists claim. Statistics are coy, but many invalids who came here for a cure never went home ('They check in, but they don't check out' as a disgruntled resident in Nice once put it). The other striking fact about the Riviera's ascent to fame and fortune is that the locals had next to nothing to do with its creation myths: the fantasy was spun by the collective desires of strangers. Not a single person in the *dramatis personae* listed below is from the Côte d'Azur, and even the most famous native is really 'from' somewhere else: a certain Giuseppe Garibaldi.

The Cast

The story begins two hundred years ago, when the French Riviera was a beautiful, isolated, impoverished place, best known as that rather awkward corridor to Italy a traveller had to tackle after sailing down the Rhône. Two Englishmen who stopped on the way changed all that.

Tobias Smollett (1721–71): doctor and novelist unforgettably nicknamed 'Smelfungus' by Lawrence Sterne for his grumpiness, Smollett spent 1763 in Nice and three years later published his best selling *Travels through France and Italy* (with prices). He occasionally deigned to put in a good word for Nice—'the plain presents nothing but gardens...blowing in full glory, with such beauty, vigour, and perfumes, as no flower in England ever exhibited'— while at the same time dismissing the locals as slovenly and slothful, poor and withered, or cheats, thieves, and bankrupts who upped prices 30 per cent for foreigners. Seeking a cure for consumption, he shocked the Niçois by indulging in the then extraordinary practice of sea bathing, which he highly recommended, although warning, prophetically it turns out, that it would be difficult for women 'unless they laid aside all regards for decorum'. Typically, the more Smollett sniped at the Riviera, the more the British wanted to go there.

Henry Lord Brougham (1778–1868): ex-Lord Chancellor and the man who gave his name to a kind of carriage, Lord Brougham added an essential touch of class to the Riviera. It all happened through chance: because of a cholera quarantine on the Italian frontier (then just west of Nice) he was forced to spend a night in Cannes in 1834, where he found the climate he thought to find in Naples there in Napoule. Soon after he bought an estate in Cannes (now, like most big properties, divided into flats), and returned every winter, encouraging his friends to do the same so he'd have someone to talk to. He amazed the locals by planting a grass lawn. Within fifty years of his arrival, Cannes had fifty hotels and the most aristocratic reputation on the coast.

The die was cast. Thousands of tubercular Brits and elderly aristocrats poured down to the Riviera to die in the winter sun. The next chapter began in 1864, when the railway was extended from Marseille to Nice, putting the coast within reach of new kind of visitor: the tourist travelling for pleasure.

Stephen Liégeard (1830–1925): a lawyer and minor poet born into a wealthy winegrowing family in Burgundy, married to a woman who owned Les Violettes, the villa adjacent to Lord Brougham's estate, Liégeard was by all accounts a most affable and charming toady of the members of the Académie Française. They still wouldn't elect him in, and Liégeard would have been forgotten if he hadn't given the coast its name in his glowing, idolizing 1887 guidebook *La Côte d'Azur*.

Queen Victoria (1819–1901): wintered on the Riviera seven times beginning in 1887, following a trail blazed back in 1875 by her frisky son the Prince of Wales, whose high jinks in France make the current royals look almost respectable. As the mightiest ruling monarch of the day, Victoria's diminutive presence was the best advertisement that newly packaged Côte d'Azur could wish for (in gratitude Nice erected her statue in Cimiez, where she liked to stay; the Germans knocked it over but it was quickly re-erected after the war). Accompanied by her Indian servants, she was popular for passing out coins to the crowds; unlike her son she studiously avoided Monaco (in London in the 1880s there was already a society for the abolition of the Casino). Her grandson who abdicated, the Duke of Windsor, was to spend much of his life on the coast pursuing a rigorous social schedule with his American duchess.

James Gordon Bennett (1841–1918): black sheep heir to the founder of the *New York Herald*, Bennett founded the *Paris Herald* (ancestor of today's *International Herald Tribune*) in 1887 and ran it from his villa in Beaulieu, using it to advertise the coast and its visitors ('Monarchs Galore!'). Bennett was one of the millionaire rogues who set the brashy tone of the Riviera in the 1880s and 1890s; if his food arrived late at a restaurant, he would buy the restaurant.

La Belle Otero (1877–1964): like Bennett, the famous *grande horizontale* Caroline Otero profited from the presence of royalty on coast, with a list of lovers that included Tsar Nicholas II, Edward VII, and Reza Shah. A stunning Andalusian gypsy dancer and child bride of an Italian nobleman, she made her fortune in Monte-Carlo in 1901 by staking her last two louis on red at *trente-et-quarante*. Knowing nothing of the game, she thought she had lost and walked away; by the time she returned red had come up 28 times and she was wealthy beyond her wildest dreams. La Belle Otero was notorious for her rivalry with the great courtesan Liane de Pougy (once in Monte-Carlo, Otero plotted to outshine Liane by making a grand entrance, blazing with every diamond she owned; Liane got word of it and followed in a simple white gown, accompanied by her dog wearing all her fabulous carats). The shape of her breasts immortalized in the cupolas of the Carlton hotel in Cannes, Otero retired in 1922 at age 45 worth 45 million francs, but gambled it away in a few years and died impoverished in a small furnished room in Nice.

The Roaring Twenties brought the first summer visitors to the Côte d'Azur. The Americans had the most money to spend and many made fools of themselves. After 1930, however, the Great Depression forced many to stay home, and in 1936 they began to be displaced by a new kind of visitor, when the French Parliament granted all workers a two-week paid holiday and cheap train tickets to the seaside. Mass tourism was on its way.

Frank Jay Gould: America's most famous scoundrel, robber baron and stock market manipulator, was, like James Gordon Bennett, excluded from respectable society in New York, but he left his son Frank Jay a cool $22 million when he died in 1892. Frank Jay was a drunk and only marginally more appetizing than his father, and made his mark on the Côte d'Azur by acquiring even more money, by buying up the casino and building the Hôtel Provençal at Juan-les-Pins in the 1920s (getting the French army to build his roads and sewers) and by constructing the enormous Palais de la Méditerranée casino in Nice to foil his rivals. His third wife, Florence Gould, redeemed him somewhat by spending his money to become one of the most beloved and generous hostesses on the coast.

Somerset Maugham (1874–1965): the British novelist was a solid fixture of the Riviera, presiding imperially at his Villa Mauresque in St-Jean-Cap-Ferrat, where he 'lived simply' to a strict routine with 13 servants, writing in the morning and using the Riviera as a background for many of his novels (he took pride in being the last professional writer to write everything out with a fountain pen). He entertained a constant stream of celebrities—Kenneth Clark, Noel Coward and Cyril Connolly were regulars—and presided over very formal dinner parties in black tie and velvet slippers, treating his guests to his cook's secret recipe for avocado ice-cream.

Colette (1873–1954): a founding figure in St-Tropez, the only big resort on the Riviera 'discovered' by the French. (Guy de Maupassant was there first, and wrote seductively about his boat trip around the coast in *Sur l'eau*, in 1887). Colette bought a little house called La Treille Muscate in 1926, met the love of her life, Maurice Goudeket, and wrote *La Naissance du jour*, the ultimate St-Trop idyll. In 1937, a victim of her own success and tired of finding her garden full of strangers from Paris, she moved to Brittany.

Isadora Duncan (1878–1927): one of the founding mothers of modern dance, Duncan sought refuge in Nice after her children were tragically drowned in the Seine and she had separated from poet Sergei Esenin, the husband she had wed in the Russian Revolution. She opened a dance studio in Nice and was one of the most popular people on the coast. No one knew what she would say or do next, and although roly-poly, she could still enchant her audience with her unique impromptu dancing in her flowing, billowing clothes. '*Adieu, mes amis, je vais à la gloire!*' were her last words before she was driven off in a Bugatti down the Promenade des Anglais; her swirling scarf got entangled in the wheel and she died instantly of a broken neck. Although Isadora had raised funds for France during the First World War, Americans were very unpopular in France in 1927 because of the Sacco and Vanzetti case, and no one attended her funeral at Père Lachaise cemetery in Paris.

Coco Chanel (1883–1971): Isadora Duncan would have lived longer had she been dressed by Chanel. Raised in rural poverty, Gabrielle Chanel was a svelte dark beauty who got her start when her aristocratic English lover Boy Capel set her up in millinery business. She soon displayed her gift as a designer in touch with the trends as well as her astute canniness as a businesswoman. In 1916, inspired by Cubism, she changed the course of fashion by making austerity and simplicity elegant, '*le luxe dans la simplicité*' as she put it, creating well cut and understated fashions and 'little black dresses' to appeal to both her *haute couture* clients and the newly emancipated working woman. A fixture of the Riviera in the 20s, with pockets full of dukes—among them Grand Duke Dimitri of Russia and the Duke of Westminster, the wealthiest man in England—she not only confirmed the new fad for sunbathing but also a whole new style of clothing: sportswear, invented for Cocteau's ballet *Le Train Bleu*. Chanel set the fashion for short hair, sailor's caps, and costume jewellery, and became one of the first designers to put her name to a scent when she discovered a perfumer in Grasse who produced a formula for subtle, intriguing long-lasting fragrance, packaged in the classic No. 5 bottle.

Aldous Huxley (1894–1963): satirical novelist Huxley spent much of his life in Sanary near Toulon. His classic *Brave New World* (1932) was in response to the rosy ideas of H.G. Wells who lived nearby; he moved to California during the Second World War.

F. Scott Fitzgerald (1896–1940): charter members of the Lost Generation, Scott and talented wife Zelda personified the madcap recklessness and escapades that people associated with the Côte d'Azur, both devoted—doomed almost—to maintaining a continual high of hedonism. When drunk, which was nearly always, Scott would be sawing bartenders in half, tossing full ash trays at people in restaurants or shotputting ice-cream down the backs of ladies; Zelda liked to lie in front of cars or dance an impromptu pirouette half-naked in the ball room at Monte-Carlo. In 1929 Zelda suffered a nervous breakdown, diagnosed as suffering from acute schizophrenia; she never recovered.

Jean Cocteau (1889–1963): a long-time resident of Villefranche-sur-Mer, gregarious painter, poet and cineaste, promoter of avant-garde musicians and artists, and a close friend of the rich and famous. Cocteau did much to define the spirit of the Côte d'Azur in its heyday, especially in *Le Train Bleu*, a work evoking the carefree sporting life by the sea (named after the legendary streamlined luxury train that linked Paris to the coast), which he wrote for Diaghilev's *Ballets Russes*, with music by Darius Milhaud, costumes by Chanel, and sets by Picasso. He would later play no small role in making sure Cannes was chosen as the venue for France's film festival, and was a frequent member of its jury.

Cole Porter (1893–1964): Porter began his career as America's best loved composer of subtle melodies and sophisticated lyrics before the First World War, when he enlisted in the French Foreign Legion and later in the French army. In Paris in the 20s, he was commissioned by Winnaretta, Princesse de Polignac and daughter of Isaac 'Sewing Machine' Singer to write a jazz ballet called *Within the Quota* ; he hung around Paris, longing to study with Stravinsky. In the summer of 1922 he rented the Château de la Garoupe in Cap d'Antibes, invited his friends down from Paris, and convinced them that summer on the Riviera was the place to be, where, as his later musical put it, *Anything Goes*.

Katherine Mansfield (1888–1923): master of the ironic, sensitive short story and married to John Middleton Murry, Mansfield spent the last five years of her life trying to find a cure for her tuberculosis, spending a good deal of time in Menton. Her letters to her husband and short stories offer an evocative view of the coast at the time.

D.H. Lawrence (1885–1930), another victim of tuberculosis and friend of Mansfield, was only 45 when after a life of wanderings he died in Vence, dismayed by what the 'vileness of man' had wrecked on the lovely coast, but commenting on the Mediterranean in a letter shortly before he died: 'It still seems as young as Odysseus, in the morning.' Another towering figure of English literature to topple on the coast was Yeats, who died at Cap Martin in 1939 and was buried at Roquebrune, where rumour has it part or all of him still remains–when his relics were transferred to Ireland they got the wrong stiff. Other Irishmen who found muses on the Côte d'Azur included Joyce, who claimed Nice was the first inspiration for his *Finnegans Wake* and film director Rex Ingram, who shot *The Four Horsemen of the Apocalypse* in Nice, based on the novel by Blasco Ibáñez, who lived in Menton.

After the War, French glumness infected even the coast, even though (with the exception of Toulon) it had escaped relatively intact. Even property prices were depressed. But it wasn't long before a new transfusion of glitter arrived and the joint was jumping all over again, although much of what was seemed glamorous and care-free was now more calculated; the new movers and shakers included the likes of Greek shipping tycoons Aristotle Onassis and Stavros Niarchos and arms dealer Adnan Kashoggi.

Grace Kelly (1929–82): Monaco Inc. was approaching bankruptcy in 1955 and Aristotle Onassis, the majority stockholder in the Societé des Bains de Mer, was manoeuvring to pull all the principality's purse strings. Prince Rainier III thwarted him by issuing more stock and marrying a glamorous American movie actress. Rita Hayworth was already spoken for: she had been living in the Château de l'Horizon in Vallauris 1947 when she married Aly Khan, son of the Aga Khan. Rainier auditioned Marilyn Monroe for the part, but Grace Kelly won the role and the dazzling society marriage that made the daughter of a Philadelphia brick magnate into a Riviera princess took place in 1956. Perhaps appropriately enough for the star of *To Catch a Thief*, the bride's mother was robbed of her jewels after the ceremony. Monaco hasn't been in the red since.

Graham Greene (1904–91): in 1966 Greene moved to Antibes, where he wrote his his auto-biographical *A Sort of Life* and *Ways of Escape*. In 1982 in righteous anger he published a booklet called *J'Accuse: The Dark Side of Nice*, lambasting the organized crime and corrup-tion that mayor Jacques Médecin's political machine turned a blind eye to or abetted; it was and still is banned in Nice. Other writers who lived in Antibes after the war include Nikos Kazantzakis and Roland Barthes; Monaco was long the address of the English-born poet of the Yukon, Robert Service (who wrote an ode in honour of Princess Grace's wedding) and Anthony Burgess; French novelist Patrick Modiano favours Nice (his *Les Dimanches d'été* about Nice, and *Voyages de Noces* about Jews taking refuge in the south during the war).

Brigitte Bardot (1934–): ever since she came down with Roger Vadim to St-Tropez to film *Et Dieu créa la femme* in 1956 Bardot has personified the myth of its free, sensuous spirit. A longtime resident of the village, married in the 80s to an extreme right wing politician, she now devotes her energy and formidable publicity machine to animal rights.

Dirk Bogarde (1920–): British screen star and increasingly respected writer, Bogarde lived for many years in a villa near Grasse. His films include the at-the-time controversial *The Servant* (1963) and *Death in Venice* (1970).

What new kind of Côte d'Azur, if any, may be wrought by its new glitterati—such famous names as Elton John, Luciano Pavarotti, Claudia Schiffer, Boris Becker and Joan Collins—still waits to be seen. One thing is certain, at least: property prices won't go down any time soon. Buy that dream villa now.

The Three Corniches

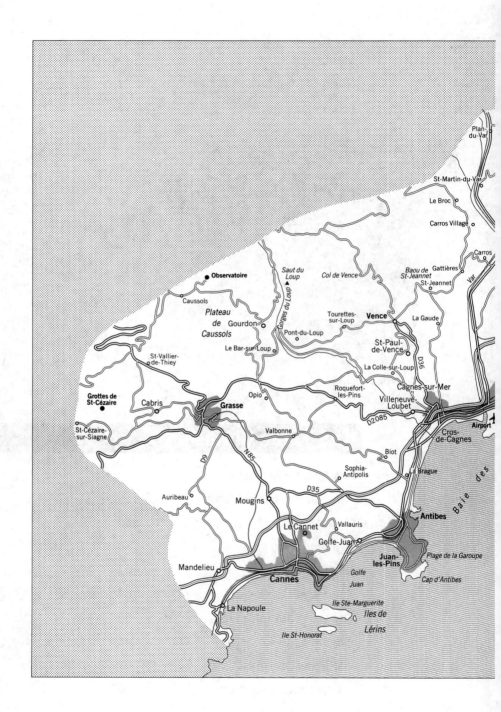

Plan-
du-Var

St-Martin-du-Var

Le Broc

Carros Village

Carros

Observatoire

Saut du
Loup

Col de Vence

Gattières

Baou de
St-Jeannet

St-Jeannet

Caussols

Plateau
de Gourdon
Caussols

Tourettes-
sur-Loup

Vence

La Gaude

Var

Gorges du Loup

Pont-du-Loup

St-Paul-
de-Vence

Le Bar-sur-Loup

St-Vallier-
de-Thiey

La Colle-sur-Loup

D36

Grottes de
St-Cézaire

Cabris

Opio

Roquefort-
les-Pins

Cagnes-sur-Mer

Grasse

Villeneuve-
Loubet

St-Cézaire-
sur-Siagne

Valbonne

D2.085

Airport

Cros-
de-Cagnes

Biot

D9

N85

Sophia-
Antipolis

Brague

Baie des

Auribeau

D35

Mougins

Le Cannet

Vallauris

Antibes

Golfe-Juan

Plage de la Garoupe

Mandelieu

Juan-
les-Pins

Cannes

Golfe
Juan

Cap d'Antibes

La Napoule

Ile Ste-Marguerite

Iles de
Lérins

Ile St-Honorat

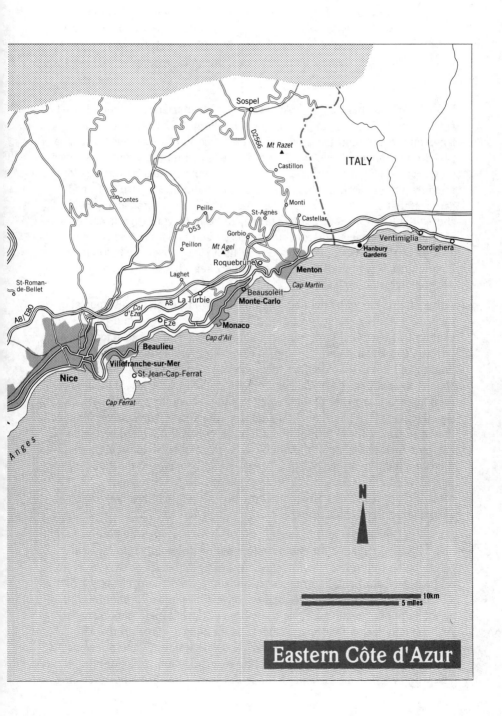

Sospel

D2566

Mt Razet ▲

Castillon

ITALY

Contes

Peille

St-Agnès

Monti

D53

Gorbio

Castellar

Peillon

Mt Agel ▲

Roquebrune

Ventimiglia

Hanbury
Gardens

Bordighera

Laghet

Menton

St-Roman-
de-Bellet

Cap Martin

Col
d'Eze

A8

La Turbie

Beausoleil

Monte-Carlo

A8/580

Eze

Monaco

Cap d'Ail

Beaulieu

Cap Ferrat

Villefranche-sur-Mer

St-Jean-Cap-Ferrat

Nice

Cap Ferrat

Anges

N

10km
5 miles

Eastern Côte d'Azur

A calcined, scalped, rasped, scraped, flayed, broiled, powdered, leprous, blotched, mangy, grimy, parboiled, country, without trees, water, grass, fields—with blank, beastly, senseless olives and orange-trees like a mad cabbage gone indigestible.

Swinburne

Just west of Italy begins that 20km swathe of Mediterranean hyperbole that represents the favourite mental image of the French Riviera, where the landscapes are at their most vertical and oranges and lemons ripen against a backdrop of snow-topped Alps. Menton, where Swinburne's senseless olives grow, is a perfect little sun-trap, rivalled only by Beaulieu a bit further along, the only place in France where bananas ripen naturally. Superb villas and gardens, that once belonged to dukes and kings, are scattered along the shore of St-Jean-Cap-Ferrat, Roquebrune, and Cap Martin. High in the mountains hang spectacular medieval villages and La Turbie, the trophy erected by the Romans to celebrate their final victory over the indomitable Ligurian tribes who until then had effectively kept the Empire from the sweet delights of Provence.

Although first tamed by the Romans, this easternmost and tastiest morsel of the Côte d'Azur long remained a world apart, ruled until the mid-19th century by the Grimaldis of Monaco, and noted above all for its lemons and poverty. Bad feelings with the French over Napoleon brought the first English and Russians, with their titles and weak lungs, to winter here, in spite of the difficult roads. They built hotels, villas and casinos in the grand, fulsome rococo spa style of the period, and to this day the spirit lingers, a slightly musty violet perfume in a semi-tropical climate. Ian Fleming summed up the bygone spirit in writing about the fate of Monaco, where high class has gone high rise: 'Part of the trouble with the Monte-Carlo rooms is that they were built in an age of elegance for elegant people, and the gambling nowadays has the drabness of a Strauss operetta played in modern dress...what used to be pastime has now become a rather deadly business of amassing tax-free capital gains.'

If most of the old glamour has faded, the scenery is as breathtaking as ever, one mighty mountain after another plummeting drunkenly into the sea, traced by hairpinning *corniche* roads zigzagging on ledges over vertiginous drops. Here continental hormones tradionally go into overdrive as the rich and famous in dark glasses race sporty convertibles down to 'Monte', although not so much to gamble these days as to visit their bank manager. And the only racing that really happens is the Monaco Grand Prix. The traffic is nearly always slow and heavy—a fact that doesn't prevent some would-be James Bonds from contributing to an appalling accident rate. The worst traffic jams inch along the lowest road, the **Corniche Inférieure**

(N98) through the seaside resorts; most of the frequent buses that ply the coast use this road, which runs parallel to the railway. To relieve the traffic, already choking in the 1920s, the most dramatic of the roads, the **Moyenne Corniche** (N7) was drilled through the rock and hung sheerly through the hills—which makes it the favourite for car chase scenes. Higher up, along the route of the Roman Via Aurelia (also called Via Julia Appia), Napoleon built the **Grande Corniche** (D 2564) with the most panoramic views of all.

Beaches

The beaches of the eastern Riviera are not renowned for their beauty. The shore is rocky—beaches are shingle, or in some cases artificial pebble. Lack of sand is more than compensated for by the spectacular settings of many beaches, backed by 200m cliffs, palm trees and some of the world's most expensive real estate.

best beaches

Monaco: chic and sharp; safe swimming.

Beaulieu (Plage des Fourmis): backed by palms, view across to Cap Ferrat.

Villefranche-sur-Mer: the trendiest beach in the region.

St-Jean-Cap-Ferrat (Plage du Passable): views to Villefranche.

Menton

The Côte d'Azur starts halfway between the fleshpots of Paris and Rome at Menton, right on the Italian frontier. Its history begins here as well, with the earliest traces of Riviera humans—folk who a million years ago already had the good sense to settle where a wall of mountains, still crowned with snow in April, blocks out the cold so that lemons can blossom all year.

Despite this early start, the Menton area wasn't inhabited again until the 10th century, when settlers clustered around the Annonciade hill, where they felt safe from Saracen pirates. The town first belonged to the Counts of Ventimiglia—little better than pirates themselves—then briefly joined Provence before it was sold to Charles Grimaldi of Monaco in 1346. The Grimaldis became rich from taxing Menton's citrus fruit up to 1848, when the town and its neighbour Roquebrune declared their independence. Unlike most of the revolts in Europe that fateful year, this puny one succeeded, and the Free Towns of Menton and Roquebrune endured until 1860, when the people voted to unite with France, and Charles III of Monaco sold his claim on the towns to Napoleon III for four million gold francs. The following year a Dr J. Henry Bennet wrote *Mentone and the Riviera as a Winter Climate*, a book that soon attracted a community of 5000 Brits, led by Queen Victoria herself in 1883. In the Second World War, the Germans wrecked Menton's port, and, when they were chased out, lobbed bombs on to it from the Italian side of the border. The damage wasn't repaired until 1956.

Nattering nabobs of negativism claim Menton has a poor beach (true) and as much atmosphere as your grandmother's antimacassar, where 30 per cent of the population are retirees (the highest percentage in France) and most of the rest are miniature poodles. On the other hand, Menton is one of the prettiest towns on the coast, magnificently situated, low on craft shops but high on relaxation compared to the hard-edged glamour-pusses to the west.

Getting There
by rail

The *Métrazur* trains that run between St-Raphaël and Ventimiglia, and all others running between Nice and Italy, stop in Menton (Menton-Centre) ✆ 93 87 50 50, Rue de la Gare. There's also a stop—Menton-Garavan—behind the port.

by bus

Buses depart from the Esplanade du Careï, between the two avenues north of the train station, every half-hour to Nice, by way of Roquebrune-Cap-Martin and Monte-Carlo. Others will take you to Ventimiglia. There are three buses daily to Castillon and Sospel, while Transports Breuleux ✆ 93 35 73 51, in Rue Masséna (near the station), have similar daily services to St-Agnès, Gorbio, and Castellar. All local Menton bus-lines pass by Esplanade du Careï.

Tourist Information

Palais de l'Europe, 8 Av. Boyer, ✆ 93 57 57 00, fax 93 57 57 00; also at the coach station, on the Esplanade du Careï, ✆ 93 28 43 27.

Post office: ✆ 93 28 64 84, on the corner of Cours George V and Rue Edouard VII.

market days

Daily, opposite the Cocteau Museum, in a pretty building with ceramic decorations; flea market on Friday.

Jean Cocteau, Love, and Lemons

Menton is squeezed between the mountains and a pair of shingle-beached bays: on the Italian side, the **Baie de Garavan**, where villas and gardens overlook the yacht harbour, while the **Baie du Soleil** (the Roman *Pacis Sinus* or Gulf of Peace) stretches 3km west to Cap Martin. In between these two bays stands a little 17th-century harbour bastion that Jean Cocteau converted into the **Musée Cocteau** ✆ 93 57 72 30 to hold his playful series of *Animaux Fantastiques*, a tapestry of *Judith et Holopherne*, while the happier love affairs of the Mentonnais are portrayed in the *Innamorati* series, also on display (*open 10–1 and 2–6 summer, 10–12 and 2–6pm winter; adm free*).

This theme of Menton's lovers was first explored by Cocteau in his decorations for the 1957 **Salle des Mariages** ✆ 92 10 50 29 (*open 9.30–12.30 and 1.30–4.30pm, closed Sat and Sun*), in the **Hôtel de Ville**, five minutes' walk away in Rue de la République. A lemon-picker weds a fisherman amid rather discouraging mythological allusions: on the right wall there's a wedding-party in Saracen costume, referring to the Mentonnais' Saracen blood, although amongst the company we see the bride's frowning mother, the groom's jilted girlfriend and her armed brother. The other wall shows Orpheus turning back to see if his beloved Eurydice is following him out of hell, condemning her to return there forever; while on the ceiling Love, Poetry (mounted on Pegasus) and Science (juggling planets) look on. Love was also a favourite theme of the original Riviera inhabitants, who carved the little Cro-Magnon Venuses now housed in the **Musée de Préhistoire Régionale**, Rue Loredan Larchey, ☎ 93 35 84 64 (*open 10–1 and 2–6 summer, 10–12 and 2–6 winter, closed Tues; adm free*). Dioramas recreate the area's cave interiors from the time when the furry animals people lived among were mammoths instead of poodles, but the star exhibit is the 30,000-year-old skull of Menton Man (found just over the border in Grimaldi) buried in a bonnet of seashells and deer teeth, long since calcified into the bone; note, too, rock carvings from the Vallée des Merveilles, high above Menton in the Roya valley of the Alpes-Maritimes.

The 1909 **Palais d'Europe** was once the casino, but is now an exhibition hall and the tourist office. In front of it is the exotic **Jardin Biovès**, the most tidied, kempt, combed and swept bit of green space you're ever likely to come across, where the elderly sit in sunshine in beige and grey to match their poodles, glumly watching life pass them by. Here the fantastical lemon-studded floats of Menton's *Fête du Citron* are parked at carnival time. A kilometre west, the summer home of the princes of Monaco, the **Palais Carnolès** (1717), is now an art museum, the **Musée des Beaux-Arts du Palais Carnolès**, Av. de la Madone, ☎ 93 35 49 71, bus 3 (*open same hours as the prehistory museum*). It holds a Byzantine-inspired *Virgin and Child* from 13th-century Tuscany, Ludovico Bréa's luminous *Madonna and Child with St Francis*, and all the previous winners from Menton's very own Biennale of painting, some of which are so awful you can only wonder what the losers were like. Other works were donated by the English landscape and portrait artist Graham Sutherland, who lived part of every year in Menton from 1947 until he died in 1980.

The Vieille Ville, and the Gardens of Garavan

The tall, narrow 17th-century houses of Menton's Vieille Ville are reminiscent of the old quarter of Genoa, knitted together by anti-earthquake arches that span stepped lanes named after old pirate captains and saints. It's hard to believe that the quiet main street, **Rue Longue**

Menton

(the Roman Via Julia Augusta), was, until the 19th century, the main route between France and Italy. According to legend, the lady at the Palais Princier (at No.123) received a secret nocturnal visit from Casanova, who crept in through the sewers.

From Rue Longue a ramp leads up to the *parvis* of the ice-cream-coloured church of **St-Michel** (1675), and its equally charming Baroque neighbour, the **Chapelle des Pénitents Blancs**, headquarters of one of the old Riviera's many religious confraternities (*see* **Nice**). The *parvis* itself has a pebble mosaic of the Grimaldi arms, used as the setting for Menton's megastar chamber music festival in August.

The Montée du Souvenir leads to the top of the Vieille Ville, where the citadel was replaced in the 19th century by the romantic, panoramic **Cimetière du Vieux Château**, curiously unmarked on the tourist map, but just a quick steep haul up from those sitting out their last years below; as if a foretaste of death, it's the one place in Menton where they can't bring their poodles. Guy de Maupassant called it the most aristocratic cemetery in Europe— the venerable names inscribed on the hierachical array of ornate tombs and little pavilions include William Webb-Ellis, the 'inventor of rugby'. Many were consumptives in their teens and twenties who, like Aubrey Beardsley, only came to Menton to die.

From the cemetery, Boulevard de Garavan leads into the neighbourhood where this dead élite would reside if they were alive today, and to the **Jardin Botanique** ✆ 93 35 86 72, planted with 700 species from around the world (*open 10–12.30 and 3–6 summer, 10–12.30 and 2–5 winter; adm*). One road off the boulevard, Av. Blasco-Ibañez, was named after the author of *The Four Horsemen of the Apocalypse* (1867–1928) who lived here in the **Villa Fontana Rosa** and decorated his garden with colourful ceramic tiles from his native Valencia; but now the house is private and it is not easy to sneak a discreet peek. **Villa Isola Bella**, on the other side of the Garavan station, was the home of another victim of tuberculosis, Katherine Mansfield (1888–1923); although ailing she was happy here, and fictionalized her experiences in a number of short stories.

To the north of Boulevard de Garavan the romantic **Jardin des Colombières**, the 40-year project of French artist and writer Ferdinand Bac (1859–1952), the flamboyant illegitimate son of Napoleon III, is unfortunately now closed.

Menton ✉ *06500*   **Where to Stay**

All but one of Menton's once grand hotels are now converted into flats, and no sparkling new ones have been built to take up the slack. If you've got the readies, the one still grand hotel is the ★★★★**Hôtel des Ambassadeurs**, 3 Rue Partouneaux, ✆ 93 28 75 75, ✉ 93 35 62 32, phoenix-new; gracious, spacious, pink and balconied, and slap bang in the middle of town. There's nearly every luxury you'd expect for the price, but no swimming pool. *Open all year.* The ★★★**Napoléon**, 29 Porte de France, ✆ 93 35 89 50, ✉ 93 35 49 22, has a heated pool covered in the winter and soundproofed, air-conditioned rooms. *Closed Nov.* The popular ★★**Le Magali**, 10 Rue Villarey, ✆ 93 35 73 78, ✉ 93 57 05 04, fills up quickly, so reserve for a room with balcony overlooking the garden. *Open all year.* Elsewhere try ★★**Claridge's**, 39 Av. de Verdun, ✆ 93 35 72 53, ✉ 93 35 42 90, or the more welcoming ★★**Bristol**, 24 Av. Carnot, ✆ 93 57 54 32, ✉ 93 28 12 62, with high ceilings and seafront rooms (cheaper ones are at the back). *Closed Nov.* Good bargains include ★**Pension Beauregard**, 10 Rue Albert Ier, ✆ 93 35 74 08, below the station, a sweet place with a quiet garden, *closed Nov*, and **★Magenta**, 8 bis Rue Guyau, ✆ 93 35 85 71, not on the sea, with ageing musty rooms but a garden terrace under the palms. *Closed Nov.*

Menton ✉ *06500*   **Eating Out**

For posh nosh, there's **La Veranda** at the Ambassadeurs (*see* above). Otherwise Menton is gastronomically a humble place. All along Rue St Michel masses of restaurants vie for your attention with tempting displays of hot pastries and baguettes spilling out into the street at lunchtime that somehow miss the mark. At No.28, try the *cassolette de rascasse* at **Le Chaudron**, ✆ 93 35 90 25, with its copious 148F menu. You'll do better between the marketplace and the sea, opposite the Musée Cocteau in the bright blue **Le Nautic**, ✆ 93 35 78 74, at 27 Quai de Monléon, serving up every possible fish dish, including *bouillabaisse*. Up at Monti, on the Rte de Sospel, the panoramic **Pierrot-Pierrette**, ✆ 93 35 79 76, complements the views with delicious fresh blue trout (133F). *Closed Mon, and evenings in winter.*

Menton ✉ *06500*   **Entertainment and Nightlife**

Menton isn't exactly a hopping place, but just in case check the Menton page in *Nice-Matin* or the glossy brochure published by the tourist office every three months. The young grumble that there's nothing to do, and head west to Monaco for nightlife; **Le Casino** with its disco **Le Brummell** (both ✆ 92 10 16 16) are disdained as a tourist ghettos. Classical music concerts take place at the **Eglise St-Michel**, especially in August during the **chamber music festival**. If you've brought the kids there's mini-golf, go-karting etc at **Koaland**, 5 Av. de la Madone, ✆ 92 10 00 40; alternatively, catch a boat from the old port for a *promenade en mer* to the Iles de Lérins, La Corniche d'Or and St Tropez, ✆ 92 10 32 57. Once in a while an undubbed film is shown on one of the three screens at the air conditioned **Eden**, 11 Rue de la République, ✆ 36 68 31 23.

North of Menton

Four narrow mountain valleys converge at Menton, the villages hanging over their slopes, linked by bus from Menton and to each other by mule-tracks. Above the easternmost valley is **Castellar** (7km from Menton), laid out on a grid plan in 1435 to replace the original 1258 village, built by the counts of Ventimiglia high on a rocky peg. An hour's hike will take you to the ghostly ruins of old Castellar; or take the less strenuous walk up the Sospel road as far as the waterfall at the **Gourg de l'Oura**. Up the second valley, the Val du Careï, the medieval monastery of **L'Annonciade** (5.5km from Menton) has gone through countless transformations over the years; best of all are its grand views and its ex votos dating back to the 1600s, including an unusual one—a piece of a zeppelin. Further up the Val du Careï, amid the viaducts of the old Menton-Sospel railway, you can wander through the scented **Forêt de Monti**, then continue up to **Castillon**, awaft with the scent of fresh concrete and artisan shops, well into its third incarnation as 'the most beautiful new village in France' after being flattened by an earthquake in 1887 and bombed in 1944.

From Menton the narrow, winding D22 noodles up to **Ste-Agnès**, at 650m the loftiest village on the entire coast. There are 3 buses a day from Menton (9.50am, 2.10pm and 4.35pm), or drive up, passing under and over the mighty viaducts of the A8, which look as insubstantial as spider's legs once you reach Ste-Agnès. The village was founded in the 900s, they say, by a Saracen who fell in love with a local girl and converted to Christianity for her sake. It certainly looks old enough—a crazy quilt of vaulted passageways and tiny squares that have unfortunately succumbed to trinketshopitis. When you can't look at another smirking *santon*, head up Rue Longue for a view that stretches to Corsica on a clear day. Come down at dusk if you can—it's the only safe way to see if anything's coming round those cliff face bends, and there's the added bonus of watching Menton light up for the evening far, far below. On foot, a path descends from Ste-Agnès to Menton in two hours, or better still, take the one-hour shortcut called the *Balcon de la Côte d'Azur* to **Gorbio** (from Menton it's 8km). Gorbio is just as picturesquely medieval as Ste-Agnès but has somehow been spared the trinkets. The best time to visit is at *Fête Dieu* (Corpus Christi) in June, when the village maintains a medieval rite called the *Procession dai limaça* when its lanes are lit by thousands of flickering lamps made from snail shells filled with olive oil, set in beds of sand.

A Dip into Italy

Just over the border, in the village of Grimaldi, the beachside **Balzi Rossi** (red caves) were the centre of a sophisticated Neanderthal society that flourished *c.* 100,000 to 40,000 BC and produced some of Europe's first art, displayed in the **Museo Preistorico** (*museum and caves open 9am–1pm and 2.30–7.30pm, closed Mon; adm*). The town of Ventimiglia has a large **market** every Friday. Also, outside Ventimiglia at Mortola Inferiore, you can visit the extraordinary **Hanbury Gardens**, a botanical paradise of acclimatized plants from around the world, founded in 1867 by Sir Thomas Hanbury (*open 10am–4pm, closed Wed; adm*). If you plan to go deeper into Italy, you can save literally thousands of lire by filling up with petrol in Menton (that's what all those Italians are doing); if you're popping over to splurge on an excellent Italian meal, it's only 12km to Bordighera and the lovely art nouveau La Via Romana, Via Romana 57 (✆ (0184) 26 66 81.

✉ *06500*   ***Where to Stay and Eating Out***

Castellar

The only place in Castellar to sleep and eat is the tranquil ★**Les Alpes**, Place Clemenceau, ✆ 93 35 82 83, with tidy little rooms and good food. *Open all year.*

Castillon

Or you can go upmarket in **Castillon** at the ★★★**Bergerie**, ✆ 93 04 00 39, 📠 93 28 02 91, with rustic but very comfortable rooms and more elaborate food. *Closed Nov.* There's also **Le St Julien** ✆ 93 04 18 04, in the Place de l'Eglise, for a traditional if unspectacular meal.

Ste-Agnès

There's **Le Saint-Yves**, ✆ 93 35 91 45, for sweet dreams, dreamy views and most notably, courtesy. *Closed mid-Oct–mid-Nov.* From April to November, ★**La Vieille**

Auberge, ✆ 93 35 92 02, is just before the entrance to the village, with a delightful garden. Full board is mandatory, but if you're not staying you can still stop by for a gargantuan feast. *Open April–Nov*. There's another warm welcome and good dining at **Le Logis Sarrasin** ✆ 93 35 86 89, offering 6 courses, including delicious *raviolis maison*; menus start at 87F. *Open all year, closed Mon*.

The Grande Corniche

Roquebrune-Cap-Martin

Nearly every potential building site in the lush mountain shore between Menton and Monaco is occupied by Roquebrune-Cap-Martin—from old Roquebrune just beside the Grande Corniche down to the exclusive garden cape of Cap Martin. Purchased by the Grimaldis in 1355 for 1000 florins, Roquebrune (like Menton) later revolted against Monaco and became a free town until joining France in 1861. The medieval village is all steep, winding, arcaded streets and over-restored houses, culminating at the top in the **Château** (*open 10am–12pm and 2–6pm, closed Fri*), with the oldest surviving *donjon* in France, erected in the 10th century by the Counts of Ventimiglia against the Saracen threat. In the 1400s, Lambert of Monaco built much of what stands today; in 1911, Sir William Ingram purchased the castle, planted the mock medieval *tour anglaise* by the gate, and donated both to the town in 1921. The antique-furnished rooms in the 3.5m thick walls are surprisingly poky—most people have bathrooms bigger than this lordling's reception hall. But the view from the top floor is huge enough for any ego. The castle guards lived below the castle in picturesque **Rue Moncollet**, carved out of the living rock; another street under the castle, Rue du Château, leads to Rue de la Fontaine and Chemin de St-Roch and a remarkable contemporary of the castle: a **1000-year-old olive tree** measuring 10m in circumference.

In 1467, as plague decimated the coastal population, the Roquebrunois vowed to the Virgin that if they were spared they would, in thanksgiving, annually re-enact tableaux of the Passion. The Virgin apparently thought it was a good deal, and the villagers have faithfully kept their side of the pact every year on 5 August. The best of the 500 roles involved in the colourful processions are jealously 'owned' by the oldest families, who pass them down to their descendants like heirlooms.

Cap Martin

In the 1890s a pair of empresses, Eugénie of France (widow of Napoleon III) and Elisabeth ('Sissi') of Austria, made Roquebrune's little peninsula of Cap Martin an aristocratic enclave, 'whispering of old kings come here to dine or die', as F. Scott Fitzgerald wrote. Churchill did the dining and Yeats, King Nikola of Montenegro and Le Corbusier the dying, the latter succumbing to a heart attack in 1965 while swimming off the white rocks beside what is now **Promenade Le Corbusier**—a lovely walk around the cape, past villas immersed in luxuriant pines, olives, cypresses and mimosas. Corby had been staying in one of villas, one of the most beautiful on the Côte d'Azur, built in 1929 by furniture designer Eileen Gray; the story goes that he loved the house so much that he got a wealthy friend to buy it an auction, helping him defeat the higher bids of Aristotle Onassis by dragging the auctioneer off at a crucial moment.

Another spectacular path leads in an hour and a half from Cap Martin to Monte-Carlo Beach. If you walk it, look back towards the Cap to see the ruined tower of the long-gone convent of

St-Martin. When it was built, the men of Roquebrune had vowed to protect the nuns from pirates, and one night in the late 1300s the tower's bell sounded the alarm; the Roquebrunois piled out of bed and ran down the hill to defend the good sisters, who laughingly confessed that they were just testing the bell's efficiency. A few nights later, pirates really did appear, and although the nuns rang like mad, their defenders only rolled over in bed. Next morning in the smouldering ruins, the older nuns were found with their throats slit, while the prettier ones were carted off to the slave markets of Barbary.

✉ 06190   *Where to Stay and Eating Out*

Affordable hotels are scarce along the **Corniches**, but if money's no object there's the ★★★★**Vista Palace**, ✆ 92 10 40 00, ✆ 93 35 18 94, the ultimate in luxury, hanging on a 305m cliff along the Grande Corniche, with a God's-eye view over Monaco straight below. Its leisure centre includes a heated pool, squash, gym, and sauna. Down on the poor sinners' level, the ★★**Westminster**, 14 Av. Louis-Laurens, ✆ 93 35 00 68, ✆ 93 28 88 50, has a pretty garden terrace near the junction of the lower and middle Corniches. *Closed Dec and Jan.*

Near **Roquebrune's** castle, in a former sheepfold cut into the rock, **Au Grand Inquisiteur**, 18 Rue du Château, ✆ 93 35 05 37, offers well-prepared Provençal dishes like *pieds et paquets* (menus at 145F and 215F). A cheaper troglodyte choice, **La Grotte**, Place des Deux-Frères, ✆ 93 35 00 04, also has tables outside at the entrance to the Vieille Ville in Roquebrune, and offers a 55F *plat du jour* and bargain menus. The well situated **Deux Frères** ✆ 93 28 99 00, with a terrace overlooking Monaco, has impressive menus at impressive prices, only *à la carte. Closed Thurs, and Fri midday, also mid Nov–mid Dec.*

Monaco

In 1297, an ambitious member of Genoa's Guelph party named Francesco Grimaldi the Spiteful dressed up like a friar and knocked at the door of the Ghibelline fortress at Monaco, asking for hospitality. The soldiers sleepily admitted him; the phoney friar pulled a knife from his robe, killed the soldiers, and let in his men. Although Francesco was the first Grimaldi to get into Monaco, the family only became lords of their rock when they purchased it outright from Genoa in 1308. They were once rulers of a mini-empire including Antibes and Menton, but the ambitions of others have reduced the Grimaldis' sovereign Ruritania to a sea-hugging 194 hectares (slightly larger than half of Central Park) under the looming mountain, Tête de Chien. Here Rainier III presides as the living representative of the oldest ruling family in Europe, and Europe's last constitutional autocrat.

For centuries the Grimaldis' main income came from a tax levied on Menton's lemons and olives, and when Menton revolted in 1848 they faced bankruptcy; Monaco was the poorest state in all Europe. In desperation, Prince Charles III looked for inspiration to the Duke of Baden-Baden, whose casino lured Europe's big-spending aristocrats every summer. Monaco, Charles decided, would be the winter Baden-Baden, and he founded the *Société des Bains de Mer* (SBM) to operate a casino and tourist industry, with the Principality as the chief share-holder. The casino was built on a rock that the prince named Monte-Carlo after himself, and he hired François Blanc, the talented French manager of the Homburg Baden casino, to create a gambling city to order, 10 per cent of all profits going to the crown. Blanc was one of the most successful financiers of the day, and he proved his worth. He loaned the French government nearly 5 million francs for the completion of Napoleon III's centrepiece, the Paris Opera, and in return assured that the French built a new railway from Nice in 1868. With transport to bring in the punters, the money poured by the bushel; in 1870 the coffers were so full that Charles abolished direct taxation in Monaco, a state of affairs that endures to this day.

'Why go to Monte-Carlo, if not to lose?' wrote the legendary Riviera courtesan, the Belle Otero. Karl Marx visited and thought it the perfect setting for a comic opera; Harpo Marx wore a black sock around his neck instead of a tie, lost 1000F then got himself thrown out for asking in a very loud voice the way to the famous cliff where losers were supposed to commit suicide. But gone are those fond days when the Monégasques could live entirely off the folly of others. France and Italy legalized gaming in 1933, ending the Principality's monopoly; the proportion of its revenue that Monaco gleans from the tables has declined from 95 per cent to a mere 4 per cent. But under Rainier III and the omnipresent SBM, Monaco has found new ways to keep its 6000 citizens and 30,000 residents from paying income tax, especially in 'offshore' banking (some 40 do business here), in the media (Télé and Radio Monte-Carlo), and 'business tourism' (the construction of Monte-Carlo's new ultra-modern congress hall). Foolish gambling pales before the deadly sin of greed: 'The promise of a penthouse, a place to park their Mercedes, and they'll sign away anything,' sighed an elderly Monégasque to *The Riviera Reporter.*

Life in an On-shore La-la Land

Here in Monte-Carlo, where you have to take amusement seriously, there is not much to laugh at.

Anthony Burgess, in *The Observer* (1978)

Big time tax-dodgers agree: it's hard to beat Monaco for comfort and convenience when the time comes to snuggle down with your piggy chips. Unlike most other tax havens, the Principality is not an island, so you can purr over to France or Italy in the Lamborghini in only a few minutes. The grub is pretty good, you can flaunt your jewels in immaculately clean streets and there's enough culture to keep you from feeling a total Philistine; beggars, the homeless and other riff-raff who might trouble your conscience are kept at bay. Security, understandably, is the prime concern and grows tighter all the time: closed-circuit cameras spy over every corner, every traffic signal records every car that goes by. In case of emergency, the whole Principality can be closed off in a matter of minutes. The undesirables and unconventional, whom the omnipresent Monégasque police can easily recognizable from the tourists playing the slots at the casinos, are quickly given the heave-ho.

Rainier III, chairman of the board of Monaco Inc., will probably go down in history as the Principality's greatest benefactor. In the dark, bankrupt 1950s he gave his little realm a fairy-tale cachet by wedding an incandescent American film actress named Grace Kelly, bringing in a much needed injection of socialites and their fat bankrolls. Through landfill and burrowing in the rock Rainier has added a fifth to his land area and on it built more (but certainly not better) than any of his predecessors, creating a

Lilliputian Manhattan. To obtain one of the precious resident's permits, you have to own or rent a flat in one of these anonymous grey towers and watch your ass. Bad-mouthing Monaco in print is a sure way to have your permit taken away. Everyone is very careful and serious and residents who still choose to work, the Luciano Pavarottis and Claudia Schiffers, are hardly ever home. Money, both legal and funny, is the main topic of conversation no matter where you go in this perfectly sanitized bolthole on the Med, this tidy suburb of reality, where a calendar of car races, circuses, fireworks, First Division football and operas puts a glittering mask over its ghoulish, acquisitive face.

Getting Around

There are no customs formalities; you can just drive into Monaco along the **Corniche Inférieure**, or take the **helicopter** from Nice airport if you're in a hurry (7mins), or a **bus or taxi** (45mins). The Monaco/Monte-Carlo **railway** station is in Av. Prince-Pierre, ✆ 93 87 50 50; **buses** every 30mins between Menton and Nice stop at several points along the Corniche.

Small as it is, Monaco is divided into several towns: Monte-Carlo to the east, Fontvieille by the port, Monaco-Ville on the rock, and La Condamine below, and there's a **public bus network** to save you some legwork. More importantly, **free public lifts and escalators** operate between its tiers of streets.

Tourist Information

2a Boulevard des Moulins, Monte-Carlo, ✆ 92 16 61 16, ✉ 92 16 60 00.

Monte-Carlo

Set back in the sculpture-filled gardens of Place du Casino rises the most famous building on the whole Côte d'Azur: the 1878 **Casino de Monte-Carlo**, ✆ 92 16 23 00, a fascinating piece of Old World kitsch known in its heyday as the 'cathedral of hell'. Anyone over 21 with a passport can visit. One-armed bandits, American roulette, craps and blackjack tables click and clatter away just as in Las Vegas or Atlantic City. For 100F you can get into the *salons privés* (open from 3pm)—quieter, more intense—where oily croupiers, under gilt, over-the-top rococo ceilings, accept limitless bets on roulette and *chemin de fer*. In the Pink Salon Bar, where naked cigar-chomping nymphs float on the ceiling, Charles Deville Wells celebrated his three-day gambling spree in 1891 that turned $400 into $40,000 and inspired the popular tune *The Man who Broke the Bank at Monte-Carlo*. Whatever you do, don't miss the thrill of flushing one of the Casino's loos.

The casino's bijou opera-theatre, the **Salle Garnier** (*open only for performances*), was designed by Charles Garnier, his part of the payback for François Blanc's loan that completed his even more elaborate Paris Opera. Inaugurated by Sarah Bernhardt in 1879 and backed by pots of SBM money, it became one of the most exciting in Europe, commissioning operas from composers like Saint-Saëns and Massenet, and after 1911, ballets from the Ballets Russes de Monte-Carlo. Since the war it's gone bland and mostly serves as an excuse for residents to go out for an evening. But in the old days its gods—Diaghilev, Nijinsky, Stravinsky, and set designers Picasso, Derain and Cocteau—held court among the dukes and flukes in the café of SBM's frothy **Hôtel de Paris**, next to the casino. Or as Katherine Mansfield put it: 'the famous Café de Paris with *real* devils with tails under their aprons cursing each other as they hand out the drinks. There at those tables sit the damned.'

If smug displays of wealth give you the misanthropic jitters, you can take comfort in the porcelain, metal, wood, and plastic people in the **Musée National de Monaco, Poupées et Automates d'Autrefois**, 17 Av. Princesse-Grace, ✆ 93 30 91 26 (*open daily Easter–Sept, 10am–6.30pm; other times 10am– 12.15pm and 2.30–6.30pm; adm*), in a pretty villa also designed by Charles Garnier. Jolliest among them is an enormous 18th-century Neapolitan *presepio* or Christmas crib, with 250 figurines from Virgin to sausage-vendor; a smaller room holds a Josephine Baker automaton in a grass skirt and Princess Caroline's Barbie and Ken. Further along Av. Princesse-Grace , you can unfray your nerves for free with a dose of Côte d'Azur Shintoism at the **Jardin Japonais** (*open daily, 9–nightfall*). Further east are beaches of imported sand, resort hotels, and that élite summertime rendezvous, the **Monte-Carlo Sporting Club**.

La Condamine and Fontvieille

The natural amphitheatre of La Condamine, the port quarter between Monte-Carlo and Monaco-Ville, has suffered the most from the speculators, their big cement brutes dwarfing the 11th-century votive chapel dedicated to Monaco's patron saint, **Ste-Dévote**. After her martyrdom in Corsica in 305, Dévote's body was put in a boat that sailed by itself, guided by a dove that flew out of her mouth, to Monaco (still known then as *Portus Herculis Monoeci*, after Hercules). In the 11th century some relic pirates snatched her bones, only to be foiled when the Monégasques set their boat on fire—an event re-enacted every 26 January amid the armada of yachts.

From Place Ste-Dévote Rue Grimaldi leads west to Place du Canton and the **Jardin Animalier** ✆ 93 25 18 31 (*open June–Sept 9am–12pm and 2–7pm, other times shorter hours*), used to acclimatize animals imported from the tropics. Or there's the Prince's very own **Collection de Voitures Anciennes**, ✆ 92 05 28 56 (*open 10–6, closed Nov*); and the **Musée Naval**, ✆ 92 05 28 48 (*hours as above*). More unusual are the prickly contents of another garden near the Moyenne Corniche, the **Jardin Exotique**, ✆ 93 30 33 65, where 7000 succulents planted in 1933 range from the absurd to the obscene (*bus 2, open 9am–7pm, until 6pm in the winter; adm*). The same ticket admits you to the adjacent **Grottes de l'Observatoire**, one of the few places in Provence inhabited in the Palaeolithic era, and curiously, the only cave in Europe that gets warmer instead of cooler as you descend into its maw. Here too is the **Musée d'Anthropologie Préhistorique**, with bones of reindeer, mammoths and hippopotami, along with some from early editions of humankind.

To the south, between the sea and the ultra-modern **Stade Louis II** ✆ 92 05 40 11 (where *AS Monaco* regularly punish the rest of the French football league), stretches **Fontvieille Park** where the charming **Princess Grace Rose Garden** is a memorial to Monaco's beloved princess, film actress, and daughter of an Irish-American brick magnate—the very same Kelly who supplied Ignatz mouse with ammo in George Herriman's classic comic strip *Krazy Kat*.

Up on the Rock: Monaco-Ville

In 1860 the principality of Monaco consisted of 2000 people living in this old Italian town, clinging spectacularly to a promontory 300m above the sea; they never dreamt it would turn into a shopping centre for Prince Rainier ashtrays or Princess Grace dolls. As scrubbed and cute as any town in Legoland, it offers devilries that in comparison make the casino seem like an honest proposition: the **Historial des Princes de Monaco**, Rue Basse (waxworks running the gamut from Francesco the Spiteful to Caroline and Stéphanie); the **Multi-vision Monte-Carlo Story**, on Rue Emile-de-Loth; the **Musée du Vieux Monaco**, and a **Musée des Souvenirs Napoléonien**, in the Place du Palais, with over 1000 items connected to the little Corsican including 'garments and toys belonging to the King of Rome!'—his ill-fated son. From June to October you can yawn your way through the plush **Palais Princier** itself, which, with its 19th-century 'medieval towers', is built around the Genoese fortress of 1215 (note the Grimaldi coat-of-arms, featuring a dagger-wielding monk). At other times when Rainier's at home you'll have to be content with the rooty-toot-toot 11.55am **Changing of the Monégasque Guard**.

Here, too, is Monaco's unattractive **Cathedral**, built in 1875 at the expense of a Romanesque chapel. From the chapel it inherited two lovely retables by Ludovico Bréa from the early 1500s: *La Pietà* (over the sacristy door) and the grand *St-Nicolas* with 18 panels in the ambulatory. The more recent princes of Monaco are buried here, including Princess Grace, whose simple tomb inscribed GRATIA PATRICIA PRINCIPIS RAINIERII III UXOR is often bedecked with nosegays from admirers, all waiting for the miracle that will sway the Vatican to beatify her.

Monaco's most compelling attraction is nearby: the remarkable **Musée Océanographique de Monaco** ☎ 93 15 36 00, in Av. St-Martin (*open July and Aug 9am –8pm, 7pm rest of summer, 10–6pm Nov to Mar; adm*), founded in 1910 by Prince Albert Iᵉʳ, who sank all of his casino profits into a passion for deep-sea exploration. To house the treasures he accumulated in his 24 voyages, he built into the cliff this museum with an 85m sheer stone façade, filling it with instruments, shells, whale skeletons, and on the ground floor a fascinating aquarium where 90 tanks hold some of the most surreal fish ever netted from the briny deep, including a mesmerizing cylindrical tank where thousands of identical fish swim in an endless circling herd. The rest of the building is taken up with research laboratories until recently headed by Jacques Cousteau, that specialize in the study of ocean pollution and radioactivity. Note that you can park directly underneath (even the car parks in Monaco are so neatly clean you can hear your tyres squeak), and get a lift straight up into the museum; but don't neglect to go out and get a view back at this remarkable building clinging to its cliff.

Besides the aforementioned path east to Cap Martin, there's a path beginning at Fontvieille's Plage Marquet that heads west along the crashing sea to the train station at **Cap-d'Ail** (Cape Garlic). A third trail begins on the D53 in **Beausoleil**, Monaco's French suburb, and ascends to the top of **Mont des Mules** in half an hour; an orientation table at the belvedere points out the sights, spread out like a map below.

Monaco ✉ *98030*   ***Where to Stay***

Monte-Carlo

Monaco's hotels have nearly as many stars as the Milky Way, so if you'd like one of the few more reasonably priced rooms in the summer, you can't reserve early enough. Tycoons can check in at the palatial ★★★★**Hôtel de Paris**, Place du Casino, ☎ 92 16 30 00, 🖃 92 16 38 49, opened in 1865 by the SBM for gambling czars and duchesses, or the beautiful Belle Epoque ★★★★**Hermitage** ☎ 92 16 40 00, 🖃 93 50 47 12, perched high on its rock in Square

Beaumarchais. For a third of the price, and a view of the sea, the top choice is the old
★★★**Balmoral** ✆ 93 50 62 37, 📠 93 15 08 69, 12 Av. de la Costa.

Monaco-Ville

The new air-conditioned ★★★**Abela**, 23 Av. des Papalins, ✆ 92 05 90 00, 📠 92 05 91
67, has a swimming pool, garden, and sea view. Cheaper choices are all here, too: the
modern, air-conditioned ★★**Terminus**, 9 Av. Prince-Pierre, ✆ 92 05 63 00, 📠 92 05
20 10, ★★**De France**, 6 Rue de la Turbie (near the station), ✆ 93 30 24 64, 📠 92 16
13 34, *closed Dec*; or ★★**Hôtel Helvetia**, 1 bis Rue Grimaldi, ✆ 93 30 21 71, 📠 92
16 70 51; ★**Cosmopolite**, 4 Rue de la Turbie, ✆ 93 30 16 95, all of which are
adequate even if they don't bubble over with charm. The **Centre de la Jeunesse
Princesse-Stéphanie**, 24 Av. Prince-Pierre, ✆ 93 50 83 20, 📠 93 25 29 82, is close
to the station, and fills up early in the day in summer.

Monaco ✉ *98030*   ***Eating Out***

In Monte-Carlo, those who make it big at the tables, or have simply made it big at life
in general, dine in the incredible golden setting of the **Louis XV**, in the Hôtel de
Paris, ✆ 92 16 36 36. This was a favourite of Edward VII as Prince of
Wales, who once while dining here with his mistress was served a crêpe
smothered in kirsch, curaçao and maraschino that its 14-year-old maker, Henri
Charpentier (who went on to fame as a chef in America) accidentally set alight,
only to discover that the accidental flambéing improved it a hundredfold. The Prince
himself suggested that they name the new dessert after his companion, hence *crêpes
Suzette*. Under Alain Ducasse, the youngest chef ever to earn three Michelin stars, the
cuisine is once again kingly—made from the finest and freshest ingredients Italy and
France can offer, as sumptuous and spectacular as the setting. In August 1996 Ducasse
is taking on a new challenge: the exclusive Paris restaurant of retiring perfectionist Joël
Robuchon, wagering that he will within three years earn another place in the record
books: as the first chef to run two three star restaurants at the same time (menus 730F
and 820F). *Closed Tues and Wed.*

The dining room of the Hermitage's **Belle Epoque**, ✆ 92 16 40 01, is a riotous pink
and silver period piece, and a historical monument to boot; the food (*feuilleté aux
langoustines*, etc.) is equally classic (menus at 190F and 430F). Just below the
Hermitage, **Le St Bénoît**, 10 Av. de la Costa (enter the car park and take the lift up),
✆ 93 25 02 34, offers superb seafood to go with the views from the terrace, high above
the port (160–225F). *Closed Mon.*

For delicious pasta dishes, there's **Polpetta**, 2 Rue Paradis, ✆ 93 50 67 84, with a
terrace and a 150F menu, *closed Tues and Sat lunch*; and for rich duck dishes straight
out of the Dordogne try **Le Périgordin**, 5 Rue des Oliviers, ✆ 93 30 06 02 (menus at
50F and 150F). *Closed Sat lunch and Sun.* To brush shoulders with Crown Prince
Albert and Boris Becker over a pizza go to **Le Texan**, 4 Rue Suffren Reymond, ✆ 93
30 34 54, just up from the port, and its vivacious, rowdy, Tex-Mex atmosphere (one of
the best value places for beer in the Principality, 80–200F). *Closed Tues.*

Entertainment and Nightlife

Nightlife in Monaco is a glitzy, bejewelled fashion parade catered for by the omnipresent SBM at the **Monte-Carlo Sporting Club**, on Av. Princesse-Grace, with its summer discotheque, Las Vegas-style floor shows, dancing, restaurants, and casino, or the similar offerings at SBM/Loews Monte-Carlo, 12 Av. des Spélugues, or at the American Bar at the Hôtel de Paris. Entrance is free at Monte-Carlo's number one dance club, the fantastical **Jimmy'Z**, 26 Av. Princesse-Grace, ✆ 92 16 22 77, favourite of U2, Sting and rich old men. Entry may be free, but the drinks require a small bank loan. **Bocaccio**, ✆ 93 30 15 22, also on the Av. Princesse-Grace, is loud and modern. Young people from all along the coast drive to **Le Stars N' Bars**, 6 Quai Antoine 1ᵉʳ, ✆ 93 50 95 95 (*open from 10pm*). Beer-drinking in a Brit-run imitation pub takes place at **Flashman's**, 7 Av. Princesse-Alice, ✆ 93 30 09 03, which remains open to the small hours.

In January the opera, theatre and ballet season begins (call ✆ 92 16 22 99 for info); in February an excellent **Circus Festival**; in April there is the International Tennis Championships and in July/August a spectacular **Fireworks Festival** and concerts at the palace. The open air **Cinéma d'été**, ✆ 93 25 88 80, 26 Av. Princesse-Grace, shows a different film in its original language every evening at 9.30pm, from June–30 Sept, or there's the 3-screen **Cinema Le Sporting** in the Place du Casino, ✆ 36 68 00 72.

Sports and Activities

Thanks to the SBM, there's always something to do in Monaco, especially if you have a few oil wells to back up your credit cards: a mountaintop 18-hole golf course high above the town at La Turbie, tennis and every imaginable water sport (but no free beaches), deep-sea tuna-fishing and cruises, helicopter tours of the coast. In January there's the **Monte-Carlo Rally**—the first one in 1902 occasioned the world's first tarmac road, designed to keep the spectators from being sprayed with dust. In April you can watch the tennis championship; the second week of May sees the famous **Monte-Carlo Grand Prix** (when even the pavements charge a hefty admission).

North of Monaco

From Monaco, the D53 ascends to the Grande Corniche, a road the Romans called Via Julia Augusta, built to link up the Urbs to its conquests in Gaul and Spain. Several hard campaigns had to be fought (25–14 BC) before the fierce Ligurians finally let the road builders through, and in 6 BC the Roman Senate voted to erect a mighty commemorative monument known as the Trophy of the Alps (the Romans called it *Tropea Augusti* or 'Augustus's Trophy') at the base of Mont Agel. The views are precipitous, and you can escape the crowds by venturing even further inland to Peille and Peillon, two of the most beautiful villages on the Côte d'Azur.

Getting Around

There are four **buses** daily from Nice to La Turbie that continue up to Peille, but never on Sundays; and 6 each a day from Monaco. Both Peillon and Peille have train stations, but they lie several steep kilometres below their respective villages.

Tourist Information

La Turbie (✉ 06320): at the Mairie, ✆ 93 41 10 10, 📠 93 41 13 99.
Peillon (✉ 06440): also at the Mairie, ✆ 93 79 91 04, 📠 93 79 87 65.
Peille (✉ 06440): also at the Mairie, ✆ 93 91 90 01.

La Turbie and its Trophy

Though hemmed in by upstart mini-villas and second homes, La Turbie (a corruption of *Tropea*) still retains its old core of narrow vaulted alleys, typical of the area. Unlike its neighbours, however, it earned a mention by Dante in *The Divine Comedy*, and has the relevant immortal lines proudly engraved on its tower. La Turbie also has an elliptical 18th-century church, **St-Michel-Archange** with a sumptuous Baroque interior of marble and agate and paintings that are attributed to, or by the schools of Raphael, Veronese, Rembrandt, Ludovico Bréa, Murillo and Ribera—not bad for a village of 2000 or so souls!

The old Via Julia Augusta (Rue Comte-de-Cessole) passes through town on its way to the **Trophy of the Alps**. This monument originally stood 45m high, supporting a 6m statue of Augustus; on its wall were listed the 44 conquered Ligurian tribes, and stairs throughout allowed passers-by to enjoy the view. When St Honorat saw the local people worshipping this marvel in the 4th century, he vandalized it; in the Dark Ages it was converted into a fort; Louis XIV ordered it to be blown up in 1705, and the stone was quarried to build St-Michel-Archange. The still formidable pile of rubble that remained in the 1930s was resurrected to 35m and its inscription replaced thanks to a rich American, Edward Tuck. The only other such trophy to survive in situ is in Romania; a small **museum**, ✆ 93 41 10 11 (*open summer 9.30–5pm, winter 9–6pm; adm*), on the site has models and drawings. From the trophy's terrace it's a dizzy 400m drop down to Monaco's skyscrapers.

Peillon and Peille

The two villages are tiny and lovely; balanced atop adjacent hilltops, both require a wearying climb to reach. But Peille and Peillon aren't quite the Tweedledee and Tweedledum of the Côte. **Peillon**, most easily reached on the D53 from Nice, is a bit more posh, complete with a foyer—a cobbled square with a pretty fountain at the village entrance. Inside are peaceful medieval stairs and arches, and the restored Baroque parish church, but Peillon's big attraction is right at the entrance: the **Chapelle des Pénitents Blancs** (*telephone the tourist office first to arrange a visit*) adorned with a slightly faded cycle of Renaissance frescoes on the *Passion of Christ*, by the charming Giovanni Canavesio (*c.* 1485), who would certainly be better known had he painted anything outside the valleys of the Maritime Alps. From Peillon, marked trails lead you to some steep but delightful countryside rambles.

One of those walks follows the Roman road in two hours to **Peille**, further up the D53. More isolated, Peille has more character, and its very own dialect, called *Pelhasc*. There's an ensemble of medieval streets like Peillon's and a church begun in the 12th century, with an interesting medieval portrait of Peille and its now ruined castle. Once, during a drought, Peille asked for help from a shepherd (in Provence shepherds often moonlight as sorcerers), and he made it rain on condition that the lord of this castle give him his daughter to wed—an event remembered in a fête on the first Sunday in September. The Church may frown at such goings-on, but Peille often had its own ideas on religion, preferring twice in the Middle Ages to be excommunicated rather than pay the bishop's tithes.

Where to Stay and Eating Out

La Turbie (✉ 06320)

Stay and eat at the **★★Le Napoléon**, 7 Av. de la Victoire, ✆ 93 41 00 54, ✉ 93 41 28 93. *Open all year.* Try to get a room on the top floor, with views of the Trophy. All rooms have baths and TVs, from 250F (good food, with menus at 115F and 145F). The only other option is the ★Cesare, 16 Av. Albert 1ᵉʳ, ✆ 93 41 16 08. *Closed Nov.*

Peillon (✉ 06440)

★★★Auberge de la Madone, ✆ 93 79 91 17, ✉ 93 79 99 36, has comfortable rooms with traditional Provençal decor and views over the valley. Inside its excellent restaurant, or out on a terrace among the olive trees, you'll find seasonal dishes like red mullet with parsley and asparagus and *tourton des pénitents* with almonds, pine nuts and herbs (menus at 130F and 210F, 190F Sundays and holidays). Rooms range between 410F–800F. *Closed Nov.*

Peille (✉ 06440)

★Belvédère, ✆ 93 79 90 45, the only hotel in the village, has five simple rooms with grand mountain views but you had better write ahead to book one. The restaurant does good ravioli and other Niçois dishes (menus from 85F). The atmosphere is so uptight, however, it's enough to make a rebel of the most good-natured soul.

The Moyenne Corniche

Eze

Between Monaco and Nice, the main reason for taking the middle road has long been the extraordinary village of Eze, the most perched, perhaps, of any *village perché* in France, squeezed on to a cone of a hill 430m over the sea. It barely avoided being poached as well as perched in a catastrophic fire in 1986 that ravaged the landscape and destroyed the pine forest that once surrounded it. Now the poaching is done on tourists; nearly every other house is a shop.

Eze, they say, is named after a temple the Phoenicians built to Isis. It then passed to the Romans, to the Saracens, and changed lords several times after. But on the whole, as you can see once inside its 14th-century gate, Eze was eminently self-reliant. Even if an enemy penetrated the walls, its tight little maze of stairs and alleys would cause confusion, the better to ambush or spill boiling oil on attackers. If they got so far as to assault what remains of the castle these days—429m above sea level—they would run into the needles of the mostly South American cacti in the **Jardin Exotique**, ℭ 93 41 10 30, ✆ 92 10 60 50 (*open every day during summer 9am–dusk, rest of year 9–12am, 2pm–dusk; adm*), a spiky paradise created on municipal initiative in 1949 by *ingénieur agronome* Jean Gastauld. The other non-commercial attraction in Eze is the **Chapelle des Pénitents Blancs**, the only unaltered building since the Middle Ages, with a 13th-century Catalan crucifix, the *Christ of the Black Death* (typical of medieval Catalan art, the sculptor emphasized Christ's divine nature, and he smiles even on the Cross); here too is a 14th-century Virgin and Child called the *Madone des Forêts*, owing to the pine-cone in Jesus' hand.

A scenic path descending to Eze-Bord-de-Mer is called the **Sentier Frédéric-Nietzsche** after the philosopher. Nietzsche, however, walked up instead of down, an arduous trek that made his head spin and inspired the third part of his *Thus Spake Zarathustra*.

Eze ✉ *06360*   ***Where to Stay and Eating Out***

Eze-Grande Corniche

A road links the three Corniches at Eze, and there are hotels on each level. For four-star treatment, go to ★★★★**Les Terrasses D'Ele Country Aurs,** Grande Corniche (1138), Rte de la Turbie, ℭ 93 41 24 64, ✆ 93 441 13 25, huge (80 rooms), expensive and '*ultra-moderne*', complete with golf simulator, conference rooms and a room for '*musculation*'. ★★**L'Hermitage**, at Col d'Eze on the Grande Corniche, ℭ 93 41 00 68, ✆ 93 41 21 11, offers priceless views (*starting at 190F*), but mundane food to go with its mundane rooms (*menus from 90F*). *Closed Dec*. From the hotel a footpath leads along the ancient *Voie Aurélienne* on to Mont Leuze, with breathtaking views over the Alps and down to the Mediterranean. Five km nearer Nice on the Grande Corniche is the **Université Canadienne en France**, ℭ 93 01 98 83, an incongruous Canadian university set in beautiful 14-hectare grounds high above the Mediterranean. The university lets its accommodation from June to September, individual villas and studios built in Provençal style, with swimming pool, tennis courts and café/bar (*studio with kitchenette from 250F a night, ideal for families or small groups*). While on the Grande Corniche, you can eat at **La Bergerie**, ℭ 93 41 03 67, which places the emphasis on meats and seafood (from 190F). *Closed Wed/midwinter*. Or try **La Croix Du Pape**, ℭ 93 41 19 00, for flame grills and pizza, starting at 130F.

Eze-Moyenne Corniche

In Eze, along the Moyenne Corniche two luxurious inns have only a handful of rooms but superb kitchens: the ★★★★**Château Eza**, Rue de la Pise, ℭ 93 41 12 24, ✆ 93 41 16 64, actually a collection of medieval houses linked together to form an eagle's nest, all sharing an extraordinary terrace, with Niçois and other Provençal specialities to match. *Closed Dec–Mar*. In a medieval castle rebuilt in the 1920s, ★★★★**Château de la Chèvre d'Or**, Rue du Barri, ℭ 93 41 12 12, ✆ 93 41 06 72, has a small park, a pool, and more ravishing views; its restaurant serves refined, light versions of the French classics, accompanied by one of the Riviera's best wine cellars (rooms start 1200–3500F, up to 4500F). *Closed Dec–April*. More modest choices in Eze include ★★**Le Golf**, Place de la Colette, ℭ 93 41 18 50, ✆ 93 41 29 93, *closed Dec–Feb*, and

✶✶Auberge des Deux Corniches, ✆/✉ 93 41 19 54, *open all year*. Turbot or *filet de bœuf aux cèpes* go down nicely at **Le Troubadour**, Rue du Brec, ✆ 93 41 19 03, and the price is nice too (menus 115F and 165F). *Closed Sun, lunch Monday*. Head to the summit of the rock, **Le Nid d'Aigle**, Rue du Château, ✆ 93 41 19 08, next door to the Jardin Exotique, for lofty seafood (*loup au pistou*, salmon; 120F and 233F menus. *Closed Wed*.

Eze-Bord-de-Mer

Down at Eze-Bord-de-Mer, there's the ultra-luxurious Riviera dream **✶✶✶✶Le Cap Estel**, ✆ 93 01 50 44, ✉ 93 01 55 20, with heated pool, *closed Oct–Mar*, or **✶✶Auberge Eric Rivot**, ✆ 93 01 51 46, ✉ 93 01 58 40, with rooms starting at 250F. *Open all year*.

The Corniche Inférieure

To the west of Eze-Bord-de-Mer another wooded promontory, Cap Ferrat, protrudes into the sea to form today's most fashionable address on the Côte d'Azur. The fascinating, wildly eclectic Villa Ephrussi de Rothschild and gardens crown the summit of Cap Ferrat, while the awful Leopold II, King of the Belgians, Otto Preminger and Somerset Maugham had sanctuaries by the sea (the most amusing way to take it all in is by way of the Côte d'Azur's equivalent of Hollywood's 'See the Homes of the Stars' bus tours: a toytown 'train' that starts on the quay at Villefranche and chugs along the roads of Cap Ferrat with a guide calling out, in French and abominable English, the names of the famous who live(d) in the villas). To the east, the peninsula and steep mountain backdrop keep Beaulieu so sheltered that it shares with Menton the distinction of being the hottest town in France, while to the west the Corniche skirts the top of the fine old village of Villefranche-sur-Mer, with a port deep enough for battleships—grey tokens from the grey world beyond the Riviera.

Tourist Information

Beaulieu (✉ 06310): Place Georges Clemenceau, ✆ 93 01 02 21, ✉ 93 01 44 04.
St-Jean-Cap-Ferrat (✉ 06230): 59 Av. Denis-Semaria, ✆ 93 76 08 90, ✉ 93 76 16 67.
Villefranche-sur-Mer (✉ 06230): Jardin François-Binon, near the Corniche Inférieure, ✆ 93 01 73 68.

market days

Beaulieu: daily exc Sunday.
Villefranche: flea market, Tues, Place de la Paix; fruit, veg and flowers, Mon–Sat, Place de la Paix; clothes, Sat–Sun, Place de L'Octroi.

Beaulieu

'*O qual bel luogo!*' exclaimed Napoleon in his Corsican mother tongue, and the bland name stuck to this lush banana-growing town overlooking the Baie des Fourmis, 'the Bay of Ants', so called for the black boulders in the sea. Beaulieu admits to a mere four days of frost a year and calls its steamy easternmost suburb La Petite Afrique, while most of its affluent population are trying to imitate Gustave Eiffel, who retired here and lived to be 90. Beaulieu's vintage casino has been renovated after four years of dilapidation, and is back to its former sparkling grandeur. The *thés dansants* held in **La Rotonde** are a further retro attraction, but the *real* magnet is a place so retro that even Socrates would feel at home there: the **Villa Kerylos**, ✆ 93 01 01 44 (*open daily 10–7pm July–Aug, and 10.30–12.30am and 2–6pm Sept–Oct*), a striking reproduction of a wealthy 5th-century BC Athenian's abode, furnishings, and garden, built in 1908 by archaeologist Théodore Reinach. Reinach spared no expense on the marbles, ivories, bronzes, mosaic and fresco reproductions to help his genuine antiquities feel at home; glass windows, plumbing and a hidden piano are the only modern anachronisms. And here, on a shore that reminded him of the Aegean, this ultimate philhellene lived himself like an Athenian, holding symposia, exercising and bathing with his male buddies, and keeping the womenfolk out of the way.

St-Jean-Cap Ferrat

Another retro-repro fantasy, the **Villa Ephrussi de Rothschild**, ✆ 93 01 33 09, ✉ 93 01 31 10 (*a 10min walk from the Corniche Inférieure, or catch the irregular bus to St-Jean; open daily 10am–6pm, 10am–7pm July and Aug*), crowns the narrow isthmus of bucolic Cap Ferrat, enjoying spectacular views over both the Baie des Fourmis and the harbour of Villefranche. The flamboyant Béatrice de Rothschild, who never went anywhere without her trunk of fifty wigs, was a compulsive art collector, and, after marrying the banker Baron Ephrussi, had this Italianate villa specially built to house her treasures—a Venetian rococo room was designed for Béatrice's Tiepolo ceiling, while other rooms set off her Renaissance furniture, Florentine bridal chests, paintings by Boucher, rare Chinese screens and furniture, Flemish and Beauvais tapestries, Sèvres porcelain, Louis-Quinze and Louis-Seize furniture, a covered Andalusian patio (a favourite location shot for James Bond and other films), a hidden bathroom and a collection of porcelain vases that ladies of yore discreetly slipped under their skirts when nature called. To create the equally eclectic gardens, the isthmus was given a crew cut, and terraced into different levels. There's a French garden with a copy of the *Amour* fountain from the Petit Trianon; a Florentine garden, with a white marble ephebe; a Spanish garden, with papyrus, dates and pomegranates; also Exotic, Japanese and English gardens, and a lapidary garden decorated with Romanesque capitals, arches, and gargoyles. For all the trouble she took to build this glorious pile, Béatrice actually spent very little time here, preferring to live in her villa in Monte-Carlo because it was closer to the gambling tables. In the summer you can take tea and cakes in the former *salon d'hiver*.

Cap Ferrat, with its lush greenery, secret villas and little azure coves is ripe territory for strolls or swims—there are numerous small beaches, albeit adorned with fine gravel. **Plage de Passable** along Chemin du Roy, west of Villa Ephrussi is popular with families and scuba divers. The 'Roy' in question was bad old King Leopold II of the Belgians, whose merciless exploitation of the Congo (see Conrad's *Heart of Darkness*) helped pay for his luxurious life here, where he took a swim every day with his beard neatly folded into a rubber whisker-protector and his valet ironed his morning newspapers. The villa (Les Cèdres) is now more democratically used for a delightful **zoo**, ✆ 93 76 04 98 (*open daily 9.30am–7pm summer, 9.30am–5.30pm winter*).

If you have fortitude you can climb up and up the steep stairway for the tremendous view from the **Phare**, the lighthouse at the south tip of the promontory, near the Sun Beach swimming pool, ✆ 93 76 08 36 (*open 9am–12pm and 3–6pm summer; otherwise 3–4pm*); if you *need* fortitude, you can find a *pastis* in the former-fishing-now-yacht-port of **St-Jean-Cap-**

Ferrat. Jean Cocteau painted the village's *Salle des Mariages*, but with hardly the same vigour as in Menton. A walking path circles around the dew-claw of land south of the port called **Pointe St-Hospice** where, in the 6th century, the Niçois saint Hospice had a hermitage (now marked by a 19th-century chapel). With one arm chained to the wall, Hospice lived off algae brought to him by pious souls, and uttered dire prophesies about barbarian invasions that came true, recorded by the Merovingian historian, Gregory of Tours. Modern-day invasions take place at nearby **Plage de Paloma**, favourite of Italian day-trippers and millionaire pensioners, and **Plage des Fosses**. Another path, the **Promenade Maurice Rouvier** leads from St-Jean's beach to Beaulieu, passing **Villa Scoglietto** and its sea-defying garden, where Charlie Chaplin spent his summer holidays, and actor David Niven lived the last years of his life.

Villefranche-sur-Mer

In the 14th century, the deep, wooded bay between Cap Ferrat and Nice was a duty-free port, hence Villefranche's name. It became an important military port for the Savoys in the 18th century, a period that saw Villefranche take on the appearance it has today: tall, brightly coloured houses, narrow lanes and stairs, some so overhung with houses that they're actually tunnels like **Rue Obscure**, 'a good place for a knifing' as William Sansom described it, although it came in handy as a bomb shelter in the last war. The streets open up to the wide quay, given over to bars and restaurants. The charm of the place, and the presence of so many brawny sailors from around the world on shore-leave, made Villefranche a popular intello-gay resort in the 1920s, with Jean Cocteau weaving his personal mythologies with opium, 'fluids' and his friends in the little Hotel Welcome: 'Poets of all kinds, speaking every language, lived there and by a simple contact of fluids transformed the extraordinary little town, whose steep chaos ends at the water's edge, into a vertiable Lourdes, a centre of legends and inventions'.

Villefranche's fishermen once stored their nets in the portside Romanesque **Chapelle St-Pierre**, Quai Courbet, ✆ 93 76 90 70, (*open 9.30–2 and 2–6 autumn, 9.30–12 and 2–5 winter, 9.30–12 and 3–7 spring, 10–12 and 4–8 summer; adm*), and in 1957, as a gift to them, Cocteau frescoed it in 'ghosts of colours' with scenes from the Life of St Peter (walking on the water with an angel's help, which astounds the fish but makes Christ smile), plus images of the fishergirls of Villefranche, the gypsies at Saintes-Maries-de-la-Mer, and angels from Cocteau's private heaven. The Duke of Savoy's **Citadelle St-Elme** has been put back to work as the Hôtel de Ville and three marginal museums: the **Musée Volti**, ✆ 93 76 33 27, with sculptures of women by a native of Villefranche; the **Musée Goetz Boumeester**, ✆ 93 76 33 44, with works donated to the city by Henri Goetz and his wife Christine Boumeester, and one with items from a 16th-century shipwreck (*all open June–Sept 10–12 and 3–7; Oct–May 10–12 and 2–5, closed Sun am, Tues and Nov*).

Where to Stay and Eating Out

Beaulieu-sur-Mer (✉ 06310)

In the 1870s, when the fabulously wealthy James Gordon Bennett, owner of the *New York Herald* and the man who sent Stanley to find Livingstone, was booted out of New York society for his scandalous behaviour, he came to the Riviera and ran the Paris edition of his paper from ★★★★**La Réserve**, 5 Bd. Général-Leclerc, ✆ 93 01 00 01, ✉ 93 01 28 99, now one of the most exclusive hotels on the Riviera, and if a touch old-fashioned, still offering its guests grand sea views, a beach and marina, heated pool and more. The neo-Renaissance restaurant (*menus 280–420F*) complements such elegance. *Closed mid-Nov–mid-Dec.* Its equally elegant *fin-de-siècle* Italianate neighbour, ★★★★**Métropole**, 15 Bd. Maréchal Leclerc, ✆ 93 01 00 08, ✉ 93 01 18 51, boasts a fine seaside garden, heated seawater swimming pool, a more relaxed atmosphere, and a superb master chef, Pierre Estival (perfect *bouillabaisse* 440F; *menus 400F and 490F*). Near the station, the modern ★★★**Artemis**, 3 Bd. Maréchal-Joffre, ✆ 93 01 12 15, ✉ 93 01 27 46, has rooms with balconies and access to a pool at the back; on the same street at No.29 ★★**Le Havre Bleu**, ✆ 93 01 01 40, ✉ 93 01 29 92, is an attractive hotel, with pleasant rooms, many with terraces. The small, simple ★**Sélect**, 1 Place Général-de-Gaulle, ✆ 93 01 05 42, near the station is convenient, yet impersonal; try the ★**Riviera** and its pretty wrought-iron balconies just up from the Basse Corniche on 6 Rue Paul-Doumer, ✆ 93 01 04 92. If it's time to eat and you're not a Rothschild, join the crowd in the garden at **La Pignatelle**, 10 Rue Quincenet, ✆ 93 01 03 37, which does delicious fish soup, and a lunch menu at 80F (*dinner menus 120F and 180F*). Wood-fired pizzas and delicious pasta abound round the corner on Bd. Maréchal-Leclerc at **Le Catalan**, ✆ 93 01 02 78 (*à la carte*). *Closed Sundays.*

St-Jean-Cap-Ferrat (✉ 06230)

Even though its villas are the most exclusive on the Riviera, Cap Ferrat has hotels in all price ranges, beginning with one of the most beautiful small hotel on the entire Côte: a charming, voluptuous Italian villa, overlooking the pleasure port, ★★★★**Voile d'Or**, ✆ 93 01 13 13, ✉ 93 76 11 17. Once owned by film director Michael Powell, who inherited it from his father (and sold it because no one ever paid their bar bills), the Voile d'Or is an ideal first or second honeymoon hotel, with a laid-back atmosphere, a garden hanging over the port, a heated pool, and rooms with every luxury a hotel could need. Its equally exceptional restaurant, favoured by the yachting set, uses only fish caught off St-Jean, giving them traditional and more exotic treatments—such as shellfish jambalaya à la Key West. The grand wine cellar is managed by an *Ancien Premier Sommelier de France* (*menus 320F and 420F*). *Closed Nov–Feb.* At the Belle Epoque ★★★★**Grand Hôtel du Cap Ferrat**, Bd. Général de Gaulle, ✆ 93 76 50 50, ✉ 93 76 04 52, the already luxurious rooms have been restored in a more airy, comfortable Riviera style, all set in acres of gardens, lawns, and palms. A funicular railway lowers guests down to an Olympic-size seawater swimming pool just over the Mediterranean. The restaurant, on a terrace shaded by parasol pines, serves delicious meals, though is decidedly unhealthy for your wallet.

More down-to-earth choices include ★★★**Brise–Marine**, Av. Jean-Mermoz, ✆ 93 76 04 36, ✉ 93 76 11 49, with a garden, terrace, and large rooms, half with sea views; or ★★**Clair Logis**, near the centre of the Cap on 12 Av. Centrale, ✆ 93 76 04 57, ✉ 93 76 11 85, a villa set in an enclosed garden. If you want traditional south coast *hauteur* with your cuisine, **Le Provençal** on Place Clemenceau, ✆ 93 76 03 97, has no menu at lunchtime—it's only *à la carte,* where you can try delicacies like violet asparagus *au jus de truffes* or thin slices of raw *daurade* (sea-bream) in balsamic vinegar (*from 560F, yes, five-six-oh*). The one star option is ★**De La Bastide**, 3 Av. Albert 1er, ✆ 93 76 06 78, is not luxurious but has a restaurant. *Closed Nov.* On the quayside, **Le**

Calablu, ✆ 93 76 01 66, serves fresh fish and tender lamb for tender prices (*100F and 120F menus*). Around the Port de Plaisance there are several nautically named but otherwise unmemorable beaneries, **Le Pirate**, ✆ 93 76 12 97; **Le Sloop**, ✆ 93 01 48 63; and **Skipper**, ✆ 93 76 01 00, being among them.

Villefranche-sur-Mer (✉ 06230)

Just beside the port, the legendary ★★★**Welcome**, Quai Amiral-Courbet, ✆ 93 76 76 93, 📠 93 01 88 81, is ideally situated, and all its finely decorated rooms are air-conditioned; those on the 5th floor are ravishing. *Closed mid-Nov–mid-Dec, half-board in season.* Or try the unpretentious, family-run ★★**Provençal**, 4 Av. du Maréchal-Joffre, ✆ 93 01 71 42, 📠 93 76 96 00. *Open all year.* For dinner, **Le Carpaccio**, Plage des Marinières, ✆ 93 01 72 97, has long been a favourite of the Rolls-Royce crowd from Monaco, yet remains affordable for a night-time splurge (count 300F *à la carte* for fish, crustaceans and, of course, *carpaccio*). *Closed Tues.* In the old town, **La Grignotière,** 3 Rue du Poilu, ✆ 93 76 79 83, serves a 149F menu of local Niçois specialities. Further on along Rue Poilu, the less expensive **La Bonne Franquette**, at No.18, ✆ 93 76 94 14, serves copious portions of fish and local pastas on its 90F and 180F menus.

Nice

Other places may be fun,
But when all is said and done,
It's so much nicer in Nice.

Sandy Wilson, *The Boyfriend*

The funny thing is, it's true. Agreeably named and superbly set on nothing less than the Bay of Angels, Nice has a gleam and sparkle in its eye like no other city in France: only a sourpuss could resist its lively old town squeezed between promontory and sea, its markets blazing with colour, the glittering tiled domes and creamy *pâtisserie* 19th-century hotels and villas, the immaculate, exotic gardens, and the famous voluptuous curve of the beach and the palm-lined Promenade des Anglais. It is the one town on the Côte that doesn't seem to need tourists, the one that stays open through the winter. You could go for the food alone, a seductive mix of the best of France and Italy; you haven't really had ravioli until you tuck into a plate in Nice, where it was invented.

The capital of the *département* of Alpes-Maritimes and France's fifth largest town (pop.400,000), Nice is the Hexagon's most visited city after Paris. The English have been coming for well over 200 years, back when 'Nizza la Bella' still belonged to Savoy, and Russian Tsarinas and Grand Dukes fleeing winter's blasts weren't far behind. The presence of so many rich, idle foreigners who stayed for months at a time formed a large part of the city's character, which hasn't always been angelic or nice: corruption, reactionary politics and organized crime are part of the famous *salade Niçoise*, along with a high density of apricot poodles and frown-faced poodle ladies. But Nice also has a university, big culture (21 museums and counting), the brilliant light that Matisse loved and a genuine identity as a city—rough, affable and informal, if clannish, defensive, and occasionally bent in a surprising number of ways.

History

Nice was a hot-spot even 400,000 years ago, when hunters who tracked mammoths and learnt how to make fires to grill their prey frequented the caves of Terra Amata. The Ligurians, around 1000 BC, were the first to move in permanently, constructing their *oppida* at the mouth of the Paillon river, and on the hill overlooking the valley. Greeks from Marseille founded a commercial colony near the seaside *oppidum* that they named Nikaïa after an obscure military victory, or perhaps after the nymph Nikaia. Beset by Ligurian pirates, the Nikaïans asked the Romans for aid. The Romans duly came, and stayed, but preferred to live near the hilltop *oppidum*, because it was closer to the Via Julia Augusta. They named this town *Cemenelum* (modern Cimiez), and made it the capital of the province of *Alpes Maritimae*. By the 3rd century AD *Cemenelum* had 20,000 inhabitants, all quickly going soft amid swimming pools and central heating.

But, by the 6th century, luxury-loving Cemenelum had collapsed with the rest of the Roman empire while Greek Nikaïa struggled on and regrouped itself in the 10th century around a cathedral. By the 1340s, with a population of 13,000, Nice was the third city in Provence after Marseille and Arles. The city's coat of arms had an eagle's head on it, and it looked to the right, to France. The Black Death and civil wars of the period soon cut it down to size, and in 1388 the city's leaders voted to hitch their wagon to a brighter star than Louis d'Anjou, and pledged allegiance to Amadeus VII, Count of Savoy. The eagle was redrawn to look left, towards Italy.

The Savoys fortified Nice and it grew rich trading with Italy. It had its own little Renaissance, thanks to Ludovico Bréa and the other members of the mid-15th-century Ecole Niçoise—Antoine and François Bréa, Jean Mirailhet, and Jacques Durandi—noted for their uncluttered, simple compositions and firm sense of line. The 17th century saw the first expansion of Nice outside its medieval walls, and in 1696 and 1705 came the first of several French interludes that interrupted Savoy rule—interludes that Louis XIV took advantage of to blow up the city's fortifications.

Cold Brits, and Absorption into the Mystic Hexagon

Although relations remained sour with France, the Savoys became firm allies with the English, and by 1755 the first trickle of milords began to discover the sunny charms of a Riviera winter. Doctor and novelist Tobias Smollett spent a year in Nice in 1763, and in his singularly grouchy *Travels through France and Italy* (1766) did what Peter Mayle has since done for Provence: made the Côte, because of, or in spite of, its quaint local characters, irresistible to the British. Even though it took at least two weeks to reach Nice from Calais, by 1787 there were enough Brits wintering here to support a casino (then a fashionable Venetian novelty), an English theatre, estate agent, and newspaper. In 1830, when a frost killed all the orange trees, the English community raised funds to give the unemployed a job: building a seafront promenade along the Baie des Anges known to this day as the Promenade des Anglais. Part of its purpose was to keep English girls away from the riff-raff, or more particularly the Niçois—the British brought with their money attitudes so arrogant that as early as the 1780s, sensitive locals left town each winter to avoid being humiliated by their visitors.

In 1860, as Napoleon III's reward for promising to help Vittorio Emanuele II of Savoy create the future kingdom of Italy, a secret treaty was signed ceding Nice and Savoy to France. To keep up appearances, a plebiscite was held. Vittorio Emanuele encouraged his subjects to vote for French union, but even more encouraging was the presence of the French army marching through Nice, and French agents bullying the majority Italian-speaking population. The final result (24,449 pro-France to 160 against) stinks even to this day. But the railway arrived shortly thereafter, and Nice settled down to its chosen vocation as the winter haven for Europe's élite. Sumptuous neo-Moorish-Gothic-Baroque follies were built to house some 20,000 wintering Britons and Russians by 1890; 20 years later the numbers of foreigners had increased to over 150,000. Queen Victoria preferred the suburb of Cimiez; her haemophiliac son, Prince Leopold, introduced croquet to Nice before dying after slipping on the marble floor in the casino. The city even made an early bid to become the Hollywood of France, when the Victorine film studios were founded in 1911 and purchased in 1925 by Rex Ingram, who brought in a constant parade of big stars and writers. During the war, Marcel Carné used them to film *Les Visiteurs du Soir* and *Les Enfants du Paradis*.

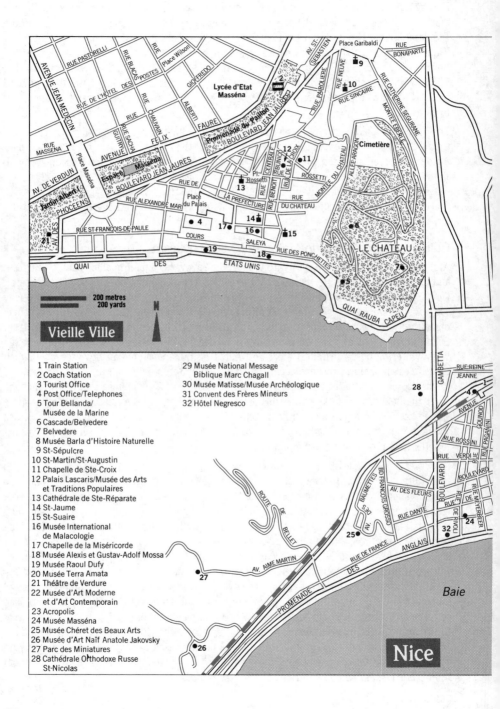

Vieille Ville

200 metres
200 yards

Nice

1 Train Station
2 Coach Station
3 Tourist Office
4 Post Office/Telephones
5 Tour Bellanda/
  Musée de la Marine
6 Cascade/Belvedere
7 Belvedere
8 Musée Barla d'Histoire Naturelle
9 St-Sépulcre
10 St-Martin/St-Augustin
11 Chapelle de Ste-Croix
12 Palais Lascaris/Musée des Arts
   et Traditions Populaires
13 Cathédrale de Ste-Réparate
14 St-Jaume
15 St-Suaire
16 Musée International
   de Malacologie
17 Chapelle de la Miséricorde
18 Musée Alexis et Gustav-Adolf Mossa
19 Musée Raoul Dufy
20 Musée Terra Amata
21 Théâtre de Verdure
22 Musée d'Art Moderne
   et d'Art Contemporain
23 Acropolis
24 Musée Masséna
25 Musée Chéret des Beaux Arts
26 Musée d'Art Naïf Anatole Jakovsky
27 Parc des Miniatures
28 Cathédrale Orthodoxe Russe
   St-Nicolas
29 Musée National Message
   Biblique Marc Chagall
30 Musée Matisse/Musée Archéologique
31 Convent des Frères Mineurs
32 Hôtel Negresco

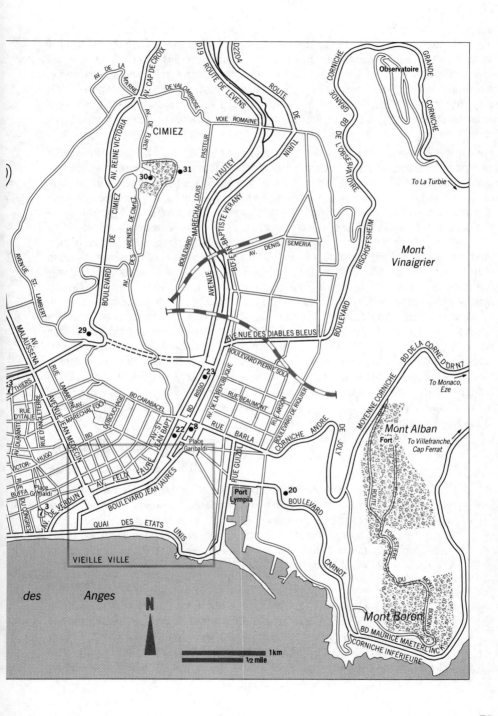

Nice Today

Since the 1930s, many of Nice's hotels and villas have been converted into furnished flats while the concrete mixers of destiny march further and further west and up the valleys. The Victorine studios are still there, but plagued by noise from jets landing in Nice airport, they are used mostly for television commercials. Rents in the city are astronomical and property values are rivalled today in France only by Paris and Cannes; wealthy, politically conservative retirees help support an equally right-wing *rentier* population. All this money floating about has attracted the corruption and underworld activities of the *milieu*, previously associated only with Marseille.

For decades Nice was ruled as the personal fiefdom of the right-wing Médecin family, who pretend to be related to the Medici, although it doesn't look as if their dynasty will endure quite as long. Jean Médecin reigned from 1928 until 1965, and was succeeded by his flamboyant son Jacques, cook, crook and anti-Semite hoster of a National Front congress no other city would have, the man who twinned Nice with Cape Town when apartheid was still on the books. Jacques Médecin had an edifice-complex nearly the size of Mitterrand's in Paris, filling Nice with huge new public complexes, and his cronies had their fingers in all kinds of pies, most spectacularly Albert Spaggiari, who had got hold of the plans of Nice's sewer system in order to steal 46 million francs from the Société Générale, and was captured by the police only to escape the courtroom by jumping out of the window on to a waiting motorcycle and making a clean getaway. In 1990 the slow, grinding wheels of French justice began to catch up with him, when it was discovered, among other things, that money for the Nice Opera was being diverted into the mayor's bank account. Médecin took to his heels and hid out in Punta del Este, Uruguay, until 1995 when he was extradited to France, where he awaits trial for abuse of public funds. His sister Geneviève barely defeated the National Front candidate in local government elections, and took his old seat on the Conseil Général of the Alpes-Maritimes *département*; his successor as mayor of Nice, Honoré Bailet, had some troubles of his own, especially in the form of a son-in-law, accused of murdering a local restaurant owner; in 1995 he was replaced by Jacques Peyrat.

Getting There and Around

by air

Nice's large, modern Aéroport Nice-Côte d'Azur is the second busiest in France, served by a wide variety of flights from around the world. Buses run every 20mins between the airport and coach station, © 93 56 35 40, while bus 23 provides links with the train station every 30mins. Flights to or from Paris go through Aérogare 2; all others through Aérogare 1. Airline numbers are Air France, © 93 18 89 89; British Airways, © 93 21 47 01; Delta © 93 21 34 87; Air Inter, © 93 21 45 38.

by train

Nice's train station is in Av. Thiers, not far from the centre (information © 36 35 35 35, reservations © 93 88 89 93). Besides *Métrazur* trains between Ventimiglia and St-Raphaël, Nice has frequent connections to Marseille and its TGV to Paris (7 hrs). The Gare du Sud, 4 bis Rue Alfred-Binet, © 93 82 10 17, is served by the little *Train des Pignes* (so called for the pine-cones that the crew used to stop to collect for pine-nuts).

by coach

The *gare routière* is on the Promenade du Paillon, on the edge of Vieux Nice, ✆ 93 85 61 81. There are frequent buses to Grasse, Vence, Cannes, Marseille, Aix-en-Provence, Avignon, Brignoles, St-Raphaël, Le Muy, Cagnes, Antibes, Menton and Monte-Carlo, as well as one a day for Plan-du-Var, Puget-Théniers and Entrevaux (on the route to Gap). Bus 17 links the coach and train stations.

by bus

Buses run by the *Transports Urbains de Nice*, or TUN, are more than nice: nearly every stop has little lights telling you how far away your bus is, at least in theory; most seem to be permanently on the fritz.

Pick up a free *Guide Horaire du Réseau Bus* with maps and schedules at the tourist office or from TUN's information centre, 10 Av. Félix-Faure, ✆ 93 16 52 10. Several tourist tickets are available, offering limitless rides for one, five or seven days. For **taxis**, call ✆ 93 80 70 70.

by ferry

In the summer SNCM has frequent sailings to Corsica. For information and reservations contact them at Gare Maritime, Quai du Commerce, ✆ 93 13 66 66, ✆ 93 13 66 81.

car, bicycle and scooter hire

Among the cheapest car hire places is **Azur Rent-a-Car**, opposite the station on Av. Thiers, ✆ 93 88 69 69, ✆ 93 88 43 36, or at 25 Promenade des Anglais, ✆ 93 87 87 37, ✆ 93 87 95 55. International giants **Avis**, at 2 Av. des Phocéens at the end of Bd. Jean-Jaurès, ✆ 93 80 63 52, ✆ 93 21 44 53, or at the airport, ✆ 93 21 36 33, ✆ 93 21 36 33, and **Hertz** at the airport, ✆ 93 21 36 72, ✆ 93 21 35 92 and 12 Av. de Suède, ✆ 93 87 11 87, ✆ 93 87 86 13, offer more expensive options.

For bike/moped/scooter hire, contact **Cycles Arnaud**, 4 Place Grimaldi, ✆ 93 87 88 55; or **Nicea Location Rent**, 9 Av. Thiers, ✆ 93 82 42 71.

Tourist Information

Av. Thiers, next to the train station, ✆ 93 87 07 07, ✆ 93 16 85 16. Other offices are near the airport, ✆ 93 83 32 64 and at 5 Promenade des Anglais, ✆ 93 87 60 60. Information on lodgings, jobs, entertainment etc. for young people is available at **CRIJ**, 19 Rue Gioffredo, ✆ 93 80 93 93, ✆ 93 80 30 33.

Main post office: near the station at 23 Av. Thiers, ✆ 93 82 65 00, although Nice's *poste restante* is in Place Wilson, ✆ 93 85 98 63.

Police: ✆ 17.

Medical: S.O.S. doctors and ambulance, ✆ 93 92 55 55. Casualty ward, Hôpital St-Roch, 5 Rue Pierre-Devoluy, ✆ 92 03 33 75.

Dismissed as a dangerous slum in the 1970s, Nice's Vieille Ville, a piquant quarter east of Place Masséna, is busy becoming the trendiest part of Nice, brimful of cafés, bistros, night-clubs, designer boutiques and galleries. And the population, once poor and ethnically mixed, is now more than half French and upwardly mobile. But the shock of the new is mitigated by the tenacity of the old-grandmotherly underwear; paint and stationery shops, and no-name working-men's bars, have so far refused to budge. Picasso liked to walk here because it reminded him of the funky Barrì Chino in Barcelona.

'Vieux' in Vieux Nice means Genoese seaside Baroque—tall, steep *palazzi*, many with opulent 17th- and 18th-century portals and windows, turning the narrow streets and steps below into chasms that suddenly open up into tiny squares, each with its chapel. To this day the old Niçois are among the most religious people on the coast, and still join the confraternities of Penitents: lay organizations dedicated to public demonstrations of penitence, founded in Italy in the 14th century during the great Franciscan and Dominican revivals. Of the city's original seven confraternities, four still survive, all in this neighbourhood.

At its eastern end, the Vieux Ville is closed by **Colline du Château**, the ancient acropolis of Nikaïa and site of the 10th- to 12th-century town and cathedral. Of the latter, a few ruins remain—the Savoyards demolished it to make way for their citadel, which was in turn blown up by Louis XIV. You can walk up the steps or pay a few *sous* to take the lift at the east end of the Quai des Etats-Unis near **Tour Bellanda** (where Berlioz composed his *King Lear Overture*) and the little **Musée Naval**, ✆ 93 80 47 61 (*open 10am–12pm and 2–5pm, summer 2–7pm, closed Mon, Tues and mid-Nov–mid-Dec*), with ships' models. Among the gardens at the top of the hill are two cemeteries, one Jewish and one grandiose Italian, where you can find the tombs of Garibaldi's mum and Mercedes Jellinek, who gained immortality in 1902 when her father chose her name for a new line of Daimlers. From the belvedere by the artificial cascade the real boats down below don't look much bigger than the models in the museum, while the shimmering, tiled, glazed rooftops of Nice curl into the distance around the Baie des Anges.

If you descend by way of the east flank of the hill, down Montée Eberlé and Rue Catherine-Ségurane (where Nietzsche lived between 1883 and 1888), you'll end up in the arcaded, 18th-century **Place Garibaldi**, named after its glowering statue of the hero of Italy's unifica-tion, who was born near the port in 1806. The Blue Penitents (all Penitents are named by the colour of their hooded robes) have their neoclassical chapel of **St-Sépulcre** on this square, while just around the corner, facing the esplanade on 60 bis Bd. Risso, is the **Musée Barla d'Histoire Naturelle,** ✆ 93 55 15 24 (*open 9am– 2pm and 2–6pm, closed Tues, holidays, and mid-Aug–mid-Sept*), where you can ponder, among other things, a 19th-century collec-tion of 7000 painted plaster mushrooms.

South of Place Garibaldi off Rue Neuve is the city's oldest parish church, **St-Martin-St-Auguste**, where a monk named Martin Luther said a mass during his momentous pilgrimage to Rome. The interior was Baroqued in the 17th century; its treasures include a fine *Pietà* (*c. 1500*) by a follower of Ludovico Bréa, and a photocopy of Garibaldi's baptismal certificate. Further south, Rue Pairolière leads into 'Babazouck', the curious nickname for the heart of Vieux Nice, and **Place St-François**, where a pungent fish market takes place every morning except Monday. Continuing south, the **Chapelle de la Croix** in Rue de la Croix is the headquarters of the Pénitents Blancs, the oldest confraternity (founded in 1306) and the most popular, perhaps because they were still into public self-flagellation in the 1750s.

A block to the west, at 15 Rue Droite, the **Palais Lascaris**, ✆ 93 62 05 54 (*open 9.30am–12pm and 2.30–6pm, closed Mon and Nov*) is a grand 1648 Genoese-style mansion. The ground floor contains a reconstructed pharmacy of 1738; the first floor or *piano nobile*, where guests would be received, is saturated with elaborate Genoese 'quadratura' (architectural *trompe-l'œil*) frescoes, Flemish tapestries, ornate woodwork, and a 1578 Italian precursor of the pianoforte. The next floor is devoted to popular traditions, furnishings, and manufacturing. Contemporary exhibitions take place at the corner of Rue Droite and Rue de la Loge, at the **Galerie Municipale Renoir**, ✆ 93 13 40 46 (*open 10.30–6, closed Mon, Sun and Aug*).

Take Rue Rossetti west to the cafés of pretty Place Rossetti, dominated by Nice's 17th-century **Cathédrale Ste-Réparate**, crowned with a joyful dome and lantern of glazed tiles in emerald bands. The uncorrupted body of Réparate, a 15-year-old virgin martyred in Caesarea in the 300s, arrived in Nice in a boat of flowers towed by a pair of angels (hence Baie des Anges). This same Réparate was the first patron saint of Florence before the city adopted intermediaries with greater heavenly clout, and here, too, in Nice, the young virgin is currently losing a popularity contest with St Rita of Cascia, whose cult has already usurped the 17th-century **Eglise Saint-Giaume**, at 1 Rue de la Poissonnerie. Here, her altar gets nearly all the business, possibly because her speciality is unhappy middle-aged housewives—Rita herself was burdened in the 14th century with a rotten husband, ungrateful children, and a smelly sore on her forehead that just wouldn't heal.

Rita's compatriot, Paganini, who died nearby in 1840 at 23 Rue de la Préfecture, had his share of troubles too, but most of them were posthumous. Ste-Réparate's bishop was convinced that the sounds Paganini made on his violin could only have been produced by the devil incarnate (the maestro liked to startle the neighbours by making it howl like a tomcat) and refused him a Christian burial. He even wanted to toss Paganini's body into the Paillon. In the end, however, the dead fiddler was shunted to Cannes and then to Genoa and Parma, where he was finally buried in 1896.

Cours Saleya

After the dark lanes of Vieux Nice, the sun pops back into the sky over Cours Saleya, an elongated little gem of urban planning, where bars and restaurants line up along the famous outdoor market, overflowing with flowers and sumptuous food displays worthy of the Riviera's gourmet vortex. The Cours is closed at one end by the 17th-century Ancien Sénat and **St-Suaire**, home of the Red Penitents, who assisted pilgrims. But the principal focal point of the Cours is the Black Penitents' **Chapelle de la Miséricorde**, designed in 1740 by Bernardo Vittone, a disciple of Turin's extraordinary Baroque architects Guarino Guarini and Juvarra. Inside (unfortunately locked except for special tours: ask at the tourist office), it's all virtuoso Baroque geometry, a gold and stucco confection with vertiginous *trompe-l'œil* paintings in the vault. A fine early Renaissance *Polyptique de la Miséricorde* (1430) by Jean Mirailhet hangs in the sacristy, painted for the confraternity, whose mission was to assure the dead a dignified burial. The Cours also has the **Galerie de Malacologie du Muséum d'Histoire Naturelle**, at No.3, ✆ 93 85 18 44 (*open Dec–Oct, Tues–Sat 10.30am–1pm and 2–6pm*). *Malakos* in Greek means soft, which describes the texture of the residents of the museum's 15,000 seashells, a few of whom are still quick in the aquarium, the rest dead on the shelf.

A double row of one-storey buildings separates Cours Saleya from the Quai des Etats-Unis, where you'll find a pair of little museums (*both open Tues–Sat 10–12noon and 2–6pm, Sun 2–6pm*): the **Musée Alexis et Gustav-Adolf Mossa** at 59 Quai des Etats-Unis, ✆ 93 62 37 11, featuring landscapes by Alexis, a native of Nice, and the exquisitely drawn mytho-morbid Symbolist works of his son Gustav-Adolf Mossa (1883–1971), who painted between 1903 and 1917 and then just stopped. At No.77 the **Musée Dufy**, ✆ 93 62 31 24, has a large collection of paintings by a much cheerier soul who spent his latter years in Nice, producing colourful 'café-society' art. Far more compelling are the handful of Dufy's early Fauve works, especially the remarkable 1908 *Bateaux à l'Estaque*, a Cubist painting predating Cubism itself, although Dufy, like many of the Fauves, never followed the direction he mapped out for others.

The Port, Terra Amata, and Hilltop Follies

To the east, Quai des Etats-Unis circles around the wind-punched hill of the Château, where it's known as Quai Rauba-Capéu ('hat thief') before it meets placid **Bassin Lympia**, the departure point for ferries to Corsica. Among the 18th-century buildings overlooking the port is the **Musée de Terra Amata**, 25 Bd. Carnot, ✆ 93 55 59 93 (*buses 1, 9, 10, from Nice Central; open 9am–12noon and 2-6pm, closed Mon*), built into the cave holding one of the world's oldest 'households', a pebble-walled wind-shelter built by hunters 400 millennia ago. A fascinating set of models, bones and tools helps evoke life in Nice at the dawn of time. Nor had things changed radically 200,000 years later, judging by the palaeolithic relics left in the nearby **Grotte du Lazaret**, ✆ 93 26 59 19 (*phone to arrange a visit, as you need to be a scholar, or in a group*).

Boulevard Carnot (the Corniche Inférieure) continues east past some extravagant Belle Epoque villas, culminating in eccentricity in the pink, turreted **Château de l'Anglais**. Built in 1858 by Colonel Robert Smith, a military engineer in India, the result weds English Perpendicular with mock-Mogul Palace to produce one of the best follies on the Riviera. Behind this rise the forested slopes of **Mont Boron**; off Route Forestière du Mont Boron, a magnificent path, the **Sentier Bellevue**, meanders to the top, capped by a fort of 1880.

A far more delightful piece of military architecture, **Fort Alban**, is just off the Moyenne Corniche, above the youth hostel (take bus 14 to Chemin du Fort, or if you're driving, turn right off Rte Forestière du Mont Boron, on to Chemin du Fort du Mont Alban). Built in 1570, it bristles with four toy turrets roofed with glazed Niçois tiles, from which the guards could see all the way to Menton. To the north, off the Grande Corniche, is an elegant **Observatoire**, Bd. Bischoffsheim, ✆ 92 00 30 11, designed in part by Charles Garnier with a dome by Gustave Eiffel (*open Saturdays; adm; bus 74 from Bd. Pierre-Sola*).

Up the Paillon

In the old days Nice's laundresses plied their trade in the torrential waters of the Paillon, and were scrubbing away in 1543, when Ottoman pirates, under the dread admiral Barbarossa, attacked. Hearing the racket on the walls, an exceptionally beefy laundress named Catherine Ségurane rushed to the highest tower, and with her hollering, enthusiasm and skilful wielding of her washerwoman's paddle galvanized the defence. When she saw that Nice was about to fall, in spite of her best efforts, she climbed a ladder, bent over and dropped her drawers. The historians write that the Turks took one look at the biggest backside they had every seen and, fearing further revelations, retreated in confusion, and raised anchor.

The often dangerous Paillon was canalized and began to vanish under the pavements in the 1830s, and now secretly gushes or trickles below some of Nice's proudest showcases and gardens. Nearest the sea, Jardin Albert Ier is the site of the open-air **Théâtre de Verdure**, while upstream, as it were, vast **Place Masséna** is generously endowed with flower-beds and benches for Nice's sun-loving retirees. Further up, the Promenade du Paillon is dominated by the hanging gardens of the bus station/multi-storey car park, a mini-Babylon with an unsavoury reputation for small-time vice—vice that pales in the face of ex-mayor Jacques Médecin's pair of dread-noughts looming beyond.

Place Masséna, Nice

The first of these, reached by sets of Aztec temple steps, is Nice's answer to the Pompidou Centre in Paris: the 282-million-franc **Théâtre de Nice**, ✆ 93 80 52 60, ✉ 93 62 19 46, and the marble-coated **Musée d'Art Moderne et d'Art Contemporain**, ✆ 93 62 61 62, ✉ 93 13 09 01 (*open 11am–6pm except Tues and Sun; 11am–10pm Fri*). Inauspiciously inaugurated in June 1990, as the public revelations of Médecin's sins and fury over his anti-Semitism reached a pitch, the ceremony was boycotted by the Niçois art community, who convinced culture minister Jack Lang to stay away as well. If you overlook the fact that the roof was already leaking four months after it was finished, or that the museum had to be closed for major repairs in December 1991 when large cracks were discovered in its foundations, the building—four concrete towers, linked by glass walkways that seem to smile and frown and afford pleasant views over the city—is an admirable setting for the works of Christo, Niki de Saint-Phalle, Warhol, Dine, Oldenburg, Rauschenberg, and other influential figures of the 1960s and 70s. The primary focus is on the artists of the 'Second Nice school': Yves Klein, Martial Rayasse, César, Arman, Ben, and Swiss-born Jean Tinguely, whose New Realist concoctions of plastic consumer junk, broken machinery, musical intruments and exploding suicide machines spoof not only society, but the artificial, rarefied and wordy world of contemporary art—especially the push-button fun house called the *Little Shop of Ben*.

The view up the Paillon is blocked by Médecin's 1985 congress and art centre and *cinémathèque* called **Acropolis**, 1 Esplanade Kennedy, ✆ 93 89 83 00, a gruesome megalithic bunker of concrete slabs and smoked glass. No design could be more diametrically opposed (stylistically and philosophically) to the acropolis in Athens, and the mass of guitars in Arman's *Music Power* at the entrance hardly redeems it. Beyond this are more mastodons: a *Palais des Expositions* and a *Palais des Sports*.

West of Place Masséna and the Promenade des Anglais

The Paillon neatly divides Vieux Nice from the boom city of 19th-century tourism, full of ornate, debonair apartments and hotels. Important streets fan out from Place Masséna and the adjacent Jardin Albert Ier: Nice's main shopping street, **Av. Jean-Médecin**, leads up to the train station; **Rue Masséna**, the centre of a lively pedestrian-only restaurant and shopping zone; and the fabled, palm-lined **Promenade des Anglais**, still aglitter through the fumes of the traffic, which is usually as strangled as poor Isadora Duncan was when her scarf caught in the wheel of her Bugatti here in 1927. The long pebble beach is crowded day and night in the summer, when parties spontaneously erupt among the many illegal but tolerated campers.

Visitors from the opposite end of the economic spectrum check into the fabled Belle Epoque **Hôtel Negresco** (No.37), vintage 1906, although they no longer roll snake eyes in the 1929 **Palais de la Méditerranée**, a masterpiece of French Art Deco built by Frank Jay Gould. In 1960 it was the most profitable casino in France; by 1979 it was bankrupt, thanks to the machinations of Jacques Médecin and his cronies who favoured the rival **Casino Ruhl**. The Ruhl reopened next to the Negresco in spring 1995, in spite of the unsolved case of the disappearance and presumed murder of Agnès Le Roux, daughter of Renée Le Roux, at the time the main owner of the Palais de la Méditerranée. Five months before disappearing in 1977 Agnès had secretly sold her share in the family business to Jean-Dominique Fratoni, owner of the Ruhl and a man with mafia and Médecin links. Meanwhile the Palais de la Méditerranée was destined for the wrecking-ball, but the speculators gave in to the protests at the last minute, on the condition that the building had all its original innards removed like an Egyptian mummy. Another gem clinging tenaciously to the Promenade among the new buildings is at No.139, a flowery Art Nouveau-style villa of 1910 built by a Finnish engineer.

Next to the Negresco is the garden of the **Palais Masséna**, © 93 88 11 34 (*open daily except Mon, Oct–Apr 10am–12pm and 2–5pm, otherwise 10am–12pm and 3–6pm*). Built in the Empire style in 1901 for Prince Victor Masséna, the grandson of Napoleon's marshal, it was left to Nice on the condition that it become a *musée d'art et d'histoire*. At the entrance, a solemn statue of Napoleon tarted up in a toga sets the tone for the ground-floor salons—heavy and pompous and stylistically co-ordinated from ceiling stucco to chair leg. The atmosphere lightens upstairs with a pair of fine retables from the 1450s by Jacques Durandi, panels from a polyptych attributed to Ludovico Bréa, ceramics, armour, and a curious 16th-century Flemish painting, the *Vierge à la Fleur* with a fly in the flower, 'a symbol of death and vanity'. The top floor displays statues of the Ten Incarnations of Vishnu, Spanish earrings, views of Nice, and rooms dedicated to hometown boys Garibaldi and the cruel and wicked Marshal Masséna, the military genius Napoleon called '*l'enfant gâté de la victoire*' whose appetite for atrocities was matched only by his greedy plundering. Then there's the obligatory Napoleana: a billiard-ball from St Helena and Josephine's bed, with a big 'N' on the coverlet.

Fine and Naïf Arts, and a Russian Cathedral

From the Masséna museum, a brisk ten-minute walk or bus 22 (get off at the foot of Rue Bassenetts and walk 100m up the path) leads to the handsome 1880 villa built by a Ukranian princess, enlarged by an American millionaire, and now home of the **Musée des Beaux Arts**, 33 Av. des Baumettes, © 93 44 50 72 (*open 10am–12pm and 2–5pm, summer 3–6pm, closed Mon and Nov*). With the Matisses, Chagalls and Dufys in Nice's other museums, the

Musée des Beaux Arts is left with 'old masters of the 19th century'—a euphemism for tired, flabby academic paintings and portraits of Madame this and Madame that, a *Portrait of an Old Man* by Fragonard and works by Carle Van Loo, a native of Nice. But there are a few meatier paintings: a 1615 *David* attributed to Tanzio da Varallo, a Lombard follower of Caravaggio; a self-portrait by Russian aristocrat Marie Bashkirtseff; and a roomful of her contemporary, Kees Van Dongen, including his entertaining 1927 *Tango of the Archangel*, which perhaps more than any painting evokes the Roaring Twenties on the Riviera—even the archangel, in his dinner-jacket, is wearing high-heels. One room is devoted to Félix Ziem, and another to the Belle Epoque's favourite lithographist, Jules Chéret, who introduced colour posters to France in 1866, most of them decorated with dancing doll-women caught in swirling pastel tornadoes of silly *putti*.

To the west, the perfume magnate Coty built the pink Château de Ste-Hélène, a building now used as the **Musée d'Art Naïf Anatole Jakovsky**, Av. Val-Marie, ✆ 93 71 78 33, bus 9, 10, 12, stop *Fabron* (*open 10am–12pm and 2–5pm, 2–6pm summer, closed Tues*). The museum is formed around 600 paintings spanning the 17th to the 20th centuries, donated by Jakovsky, a tireless promoter of naïve art. The Yugoslavs are especially well-represented, with an enthusiasm for the genre that perhaps in some way counterbalances the unsolvable, nightmarish imbroglio of their politics. But even among the scenes of jolly village fêtes and fairs the surreal is never far, especially in *The Clock* by Jules Lefranc, and in the funny *Sodom and Gomorrah*, where the columns go flying every which way.

Three new commercial attractions have sprouted at the western end of Nice: the **Parc des Miniatures**, ✆ 93 44 67 74; bus 22 (*open every day; adm*) on Bd. Impératrice-Eugénie, where Côte landmarks from the Terra Amata caves to Nice's Museum of Contemporary Art have been shrunk down to a 1:25 scale. Also new, presumably to provide transport between the little buildings, is the **Musée des Trains Miniatures**, ✆ 93 97 41 40. Near the airport you may already have noticed the mega-greenhouse of **Parc Floral Phœnix**, 405 Promenade des Anglais, ✆ 93 18 03 33; bus 9, 10, 23, 24, 26 (*open every day 9am–7pm, 9am–5pm in winter*), a Disneyland for botanists or garden lovers: its diamond dome supports 2500 different plants in 7 different tropical climates—7 hectares of it .

In 1865, the young Tsarevich Nicholas was brought to Nice, and, like so many consumptives who arrived in search of health, he met the grim reaper instead. The luxurious villa where he died was demolished to construct a mortuary chapel and the great **Cathédrale Orthodoxe Russe St-Nicolas** (or **Eglise Russe**), located a few blocks from the west of the train station at 17 Bd. du Tzarévitch, just off Bd. Gambetta (*open Mon–Sat 9am–12pm and 2.30–6pm; no shorts or sleeveless shirts; adm*), modelled on the five-domed church of Jaroslav near Moscow. Paid for by Tsar Nicolas II and completed only five years before the Bolshevik Revolution, its five onion domes shine with a colourful coating of glazed Niçois tiles; inside are lavish frescoes, woodwork and icons.

Cimiez: Chagall, Matisse, and Roman Ruins

On the low hills west of the Paillon, where wealthy Romans lived the good life in *Cemenelum*, modern Niçois do the same in Cimiez, a luxurious 19th-century suburb dotted with the grand hotels of yesteryear. Bus 15 or 15a from the *gare routière* will take you to the main attractions, beginning with the **Musée National Message Biblique Marc Chagall**, at the foot of Cimiez hill on Av. du Docteur Ménard, west of Bd. de Cimiez, ✆ 93 81 75 75 (*open Oct–June*

10am–12.30pm and 2–5.30pm, July–Sept 10am–7pm, closed Tues; adm). Opened in 1971, the airy, specially designed building incorporates stained-glass windows and mosaics by Chagall while 17 large canvases on Old Testament subjects glow on the walls, especially the red, red, red series of the *Song of Songs*. There are often temporary exhibits on Jewish art and studies, and a suitably biblical garden of olives and cypresses with an outdoor café.

Cimiez owed much of its original cachet to Queen Victoria, and she's gratefully remembered with a statue in front of her favourite lodging, the Hôtel Excelsior Regina Palace on Av. Regina, off Av. Reine-Victoria. After the Second World War, the same hotel became headquarters for Henri Matisse, who died here in 1954, leaving the city a priceless collection of his works, displayed in the **Musée Matisse**, an exquisite late 17th-century Genoese villa at 164 Av. des Arènes-de-Cimiez, ✆ 93 81 08 08 (*take bus 22 from the Promenade des Anglais or Av. Jean-Médecin; open 11am–7pm, 10am–5pm Oct–April, closed Tues*). It contains all the bronzes Matisse ever made, and other works of every period—from one of his first oil-paintings, done in 1890, to his paper cut-outs of the 1950s; among the best known works are *Nature Morte aux Grenades*, *Rococo armchair*, designs for the chapel in Vence (*see p.99*), illustrations made for Joyce's *Ulysses*, and the world's largest collection of his drawings.

Adjacent to the Matisse Museum is the new **Musée Archéologique** (*open 10am–12pm and 2–6pm, October and May 2–5pm, closed Sun am and Mon*), entered through the excavations of *Cemenelum*. These include the baths, with a marble summer pool, and the amphitheatre, with seating for 4000 (unusually small for a population of 20,000, but perhaps the posh Romans here were too couth for gladiators). The museum houses vases, coins, statues, jewels, and models of what Cimiez looked like 2000 years ago.

From the archaeology museum it's a short walk across the Jardin Public to the Franciscan **Musée Franciscain Eglise et Monastère de Cimiez**, ✆ 93 81 00 04 (*guided tours; open 10–12pm, 3–6pm, closed Sun*). The Franciscans have been here since the 1500s, but their church was heavily restored in 1850, although it still has two beautiful altarpieces by Ludovico Bréa: the *Vierge de Piété* and a *Crucifixion* on a gold background, together with other less explicable 17th-century paintings in the cloister that some scholars think may have alchemical meanings. There's a museum documenting Franciscan life in Nice from the 13th–18th centuries, including both documents and art. Dufy and Matisse are buried in the adjacent cemetery, and there are fine views over the valley of the Paillon.

The Ministry of Culture sponsors the doings in the 18th-century **Villa Arson**, 20 Av. Stephen-Liégeard, ✆ 92 07 73 73 (*open summer 1–7pm, winter 2–6pm except Mon and Tues*)—not headquarters for a pyromaniac club, but a centre for contemporary art, with students, studios for working artists, exhibitions, a library, and thankfully, a café, surrounded by 1960ish concrete terraces decorated with pebbles.

Nice ✉ *06000* **Where to Stay**

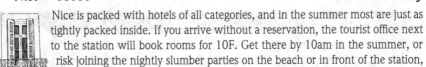 Nice is packed with hotels of all categories, and in the summer most are just as tightly packed inside. If you arrive without a reservation, the tourist office next to the station will book rooms for 10F. Get there by 10am in the summer, or risk joining the nightly slumber parties on the beach or in front of the station, where you'll encounter giant cockroaches from hell. Come instead in the off season, when many of the best hotels offer the kind of rates the French would call *très intéressant*.

Nice has luxury grand hotels galore, but for panache none can top the fabulous green-domed ★★★★**Negresco**, 37 Promenade des Anglais, ✆ 93 16 64 00, 🖷 93 88 35 68. A national historic monument, it was designed for Romanian hotelier Henri Negresco (who started his career as a gypsy violinist) by Edouard Niermans, architect of the Moulin Rouge and the Folies Bergères. The one hotel in Nice where a Grand Duke would still feel at home, and the last independent luxury hotel on the coast, its 150 chambers and apartments have all been redecorated with Edwardian furnishings and paintings by the likes of Picasso and Léger. Most spectacular of all is the *salon royal*, lit by a Baccarat chandelier made for the Tsar.

If hobnobbing with the rich and famous in the Negresco is out, there's the elegant Art Deco ★★★★**Beau Rivage**, 24 Rue St-François-de-Paule, ✆ 93 80 80 70, 🖷 93 80 55 77, on a pedestrian street in Vieux Nice overlooking the sea and Beau Rivage beach; Matisse spent two years here and Chekhov, during his stay, wrote *The Seagull*. The rooms are as luminous and beautiful as a Matisse and there's direct access to the beach. Or you can choose the modern comforts, roof-top pool, sauna, and many other amenities of the artsy, stylish ★★★★**Elysée Palace**, 59 Promenade des Anglais, ✆ 93 86 06 06, 🖷 93 44 50 40, with a façade dominated by an enormous bronze silhouette of a woman.

Best among the tri-star choices is the idiosyncratic ★★★**Windsor**, 11 Rue Dalpozzo (behind the Negresco), ✆ 93 88 59 35, 🖷 93 88 94 57, in the midst of a tropical garden, featuring a pool, an English-style pub, a Turkish hammam, a Thai sitting room and dreamy frescoes in the rooms. Another choice with character, ★★★**Vendôme**, in the centre of town at 26 Rue Pastorelli, ✆ 93 62 00 77, 🖷 93 13 40 78, has prettily-renovated, air-conditioned rooms, a superb stairway, and a garden. More reasonable but still stylish choices include the handsome ★★**Nouvel Hôtel**, 19 bis Bd. Victor-Hugo, ✆ 93 87 15 00, 🖷 93 16 00 67, Belle Epoque in style, but with air-conditioned rooms, each with its own bath.

In quiet Cimiez, ★★**Le Floride** has lost some of its former charm, but is still an attractive old villa with a shady garden at 52 Bd. de Cimiez, and each blue room has a colour TV and bath (✆ 93 53 11 02, 🖷 93 81 57 46; the restaurant now only serves lunch). Up beyond Cimiez, at the northern exit to Nice, ★★**Le Relais de Rimiez** at 128 Av. de Rimiez, ✆ 93 81 18 65, 🖷 93 53 51 23, has terraces overlooking the city and the sea. *Closed Jan–mid-Feb.*

For long-term stays, there are three comfortable apartment-hotels just off the Promenade des Anglais, run by the Citadines group: **Nice Avenue des Fleurs,** 17 Av. des Fleurs, ℭ 92 15 51 51, ✆ 92 15 51 00; **Nice Buffa,** 21 Rue Meyerbeer, ℭ 93 16 54 54, ✆ 93 16 18 32; and **Nice Promenade,** 3–5 Bd. F.-Grosso, ℭ 93 37 26 26, ✆ 93 44 93 88.

inexpensive

There are plenty of cheaper choices; perhaps the one most likely to bring happiness is the 11-room **Porte Bonheur,** with its little garden at 146 Av. St-Lambert, ℭ 93 84 66 10, undignified even by a star but the only cheap hotel in this list to be featured on French TV for its charm. Double rooms with bath are 135F plus, but book well in advance to get one (it's north of the station near the interesting 1930s church of Ste-Jeanne d'Arc, bus 1, 2, 22, 24 to Av. Borriglione).

A stone's throw from the station the friendly ★**La Belle Meunière,** 21 Av. Durante, ℭ 93 88 66 15, is a long-time favourite of budget travellers in Nice—it even has parking and a little garden for breakfast. Another choice is **Soleil d'Or,** 16 Av. des Oranges, ℭ 93 96 55 94, which has 11 rooms and a restaurant. In Vieux Nice, near the coach station, ★**Au Picardy,** 10 Bd. Jean-Jaurès, ℭ 93 85 75 51, has pleasant soundproof rooms in a family pension atmosphere.

The **Auberge de Jeunesse** is 4km east of town (bus 14, stop *L'Auberge*) on Rte Forestière du Mont-Alban, ℭ 93 89 23 64, but beware that the last bus leaves at 7pm. Even further afield is Cimiez's **Clairvallon Relais International de la Jeunesse,** 26 Av. Scudéri, ℭ 93 81 27 63 (bus 15 or 22), although it has the added plus of a pool. There are dormitory rooms in the **Espace Magnan,** west of the centre at 31 Rue Louis-de-Coppet (bus 3, 9, 10, 12, 22 stop: *Rosa Bonheur*), ℭ 93 86 28 75; or individual ones in the university residence halls at **Les Collinettes** during July and August, 3 Av. Robert-Schumann, ℭ 93 97 06 64 (bus 14 or 17, stop: *Châteauneuf*).

Nice ✉ *06000*   ***Eating Out***

Although now a solidly French-speaking corner of the Hexagon, Nice's cuisine still has a heavy Ligurian accent, with a fondness for seafood, olive oil and olives, chick peas, fresh basil, and pine-nuts. A typical first course consists of pasta (ravioli filled with seafood or artichoke hearts, or served with a delectable walnut sauce) or, in the summer, *soupe au pistou*, a hearty soup of courgettes (zucchini), tomatoes, beans, potatoes, onions and vermicelli, served with *pistou*, a sauce based on basil, pine-nuts, and garlic. Another Niçois favourite is *bourride*, a fish soup served with *aïoli* that many prefer to the more elaborate Marseille *bouillabaisse*, and teeny-tiny fish called *poutines*, by law only caught between Beaulieu and Cagnes, and which local cooks fry in omelettes or pile on top of pasta.

Another popular first course is the world-famous *salade Niçoise*, which even in Nice is made in as many 'true and genuine' ways as *bouillabaisse* in Marseille—with quartered tomatoes, capers, black olives, spring onions, anchovies or tuna, green beans, and with or without hard-boiled eggs and potatoes. Main courses are often from the sea: grilled fish with herbs or, more of an acquired taste, *estocaficada*, wine-dried cods and guts, stewed in *eau-de-vie*, with potatoes, garlic, onions, and peppers. Favourite side dishes include *ratatouille* (another famous dish of Niçois origin) or boiled Swiss chard (*blette*) in vinaigrette.

expensive

Gastronomic Nice is dominated by the Belle Epoque magnificence of the **Chantecler**, 37 Promenade des Anglais, ✆ 93 16 64 00, the restaurant snuggling into the opulent arms of the Negresco. Here Dominique Le Stanc, successor to the flamboyant chef Jacques Maximin, has succeeded in seducing the Niçois with his own fabulous versions of Chantecler favourites like ravioli bursting at the seams with *langoustines*, asparagus tips, and artichokes, pigeon roast with cumin and and a melt-in-your mouth *marbre de chocolat chaud* with a delicate almond cream (*lunch menus from 250F including wine*). **Don Camillo**, 5 Rue des Ponchettes, ✆ 93 85 67 95, was opened by a former pupil of Maximin and Paul Ducasse, already celebrated for its homemade ravioli filled with Swiss chard *en daube* and fabulous Italian desserts (*à la carte only, around 320F*).

moderate

The best restaurant-hunting territory is Vieux Nice and, especially for fresh fish, around the port, where you'll find the charming **Les Préjugés du Palais**, 1 Place de Palais, ✆ 93 62 37 03, serving up delicious French classics with a seafood emphasis, followed by luscious desserts; the 160F menu is excellent value. *Closed Sun.* **Atmosphère**, 36 Cours Saleya, ✆ 93 62 32 50, enjoys a privileged spot and offers good but hardly exceptional seafood, not always served with a smile (*menus from 100F to 350F*). Also in Vieux Nice, with a terrace near the sea at 50 Bd. Jean-Jaurès, **McMahon**, ✆ 93 51 84 82, was named after the Irish family fleeing Ireland, later becoming the Duke of Magenta. Elsewhere, **Restaurant Flo**, 4 Rue Sacha-Guitry, ✆ 93 13 38 38, offers oysters and fish for late-night theatre crowds (*last orders 1.30am, menus from 99F*).

inexpensive

Less expensive choices abound. One of the best is up in Cimiez: **Auberge de Théo**, 52 Av. Cap de Croix, ✆ 93 81 26 19, where on a large terrace overlooking Nice, you'll find genuine Italian pizzas, salads with *mesclun* (Nice's special mixed salad), and Venetian *tiramisù* for dessert (*70–150F*). Best near the station is **Aux Voyageurs Nissart**, 19 Rue d'Alsace-Lorraine, between the station and Av. Jean-Médecin, ✆ 93 82 19 60, which has a wide-ranging 62–90F menu.

For snacks and somewhere to sit, Vieux Nice's **René Socca**, 2 Rue Miralhetti, ✆ 93 92 05 73, offers *socca*, *pissaladière*, pizza by the slice and much more, which you can down with a beer or wine at the bar across the street; **Cave Ricord**, 2 Rue Neuve, near Place Garibaldi, ✆ 93 85 30 87, a funny old-fashioned wine bar with *socca*, pizza, and *pan-bagnats* and other inexpensive dishes serving a slightly too touristy crowd; or the popular **La Taverne de L'Opéra**, 10 Rue St-François-de-Paule, ✆ 93 85 72 68, with excellent *socca* and other delights, plus jazz on Friday nights (*70–90F*). For Italian, try the small and cheap **Spaghetti Ssimo**, 3 Cours Saleya, ✆ 93 80 95 07 (*49–109F, closed Sunday evening*). For good traditional French bistro food, try **St. Germain**, 9 Rue Chauvin, ✆ 93 13 45 12.

Vieux Nice is the most attractive place to shop, for art, cheap clothes and glorious food at the outdoor markets and local shops. In Cours Saleya, the morning **food and flower market** (*daily exc Mon*) is supplemented on Monday by old books, clothes, and bric-à-brac; arts and crafts appear on Wednesday afternoon, and paintings on Sunday afternoons. At Place St-Francis is the **Fish Market** (*6am–1pm every day exc Monday*) and many Niçois gourmets swear that the olive oil from **Alziari Nicolas**, 14 Rue St-François-de-Paule, is the best in the world; on the same street at No.7, **Henri Auer** is famous for its chocolates and crystallized fruits. The pedestrian zone around Place Masséna has scores of clothes shops and boutiques, while in Av. Jean-Médecin you'll find Nice's biggest department store, Galeries Lafayette, and Marks & Spencer, as well as *Nice Etoile*, a centre with useful shops like the bookshop FNAC (which sells tickets to concerts and other events) and the Body Shop. For antiques, try the shops around Rue Antoine-Gauthier (by the port) or the antique market, **Villa Ségurane**, at 28 Rue Catherine-Ségurane. For santons try **La Couquetou**, 8 Rue St-François-de-Paule; or **Les Poupées Yolandes**, ✆ 4 Rue A.-Gauthier. Provençal fabrics can be found at **Sainte Réparate Provence**, 1 Rue Ste-Réparate, ✆ 93 13 03 14. **Papeterie Rontan**, 5 Rue Alexandre-Mari, ✆ 93 62 32 43, an old-fashioned, wood-floored shop, sells delicious paper of every sort, and maps a-plenty. Books in English are sold at **The Cat's Whiskers**, 26 Rue Lamartine.

Entertainment and Nightlife

You can find out what's happening in Nice in the daily *Nice-Matin*, though it's not much good for anything else except lining the canary's cage. Other sources covering the entire Côte are *7 jours/7 nuits*, distributed free in the tourist offices, or the *Semaine des Spectacles*, which appears Wednesdays in the news-stands, or Radio Riviera, the coast's English language station broadcast out of Monaco at 106.3 and 106.5. Local news, hours of religious services in English and more are in the monthly English-language *Blue Coast Magazine*, a new, glossy look at life on the Riviera, distributed in newsagents and English bookshops. If you need a **babysitter**, contact the baby-sitting service at 54 Bd. René-Cassin, ✆ 93 21 62 01.

The movie-goer in Nice is spoilt for choice: there's the **Pathé Paris**, 54 Av J.-Médicin, ✆ 36 68 20 22; **Pathé Masséna**, with the same phone number as Pathé Paris, and just down the road; **Variétés**, 7 Bd. Victor-Hugo, ✆ 93 87 74 97; or for films in their original language at the **Rialto**, 4 Rue de Rivoli, one block from the Negresco, ✆ 93 88 08 41; **Le Nouveau Mercury**, 16 Place Garibaldi, ✆ 93 55 32 31; and **Cinémathèque de Nice**, 3 Esplanade Kennedy, ✆ 93 04 06 66. The Belle Epoque **Opéra de Nice**, 4–6 Rue St-François-de-Paule, ✆ 93 85 67 31, puts on operas, concerts and recitals at various locations including the **Acropolis** (1 Esplanade Kennedy); the **Théâtre de Nice** (Esplanade des Victoires); and the **Théâtre de Verdure** (on the Promenade des Anglais). Classical music concerts are organised by **La Fondation Sophia-Antipolis à l'Hôtel Westminster**, 27 Promenade des Anglais, ✆ 93 88 29 44, **Fondation Kosma**, at the Conservatoire de Nice, ✆ 93 53 01 17; free at the **Musée Chagall** (*Sept–May*), and also Musée des Beaux-Arts, 33

Av. des Baumettes, ✆ 93 44 50 72 (*once a month, October–May*) Music, from ancient to avant-garde, and art videos are the fare in the auditorium of the **Musée d'Art Moderne et d'Art Contemporain**, ✆ 93 62 61 62. Big-league musicians and dancers perform at **CEDAC de Cimiez**, 49 Av. de la Marne, ✆ 93 81 09 09, while **Forum Nice Nord**, 10 Bd. Comte-de-Falicon, just off the A8 at Nice-Nord, ✆ 93 84 24 37, is a major venue for modern dance. From April onwards rock, jazz, and other concerts take place in the outdoor **Théâtre de Verdure** in Jardin Albert Ier. There are several small theatres in Vieux Nice with imaginative productions, such as **Théâtre du Cours**, 5 Rue de la Poissonnerie, ✆ 93 80 12 67, and **Théâtre de La Semeuse**, 21 Rue St-Joseph, ✆ 93 92 85 08. Molière and other classics are showcased at **Théâtre de l'Alphabet**, 10 Bd. Carabacel, ✆ 93 13 08 88, and in the new **Théâtre de Nice**, by the contemporary art museum, ✆ 93 80 52 60.

Nice's nightlife is divided between expensive clubs and bland hotel piano bars, and the livelier bars and clubs of Vieux Nice, which come and go like ships in the night. Some of the most jumping joints are the ex-pat havens in Vieux Nice, noisiest of which is the British-owned **Chez Wayne**, 15 Rue de la Préfecture, ✆ 93 13 46 99 (*open 10 am–midnight, reservations obligatory at weekends*), a pub and restaurant with live music every night . Fiddlers fiddle at the **Scarlett O'Hara**, 22 Rue Droite, ✆ 93 80 43 22. The Dutch go boozing at the funky **De Klomp**, 6 Rue Mascoïnat, near Place Rossetti, ✆ 93 92 42 85, with live jazz and a hedonistic atmosphere not for tee-totallers or anti-smokers. Other night music in Vieux Nice is Brazilian, at the **Ship**, 5 Rue Barillone, ✆ 93 80 46 76, accompanied by cuisine from the Americas (135F menu) and Californian wines, of all things. **Hole in the Wall**, at 3 Rue de l'Abbaye, ✆ 93 80 40 16, is just that: a small hole serving large beers, big fresh burgers, and live music on an unfeasibly small stage. To the north of Vieux Nice, **Jonathan's** beer cellar serves food, lit by candles, and the 1970s-inspired 'live' music is hosted by Jonathan himself: wait long enough and he might treat you to his Rolf Harris impersonation. For clubbing and dancing, **Alizé**, Quai des Etats-Unis, ✆ 93 92 37 08, is fast, and full of sailors, of course; and **Le Forum Music**, 45 Promenade des Anglais, ✆ 93 85 05 06, which, perhaps due to its location, has more tourists and too many prostitutes for its own good; **Le News Rock**, 9 Passage E. Négrin, ✆ 93 87 76 30, is much younger, both in its music and clientele.

Other tempting places for a drink or snack include the 19th-century **Grand-Café de Turin** (or **Chez Jo L'Ecailler**), 5 Place Garibaldi, ✆ 93 62 66 29, serving some of the best, cheapest oysters in town (and other shellfish in non-R months, *open until 11*).

Festivals

Nice is famous for its **carnival** in the two weeks before Lent, first mentioned in the 13th century. It died out in the early 1800s, and subsequent attempts to revive it to amuse the tourists only succeeded in 1873, when the painters Alexis and Gustav-Adolf Mossa took over the show. They initiated a burlesque royal cortège to escort the figure of King Carnival, *Sa Majesté Carnaval*, down Av. Jean-Médecin, accompanied by comical *grosses têtes*—masqueraders with giant papier-mâché heads. During the subsequent parades, dances and battles of flowers and sweets, King Carnival reigns from Place Masséna, only to be immolated on the night of Mardi Gras to the explosive barrage of fireworks. As mayor, Jacques Médecin was a big supporter of the carnival, much to the annoyance of many residents, especially since it cost more money to put on than it brought in, and was generally agreed to be a commercial rip-off; future carnivals will, it seems, be on a smaller scale. The second and third weeks of July see the excellent **Festival de Jazz** in the Jardin Public de Cimiez; from the end of July to the beginning of August there are the **Festival International du Folklore** and more *Bataille des Fleurs*, and in September there's the **Fête de la Vigne**, when Bacchus is not forgotten. The Comité des Fêtes handles all festival information at 5 Promenade des Anglais, ℂ 93 87 16 28.

Vin de Bellet AOC

'The wine-merchants of Nice brew a balderdash, and even mix it with pigeon's dung and quick-lime' wrote Tobias Smollett. But they never dared to mess with Vin de Bellet, the rare and costly elixir produced in the steep, sun-soaked hills west of Nice. The vineyards owe their special quality to the alternating currents of sea and mountain air and to their original varieties of grapes: *braquet, folle noire* and *negrette de Nice*, all of which combine to create a noble wine with a bouquet of wild cherry that can be aged up to 30 years. The rosés, from the same grapes, are one of the best accompaniments to *loup*, the most delicate Mediterranean fish. Vin de Bellet *blanc*, reminiscent of chablis, is a blend of *rolle, spagnou, roussan* and *mayorquin*.

Only 1200 hectolitres are produced each year, and most of it never gets much further than the cellars of the Riviera's top restaurants. Alternatively, pick up a bottle of your own by ringing ahead and following the Route de Bellet north of Rue de France (parallel to the Promenade des Anglais) to St-Roman-de-Bellet and the 18th-century **Château de Bellet,** ℂ 93 37 81 57. The second estate, **Château de Crémat,** just south of the *autoroute* A8, off Av. Durandi, ℂ 93 37 80 30, is a fantasy castle, built in 1850 in a pseudo-medieval style called *style troubadour*.

St. Paul de Vence

West of Nice: Cagnes to Cannes

The deep Greek of the Mediterranean licked its chops over the edges of our febrile civilization.

Zelda Fitzgerald

The stretch of the Riviera between Nice and Cannes is just about as dense and febrile and excessive as old Europe ever gets—'one vast honky-tonk' declared Noel Coward back in 1960: too many cars, villas, theme parks, and marinas full of yachts the size of tankers, too many gift shops in the lovely *villages perchés*, too many Parisians and movie stars in Cannes and too many technocrats in Sophia-Antipolis, the 'Silicon Valley of the Riviera'. The scenery, especially up around the Gorges du Loup, is decidedly excessive, and you can be bedazzled by the perfumes at Grasse and surplus of art that crowds the coast: Renoir in Cagnes, Léger in Biot, more Matisse in Vence, Picasso in Antibes and Vallauris, and all the contemporary greats up at the dazzling Fondation Maeght. There are so many good restaurants at Mougins, you hardly dare go out for a walk. Nothing succeeds like excess.

For a map of the region *see* pp.46–7.

___

Beaches

Between Nice and Antibes the shore is as rocky as the eastern side of the Côte. But purists should make for Antibes, where the sand starts in earnest. There are two public beaches in Antibes: the best lie south of the town centre, just before the Cap, with views back across the Baie des Anges to the Alps.

Juan-les-Pins, blessed with fine sand, is also cursed with countless private beach clubs. Public beaches exist here—try further west towards Golfe-Juan. Cannes has even more snooty beach clubs, but here too there is a public beach right in front of the Palais des Festivals. Further west towards Mandelieu the beach is beautifully sandy, and free.

best beaches

Antibes: Port and south of centre on D2559.

Cannes: Palais des Festivals and west to Mandelieu.

Cagnes

West of Nice runs the river Var, the wet but politically prickly border between France and Savoy, whose dukes were usually allied to France's rivals—England, Spain, or Austria. As bridges over the Var were periodically blown up, for centuries people crossed the water sitting on the shoulders of two strong men. Nowadays in the maelstrom of traffic and overbuilding it's hard even to notice the Var at all. Across the river lies the bloated amoeba of Cagnes, divided into three cells—overbuilt Cros-de-Cagnes by the sea with a Hippodrome; Cagnes-sur-Mer, further up, site of Renoir's house, the happiest of all artists' shrines in the south; and medieval Haut-de-Cagnes on the hill, notorious in the 17th and 18th centuries for the indecorous pastimes and the brilliant parties held in its castle before the Revolution—beginning a long tradition of artsy decadence and futility chronicled in Cyril Connolly's *The Rock Pool* (1936), in which Zelda Fitzgerald's carnivorous Greek Mediterranean becomes merely 'the tideless cloaca of the ancient world'.

Getting Around

There are **train stations** in both Cagnes-sur-Mer and Cros-de-Cagnes (for information, call ✆ 93 22 46 47) and eight **minibuses** a day from Cagnes-sur-Mer station up the steep hill to Haut-de-Cagnes. There's a massive **underground car park** just outside the village entrance, and restricted parking in the serpentine streets of the old village (beware of parking by the police station at the back of the château). **Buses** from Nice to Vence stop in Cagnes-sur-Mer, where you can also **hire a bike** at Cyclette Marcel, 5 Rue Pasqualene, ✆ 93 20 64 07.

Tourist Information

Cagnes-sur-Mer (✉ 06804): 6 Bd. Maréchal-Juin, ✆ 93 20 61 64.

market days

Cagnes-sur-Mer: Wednesdays.
Cros de Cagnes: Tuesdays and Thursdays.

Cagnes-sur-Mer: Musée Renoir

Av. des Colettes, open 10am–12pm and 2–5pm, summer 2–6pm, closed Tues and 15 Oct–15 Nov; adm; ✆ 93 20 61 07.

There is only one thing to do in sprawling Cagnes-sur-Mer: from central Place Général-de-Gaulle follow Av. Auguste-Renoir up to Chemin des Colettes, to Les Colettes, where Renoir spent the last 12 years of his life. Stricken with rheumatoid arthritis, Renoir followed his doctor's advice to move to warmer climes and chose Cagnes, where 'one's nose is not stuck in the mountains'; in 1903 he purchased an ancient olive grove to build a villa in. Rejuvenated by the climate, Renoir produced paintings even more sensuous and voluptuous than

93

before, and there's no contrast more poignant than that of colour-saturated *Grandes Baigneuses* (in the Louvre) and the photograph in the museum of the painter's hands, so bent and crippled that they're painful even to look at. 'I pay dearly for the pleasure I get from this canvas,' he said of one portrait that he especially liked, painted with brushes strapped to his hands. It was also in Cagnes that Renoir first experimented with sculpture, by proxy, dictating detailed instructions to a young sculptor.

In 1989, the museum's collection of portraits of Renoir by his friends was supplemented with ten canvases the master himself painted in Cagnes. The north studio, with his wheelchair and easel, looks as if Renoir might return any minute—even the chicken wire he put over the window to keep out the children's tennis balls is in place. You can wander freely through the venerable olive grove; the only drastic change from Renoir's day is the view down to the sea.

Haut-de-Cagnes

Spared the worst of the tourist shops, intricate, medieval Haut-de-Cagnes has become instead the fiefdom of contemporary artists, thanks to the UNESCO-sponsored *Festival International de la Peinture*. The crenellated **Château-Musée Grimaldi**, ✆ 93 20 85 57 (*open daily exc Tues, 10am–12pm and 2–5pm in winter, 10am–12pm and 2.30–7pm in summer, closed 15 Oct–15 Dec; adm*) was built by the first Rainier Grimaldi in the 1300s, at a time when there were a hundred excess male Grimaldis prowling the coast, looking for a castle to call home. This particular branch of the family held on to Cagnes until the Revolution; its most famous twig was Henri, a good friend of Louis XIII, who convinced his cousin in Monaco to put himself under the protection of France rather than Spain.

A handsome inner courtyard tiered with galleries provided all the castle's light and air. In the vaulted halls on the ground floor there's a **Musée de l'Olivier**, where among the presses you may find a small machine for pressing coins, not olives, used by the Marquis to counterfeit the king's coin (he was arrested in 1710, by the Comte d'Artagnan of the Musketeers). Upstairs are Henri Grimaldi's ornate reception rooms, topped by *The Fall of Phaeton* (1624) by the Genoese Giovanni Andrea Carlone, one of those hysterical *trompe-l'œil* ceiling paintings of floating horse stomachs and testicles that the Italians were so fond of. In another room, the **Donation Suzy Solidor** contains 40 paintings donated by the free-living chanteuse and cabaret star, each a portrait of herself, each by a different artist—Van Dongen, Dufy, Kisling, Friesz, Cocteau, and so on. On the next floor, the **Musée d'Art Moderne Méditerranéen** is dedicated to the above and other painters who have worked on the coast.

Besides the château, Henri hired the Genoese to fresco the walls of the **Chapelle Notre-Dame de la Protection**, just below (*open 2.30–6pm July, Aug, Sept, otherwise 2–5pm, closed Tues and Fri*). Later whitewashed over, the frescoes were only rediscovered by accident in 1936, and are full of quirky perspective tricks that make the babies as big as some of the mothers in the *Massacre of the Innocents*.

Villeneuve-Loubet and Escoffier

To the southwest of Cagnes, on another hill dominated by another medieval castle, Villeneuve-Loubet is a small village known for its fishing, a visit by François Ier (where he signed a ten-year peace treaty with Charles V in 1538) and Marshal Pétain, hero of the First World War, who was working as a farmer and wine grower before accepting the summons to govern France from Vichy. The event that really put it on the map, however, happened in

1846, when Auguste Escoffier came into the world here to become 'the chef of kings and the king of chefs'—the king in question being Edward VII, who encouraged Escoffier and the hotelier César Ritz to move to London, thus making the Savoy and the Carlton citadels of class and cuisine. Escoffier's birthplace is now the **Musée de l'Art Culinaire**, 3 Rue Escoffier, © 93 20 80 51, (*open 2–6pm, 2–7pm summer, closed Mon, holidays, and Nov*), but don't come looking for nibbles or scratch-and-sniff exhibits of his creations. Instead there's a 19th-century Provençal kitchen; an autographed photo of soprano Nellie Melba, thanking Escoffier for calling his new peach dessert after her; a collection of the chef's radical light menus which seem incredibly elaborate nowadays; and the sugar sculptures Escoffier loved, still prepared by local *pâtissiers* for saccharine competitions that put the kitsch back in kitchen. There's also a **Musée Militaire**, Place de Verdun, © 93 22 01 56 (*open 10–12 and 2–7, closed Mon*).

Villeneuve-Loubet-Plage is another kettle of fish, home of those concrete ziggurats you may have already noticed, looming over the Bay of Angels with all the charm of totalitarian Mesopotamia. They are part of the **Marina Baie des Anges** built in the 1970s, before the French regulated building on the coast—too late indeed for the once beautiful stretch between here and Cannes.

Cagnes ✉ *06800*   ***Where to Stay and Eating Out***

Haut-de-Cagnes

The luxury choice for this niche of the coast is Haut-de-Cagnes's ★★★**Le Cagnard**, Rue Pontis-Long, © 93 20 73 21, 📠 93 22 06 39, with sumptuous comforts discreetly arranged to fit in with the 12th-century architecture. Nearly every room has a private terrace, but the largest and most magical belongs to the hotel's excellent restaurant, serving delicacies such as pigeon stuffed with morels and *foie gras* (*but for a price—menus begin at 300F*). *Open all year*. You can dine for less at **Les Peintres**, 71 Montée de la Bourgade, © 93 20 83 08, where the walls are covered with paintings and the tables with warm homemade bread and Provençal dishes (*menus 200, 300 and 420F*). *Closed mid-Nov–mid-Dec, Wed*.

Cagnes-sur-Mer

In Cagnes-sur-Mer, modern ★★**Les Colettes**, Chemin des Colettes, © 93 20 80 66, is the best choice, with a pleasant welcome, a pool overlooked by balconies with deckchairs, and kitchenettes in most rooms. *Closed Nov–26th Dec*. None of the restaurants here stands out, but the 40 different kinds of fresh chocolates do at **L'Oiseau d'Or**, 2 Place Général-de-Gaulle, © 93 20 80 54, including *grimaldines*, flavoured with fresh orange juice.

St-Paul-de-Vence and Vence

Inland from Cagnes are two towns as bound up with contemporary art as any in France. St-Paul-de-Vence is the home of the wonderful Fondation Maeght, while Vence has a unique **chapel** painted by **Matisse** (*open only Tues and Thurs, closed Nov*). D.H. Lawrence and Marc Chagall died in Vence, a pleasant enough old town where real people still live amongst the writers, artists, and perfectly tanned Martians with faces lifted, stretched, and moulded into tautly permanent supercilious frowns.

There are frequent **buses** from Cagnes-sur-Mer to La Colle-sur-Loup, St-Paul-de-Vence and Vence, and connections nearly every hour from Nice. La Gaude can be reached by bus from St-Jeannet and Cagnes-sur-Mer (but not from Vence); Tourrettes-sur-Loup and Le Bar-sur-Loup are on the Vence–Grasse bus route.

Tourist Information

St-Paul-de-Vence (✉ 06570): Maison de la Tour, ✆ 93 32 86 95.
Vence (✉ 06140): Place du Grand Jardin, ✆ 93 58 06 38, 📠 93 58 91 81.

market days

Vence: Tuesday to Friday: fruit,vegetables and flowers, Place Surian et Place du Grand Jardin; Tuesday and Friday: clothes, Place Clemenceau; Wednesday: flea-market, Place Clemenceau; Saturday (*all day*): arts and crafts, Place Clemenceau.

St-Paul-de-Vence

Between Cagnes and St-Paul the D6 winds above the river Loup, passing through **La Colle-sur-Loup**, a village once famous for its roses, that now earns its keep from the overspill of tourists from St-Paul-de-Vence, its mother town. For La Colle was founded in 1540, when François Ier showed his gratitude to St-Paul-de-Vence for standing up to the assaults of his arch-rival, Emperor Charles V, by financing a rampart around the town. Some 700 houses had to be demolished to make room for the king's gift, obliging the displaced populace to move elsewhere.

Reduced in size, **St-Paul-de-Vence** became the '*ville fortifiée*' and still preserves a *donjon* watchtower dating from the 12th century, as well as François's costly ramparts. A cannon captured from Charles V is embedded near the town gate, a gate much more accessible these days than the simple wooden door of the restaurant **La Colombe d'Or**, down in the square. Its first owner, an unschooled farmer named Paul Roux, fell in love with modern art and for 40 years accepted paintings in exchange for hospitality from the impoverished artists who flocked here after the First World War—including Picasso, Derain, Matisse, Braque, Vlaminck, Léger, Dufy, and Bonnard. By the time he died he had accumulated one of France's greatest private collections—but strictly for the viewing by those who can at least afford a meal.

If you're prone to claustrophobia, visit St-Paul early, before its little lanes are clogged with visitors and baskets of artsy trinkets. From its ramparts, to the north, you can see the odd, sphinx-shaped rock called the **Baou de St-Jeannet**, that was painted into the uncanny landscape of Nicolas Poussin's *Polyphème*. There's a handsome fountain along Rue Grande, and the church of the **Conversion de St-Paul**, sumptuously furnished with Baroque stuccoes, woodwork and paintings—including one of St Catherine of Alexandria in the left aisle, attributed in part to Tintoretto.

Fondation Maeght

> *Here is an attempt at something never before undertaken: creating a world with which modern art can both find its place and that otherworldliness which used to be called supernatural.*
>
> The Foundation's inaugural speech by André Malraux, 1964

Set back in the woods up on Route Passe-Prest, the **Fondation Maeght**, ✆ 93 32 81 63, 📠 93 32 53 22 (*open daily July–Sept 10am–7pm, Oct–Jun 10am–12.30pm and 2.30–6pm; adm*) is the best reason of all for visiting St-Paul. Its fairy godparents, Aimé and Marguerite Maeght, were art dealers and friends of Matisse and Bonnard who decided, in the early 1960s, to create an ideal environment for contemporary art, and for its creators. They hired Catalan architect José-Luis Sert, a pupil of Le Corbusier and good buddy of Joan Miró, to design the setting—'building' seems too confining a term for these walls that are 'a play between the rhythms of the interior and exterior spaces', as Sert himself described them. The various levels of the building follow the changes in ground level; the white 'sails' on top collect rainwater for the fountains; 'light traps' in the roof are designed to distribute natural light evenly, although the quality of light varies from room to room.

The permanent collection, which includes nearly every major artist of the past 50 years, is removed during the Foundation's frequent exhibitions of young artists and retrospectives of established ones. But you'll always see the works incorporated into the walls, windows and gardens—Miró's *Labyrinth*, a garden path lined with delightful sculptures and a ceramic half-submerged Egg; a wet and wobbling tubular fountain by Pol Bury, a mobile by Calder, mosaics by Chagall, Tal-Coat, Braque and Ubac, Léger's *Flowers, Birds and Bench*, and Giacometti's stick-figured cat and elongated people, reminiscent of Etruscan bronzes at their quirkiest. The Foundation also has a cinema and a studio for making films, art workshops, and one of the world's most extensive art libraries.

St-Paul-de-Vence ✉ *06570*　　　　　　**Where to Stay and Eating Out**

 To stay in St-Paul-de-Vence, have buckets of money and book months in advance in the summer, especially to sleep among the 20th-century art in ★★★**La Colombe d'Or**, Place des Ormeaux, ✆ 93 32 80 02, 📠 93 32 77 78. The rooms are full of character, the pool is heated, the terrace lovely. The restaurant, where Yves Montand and Simone Signoret celebrated their wedding, and Arnold Schwarzenegger hosted his 1993 Cannes Film Festival bash, is more a feast for the eyes than for the stomach, but you won't go wrong with its traditional groaning platters of hors-d'œuvres and grilled meats (*à la carte only, around 400F*). *Closed Nov–mid Dec.* In the centre, in the 16th-century ★★★★**Le St Paul**, 86 Rue Grande, ✆ 93 32 65 25, 📠 93 32 52 94, the interior designers let their hair down to create unusual but delightful juxtapositions of medieval, surreal, Egyptian and Art Deco elements. Its equally attractive restaurant has a summer terrace, where you can try delicacies such as *sashimi de saumon* with ginger and citrus fruits (*lunch menus from*

290F). The more moderately priced ★★★**Le Hameau**, 528 Rte de La Colle, ✆ 93 32 80 24, 🖳 93 32 55 75, has lovely views over the orange groves and a swimming-pool (no restaurant). *Closed mid-Nov–mid-Feb*. Cheapest of all is ★★**Les Remparts**, 72 Rue Grande, ✆ 93 32 09 88: pleasant rooms with baths, and a good affordable restaurant with a superb terrace (*menus from 280–480F*). A couple of minutes by car from St-Paul, **Le Ste Claire**, Espue St Clair, ✆ 93 32 02 02, is traditional but not dull, particularly the *foie gras* in pastry.

Vence

> *I live among rocks, which happy fate*
> *Has sprinkled liberally with roses and with jasmine,*
> *Trees carpet them from foothill to summit,*
> *Rich orange groves blossom in the plains;*
> *The emerald in their leaves reveals its hue,*
> *On the fruit shines gold, and silver on the flower.*
>
> Antoine Godeau, on Vence

Sister city of Ouahigouya in Burkina Faso, Vence lies 3km from St-Paul and 10km from the coast, sufficiently far to seem more like a town in Provence than a Riviera fleshpot. Roman *Vintium*, it kept up its regional prestige in the Middle Ages as the seat of a bishopric (albeit the smallest in France) with a series of remarkable bishops. Two are now Vence's patron saints: Véran (449–481), an alumnus of the seminary of St-Honorat near Cannes, and Lambert (1114–54). Lambert had to confront the claims of the new baron of Vence, Romée de Villeneuve, knighted by Raymond Bérenger V of Provence after Romée arranged for Bérenger's daughters the four most strategic marriages of all time—to the kings of England, France (St Louis) and Naples, and the German emperor. Although Romée earned a mention in Dante's *Paradiso* (an apocryphal story telling how he began and ended his career as an impoverished pilgrim), as baron he set a precedent of quarrelling with the bishop of Vence that lasted until the Revolution abolished both titles. Alessandro Farnese was head of Vence's see from 1508 to 1511—one of the 16 absentee bishoprics he accumulated thanks to his beautiful sister Giulia, the mistress of Pope Alexander IV, who slept with enough cardinals to get her brother elected Paul III. But best-loved of Vence's bishops was Antoine Godeau (1639–72), a dwarf famed for his ugliness, a gallant poet and 'the wittiest man in France'. Appointed the first member of the Académie Française by Cardinal Richelieu, Godeau tired of it all by the time he was 30, took holy orders and devoted himself to reforming his see—rebuilding the cathedral, and founding tanneries and scent industries.

Although a fair amount of villa sprawl extends on all sides, the **Vieille Ville** has kept most of its medieval integrity. Enter the walls by way of the west gate, the fortified **Porte du Peyra**: the **Place du Peyra**, just inside, was the Roman forum and is still the site of the daily market. Roman tombstones are incorporated in the walls of the **Ancienne Cathédrale**, a rococo church full of little treasures—the pre-Christian sarcophagus of St Véran; the tomb of Bishop Godeau; Merovingian and Romanesque fragments of stones and birds, especially in the chapel under the belfry; a spluttery mosaic by Chagall; reliquaries donated by Alessandro Farnese; and, best of all, the stalls with lace-fine carvings satirizing Renaissance customs and mores, sculpted by Jacques Bellot in the 1450s. Also in and around the Vieille Ville is the **Centre d'Art Vaas**, ✆ 93 58 29 42, which boasts an art school, sculpture garden, and *boutique* or shop.

West, outside the walls, **Place du Frêne** is named in honour of a majestic ash tree planted here in 1538 to commemorate visits by François Ier and Pope Paul III; the 17th-century château built here by Vence's plucky barons is now used for exhibitions. Vence's **Saturday market** spills beyond the confines of the city, and all that's home grown, crafted or made is exhibited with worthy pride. Trawl the stalls and you may well find something way above the ordinary (Olivier de Celle hunts out his woods with the passion of a truffle-hunter, and carves them into fruits so beautiful they're hard not to touch). You'll be hurried by the crowds and the sweet stench of bakeries browning new wares, and pancakes hissing and crisping from trollies on the corners.

Matisse's Chapelle du Rosaire

From Vence, follow Av. des Poilus to the route for St-Jeannet/La Gaude. Open Tues and Thurs 10–11.30am and 2.30–5.30pm.

Matisse arrived in Vence in 1941 to escape the bombing along the coast, and fell seriously ill. The 'White' Dominican sisters nursed him back to health, and as a gift he built and decorated the simple **Chapelle du Rosaire** for them. Matisse worked on the project well into his 80s, from 1946 to 1951, using long bamboo poles to hold his brushes when he was forced to keep to his bed, designing every aspect of the chapel, down to the priest's robes. He considered the result his masterpiece, an expression of the 'nearly religious feeling I have for life', the fruit 'of a life consecrated to the search for truth'. The truth he sought, however, was not in Christianity, but in the essentials of line and light.

Probably the most extraordinary thing about these decorations by the most sensual of Fauves is their lack of colour, except in the geometrically patterned stained glass windows that occupy two walls and which give the interior an uncanny glow. The other walls are of white faïence, on which Matisse drew black line drawings of St Dominic holding a Bible, and the Virgin and Child, the Crucifixion and the fourteen Stations of the Cross. None of the figures has a face, but they're powerfully drawn and compelling in their simplicity.

Vence ✉ *06140*   ### Where to Stay and Eating Out

Vence has more choice and lower prices than St-Paul—unless you check into the opulentissimo ★★★★**Château St-Martin**, 3km from Vence on Rte de Coursegoules, ✆ 93 58 02 02, 🖷 93 24 08 91, a set of villa-*bastides* built around a ruined Templar fortress. The 12-hectare park has facilities for riding, fishing, tennis and a heart-shaped pool installed at the request of Harry Truman, who never had such luxuries back in Independence, Missouri. The restaurant is equally august, with prices to match (*lunch menu 400F*). *Closed mid Oct–mid April.*
★★★★**Relais Cantemerle**, 258 Chemin Cantemerle, ✆ 93 58 08 18, 🖷 93 58 32 79, is decorated with Art Deco bits and pieces from the gutted Palais de la Méditerranée in Nice. Set in its piney garden, with terraces and a pool, the Cantemerle's restaurant serves some of the finest food in Vence (try the *terrine de rascasse aux pointes d'asperges; menu 230F*). *Closed Oct–April.*

★★**La Roseraie**, 14 Av. H.-Giraud, ✆ 93 58 02 20, 🖷 93 58 99 31, offers a garden of magnolias and cedars, with an enormous home-made breakfast, by an impeccable pool. Sadly there's no longer a restaurant, but the owner's passion has been channelled into antiques, Salernes tiles a-plenty, and lovely ironwork. Even the bicycle provided to pedal off to the Matisse Chapel is picturesque. Beware the two top-most rooms which are noisy and cramped.

Hidden away in the centre of Vence, the charming yet unpretentious **★Closerie des Genêts**, 4 Impasse Marcellin-Maurel, ✆ 93 58 33 25, has quiet rooms, a garden and a decent restaurant (*rooms 160–260F*). For gastronomy, you won't go wrong or hungry at **Auberge des Templiers**, 39 Av. Joffre, ✆ 93 58 06 05, which although not innovative, is just elegant and traditional French—lamb, *foie gras* and fish (*menus 200–300F*). *Closed Sunday evenings and Monday.* More Provençal regional cuisine and good fresh fish can be found at **La Farigoule**, 15 Av. Henri-Isnard, ✆ 93 58 01 27 (*menus 115–140F*). *Closed Friday and Saturday lunchtimes, annual closing Nov 10th–Dec 15th.* In the Vieille Ville, the quaint **Le Pigeonnier**, Place du Peyra, ✆ 93 58 03 00, makes its own pasta and ravioli, as well as fish. C*losed Sat lunch and Mon.* **Le Pêcheur du Soleil**, on Place Godeau (behind the church), is fine; as long as you won't be dazzled by the choice of 400 different pizza toppings; but at the unprepossessing-looking **Crêperie Royale**, 14 Rue Isnard, over the warm breath of strong spirit you will be served—a rarity in France—real tea, made and brewed with sweet leaves from a tin. Don't be tempted by the plaque on the door of **La Vieille Douve**, Av. Henri-Isnard, as '*douve*' means ditch.

Excursions around Vence, and the Gorges du Loup

Vence makes an excellent base for exploring the countryside, especially if you have your own car—otherwise the only connections are the once- or twice-daily buses from Nice to St-Jeannet and Gattières.

Ten km beyond the Chapelle du Rosaire, the wine-making village of **St-Jeannet** balances on a terrace beneath the distinctive *Baou*, a sheer 400m rock that dominates the surrounding countryside. A two-hour path from the Auberge de St-Jeannet leads to the summit, with views stretching to the Alps. A narrow road continues south to the *village perché* of **La Gaude**, unspoiled despite the giant Y-shaped IBM research centre along the way. Alternatively, continuing northeast on D2210, are three other *villages perchés* that have yet to sell their souls to Mammon: **Gattières**, **Carros** on a 300m rock over the Var crowned by a 13th-century château, and **Le Broc**, 4km up the Var on D2209, with a Canavesio in its church. Another excursion from Vence takes you through the austerely beautiful **Clues de Haute Provence** by way of the **Col de Vence**, 975m up and affording an incomparable view of the coast from Cap Ferrat to the Esterel (take D2 north).

The most popular excursion of all is to loop-the-Loup, so to speak, around the upper valley of the Loup river, starting on D2210. On the way you can call at the **Château Notre-Dame des Fleurs**, 2.5km from Vence on Route de Grasse, ✆ 93 24 52 00 (*open 11–7pm every day except Sun, all year*), a 19th-century castle built over the ruins of an 11th-century Benedictine abbey, which used to be home to the deliciously named Musée du Parfum et de la Liqueur, but is now sadly yet another contemporary art gallery.

Some essential oils, especially of violets, originate in **Tourrettes-sur-Loup**, 2.5km further on. Its medieval core of rosy golden stone has often been compared to an Algerian town, the houses knitted together so that their backs form a wall defended by the three small towers that give the village its name. Tourrettes grows more violets than any town in France, and in March all the façades are covered with bouquets for the *Fête des Violettes*. But in the summer Tourrettes turns into a veritable *souk*, where you can purchase handmade fabrics, jewellery, marionnettes, ceramics, household items and more. The village **church** has a triptych by the school of Ludovico Bréa and a Gallo-Roman altar dedicated to Mercury, while the **Chapelle St-Jean**, at the village entrance, has naïve frescoes mixing biblical tales with local life, painted by Ralph Souplaut in 1959.

Before heading into the Gorges du Loup, take a short detour south at **Pont-du-Loup** to **Le Bar-sur-Loup**, scented by its plantations of oranges, jasmine, roses and violets. The village surrounds the château of the lords of Bar, a branch office of the counts of Grasse (one of whom grew up here to become the Admiral de Grasse, who chased the British out of Chesapeake Bay, so Washington could blockade Yorktown and win the American War of Independence). Legend has it that one of his 15th-century ancestors held a wild party here in the middle of Lent, during which the guests all dropped dead. Mortified, the lord commissioned an itinerant artist from Nice to commemorate the event by painting a curious little *Danse Macabre*, now in the tribune of the church of **St-Jacques**: the elegant nobility dance to a drum, unaware that tiny demons of doom echo the dance on their heads. Death, grinning, mows them down, while busy devils extract their souls in the form of newborn babies and pop them into the mouth of Hell. The church also has a retable by Ludovico Bréa and, on the door, beautiful Gothic/Renaissance panels representing St Jacques, carved by Jacques Bellot of Vence. Not to be missed in **Pont du Loup** is the **Confiserie des Gorges du Loup**, ✆ 93 59 32 91 (*open every day 9–12pm and 2–6pm except Sun*), where jams, jellied fruits, crystallised flowers, chocolates and sweets are made before your eyes, by men in white hats and blue aprons. The factory's quaint and full of antique kitchen furniture, but best is the free tasting at the end of each tour.

North of Pont-du-Loup, D6 leads into the steep, fantastical cliffs of the **Gorges du Loup**, cooled by waterfalls—one next to the road falls a sheer 45m—and is pocked by giant *marmites*, or glacial potholes. The largest of these is up at **Saut-du-Loup**, and in spring the river broils through it like a witch's cauldron. At Pont de Bramafan you can cross the gorge and head back south. Looming ahead is **Gourdon**, 'the Saracen', a brooding eagle's nest converted into yet another rural shopping-mall of crafts and goodies. Its massive rectangular **château** was built in the 1200s over the Saracen citadel, and heavily restored in 1610. Inside are a pair of museums (✆ 93 09 68 02; *open 11am–1pm and 2–6pm summer, 2–6pm only in winter, closed Tues; adm*): the **Musée Historique** with antique arms and armour, the odd torture instrument in the dungeon, a Rembrandt self-portrait, and Marie-Antoinette's writing-desk, while upstairs, a **Musée de Peinture Naïve** features a small portrait by the Douanier Rousseau and works by his French and Yugoslav imitators. The panoramic three-tiered castle gardens were laid out by Le Nôtre, although now most of the plants are alpine. You can take a spectacular two-hour walk on the **Sentier du Paradis** from Gourdon to Pont-du-Loup, or sneak a preview of lunar travel by driving up the D12 (or walk along the GR4 from Grasse) on to the desolate **Plateau de Caussols**, boasting the driest, clearest air in France—hence an important observatory. French film directors often use it for Western or desert scenes, the very kind used these days for selling French cars and blue jeans.

Gattières (✉ 06510)

The small **★★Beau Site**, Rte des Serres Gattières, ✆ 93 08 60 06, has a lovely view down the Var, a garden, and a pleasant restaurant with a 98F menu. **L'Hostellerie Provençale**, at the entrance of the old town, ✆ 93 08 60 40, offers excellent value for hungry travellers with its 98, 140F and 160F menus—masses of hors-d'œuvres, homemade ravioli, *daube* and much more. *Open all year.*

Tourrettes-sur-Loup (✉ 06140)

★★Auberge des Belles Terrasses, Rte de Vence, ✆ 93 59 30 03, ✆ 93 24 19 86, has basic but pleasant rooms with views from its terraces and a good little restaurant (*menus 85, 145F*). For comfortable, clean rooms and a view of orange trees and distant sea, head for **★★La Grive Dorée**, 11 Route de Grasse, ✆ 93 59 30 05. Its simple restaurant offers *coq au vin* and *truite aux amandes* (*menus 98F, 175F*).

Le Bar-sur-Loup (✉ 06140)

Stop for lunch with local shopkeepers and *gendarmes* at **L'Amiral**, 8 Place Francis-Paulet, ✆ 93 09 44 00, in an impressive 18th-century house that belonged to Admiral de Grasse. The dishes on the menu change daily, and are always spot on for freshness and value (*menus at 98 and 150F*). Be sure to reserve for dinner in the summer.

Back towards the Coast: Biot

Between Cagnes and Cannes, the *résidences secondaires* battle for space with huge commercial greenhouses and fields of flowers destined for the scent distilleries of Grasse, a paroxym of fragrance and colour powerful enough to make a sensitive soul swoon. Set in a couple of miles from the sea, Biot (rhymes with yacht) is a handsome village endowed with first-rate clay—in Roman times it specialized in wine and oil jars large enough to contain Ali Baba's forty thieves. In 1955, Fernand Léger purchased some land in order to construct a sculpture garden of monumental ceramics—then died 15 days later. In 1960 his widow used the land to build a superb museum and garden to display the works he left her in his will. Come late in the day if you want to see more of Biot and less of the human race.

Getting There

Biot's train station is down by the sea at La Brague, and you will have a steep 5km walk from here up to the village. Buses approximately every hour from Antibes stop at the station en route to Biot.

Tourist Information

6 Place de la Chapelle, ✆ 93 65 05 85, ✆ 93 65 18 09.

Musée National Fernand Léger

Open 10am–12pm and 2–6pm, 2–5pm winter, closed Tues; adm; ✆ 93 65 63 61.

To the right of the entrance to Biot, Léger's museum (at Chemin du Val de Pome) is hard to mistake behind its giant, sporty ceramic-mosaic designed for the Olympic stadium of Hannover. Opened in 1960, the museum was enlarged in 1989 to provide more space for the 348 paintings, tapestries, mosaics and ceramics that trace Léger's career from his first flirtations with Cubism back in 1909—although even back then Léger was nicknamed the 'tubist' for his preference for fat noodly forms. After being gassed in the First World War, he recovered to flirt with the Purist movement founded by his buddies Le Corbusier and Amédée Ozenfant around 1918, a reaction to the 'decorative' tendencies of Cubism. Purism was to be the cool, dispassionate art of the machine age, emotionally limited to a 'mathematical lyricism', and Léger's scenes of soldiers and machines fitted the bill. After teaching at Yale during the Second World War, he returned to France with a keen interest in creating art for the working classes, using his trademark style of brightly coloured geometric forms to depict workers, factories, and their pastimes. The new wing of the museum contains Léger's ceramics, mosaics and other works—most notably the tapestres called *La Création* (1922) and *Liberté*, the latter illustrating the eponymous poem by his friend Paul Eluard. The presence of the museum has boosted the local ceramic and glass industry; across from the museum at **La Verrerie de Biot**, Chemin des Combes, ✆ 93 65 03 00, you can watch workers make glass suffused with tiny bubbles (*verre à bulles*).

Guarded by 16th-century gates, Biot itself has retained much of its character, especially around central **Place des Arcades**. A hundred years ago, the accents in this charming square would be Genoese—Biot's original population was decimated by the Black Death, and the village was only resettled in 1460, when the Bishop of Grasse invited in 50 families from Genoa. The church they built among the arcades has two excellent 15th-century altarpieces: the red and gold *Retable du Rosaire* by Ludovico Bréa and the recently restored *Christ aux Plaies* by Giovanni Canavesio, who was married to a Biotoise.

With his bright colours and often playful forms, Léger is one artist children usually like. Afterwards you can take them to **La Brague** by the sea, to watch the performing dolphins and other sea creatures at **Marineland**, the oldest of its kind in Europe (*open daily from 11am, with nocturnal performances at 9.30pm in July and Aug, adm*). Next door to it at **Aquasplash**, you can play otter yourself on the slides (*open daily in summer, 10am–7pm, ✆ 93 33 49 49 for both attractions*), or watch the silent pretty creatures at **La Jungle des Papillons**, a live butterfly zoo, ✆ 93 33 55 77 (*open all year, 10–5pm*).

Biot ✉ 06410

Where to Stay and Eating Out

There aren't many choices in Biot, but on the other hand there aren't many nicer places in which to escape the maddening Riviera crowds than ★★★**Hostellerie du Bois Fleuri**, 199 Bd. de la Source, ✆ 93 65 68 74, 🖷 92 94 05 85, in the forest between Biot and Valbonne, offering tranquillity, views, swimming, tennis and large rooms in a rose-coloured castle. In the medieval centre of Biot, ★**Arcades**, 16 Place des Arcades, ✆ 93 65 01 04, is a delightful old hotel in a 15th-century building, furnished with antiques. The amiable restaurant below does a genuine *soupe au pistou* and other Provençal favourites (*160F*); but for a special feast, reserve a table at least a week in advance at ★★**Auberge du Jarrier**, Passage de la

Bourgade, ☎ 93 65 11 68, in an old jar-works, with a magical terrace, friendly service and a superb four-course seasonal 200F menu that puts the Côte's *haute cuisine* budget-busters to shame. *Closed Monday evening, Tues.*

Antibes, Juan-les-Pins and Vallauris

Set on the largest of the Côte's peninsulas, Antibes started out as the Greek trading colony of *Antipolis*, 'the city opposite' Nice. But these days it's also the antithesis of the Nice of retired folks soaking up the rays: Antibes belongs to the young, who scoot, bike and skate like their counterparts in California to *collège* and *lycée*, and the aspiring young who frequent the mega-white boats that measure over a hundred yards long, moored shoulder-to-shoulder, vying to see which has the most high-tech communications systems or the most advanced surface-to-air missile launcher. Here the *de rigueur* Riviera poodle has been supplanted by the seadogs' terriers, labradors and spaniels, or the even more exotic breeds kept by the chi-chi employees at Sophia-Antipolis. On the other side of luxurious Cap d'Antibes are the sandy beaches of Juan-les-Pins, where you can swing all night, especially to the tunes of the Riviera's top jazz festival. Inland from here is Vallauris, another ceramics village, this one synonymous with Picasso.

Getting Around

Antibes' **train station**, is near the edge of town, along the Av. Robert-Soleau towards Nice at Place P. Semard, ☎ 93 99 50 50, and has frequent trains to Nice and Cannes. **Buses** (☎ 93 34 37 60) for Cannes, Nice, Nice airport, Cagnes-sur-Mer, and Juan-les-Pins depart from Place de Gaulle; others leave from Rue de la République. From Golfe-Juan buses leave every 20 mins for Antibes.

Tourist Information

Antibes (✉ 06600): 11 Place de Gaulle, ☎ 92 90 53 00, 🖷 92 90 53 00.
Juan-les-Pins (✉ 06160): 51 Bd. Guillaumont, ☎ 92 90 53 05 (*write to them to book tickets for the jazz festival*).
Golfe-Juan (✉ 06220): 84 Av. de la Liberté, ☎ 93 63 73 12.
Vallauris (✉ 06220): Square du 8 Mai 1945, ☎ 93 63 82 58 (*open all year*).

market days

Antibes: Cours Masséna: fruit and veg, flowers, rolls of fabric, wicker-work a-plenty (*6am–1pm sharp, every day July–Aug, otherwise daily except Mon*); Place Audi Berti: fleamarket, other people's bits and pieces (*Thursdays, 7am–6pm*); Port Vauban: clothes market (*Thursday am*).

Antibes and the Musée Picasso

> *Now all the gay decorative people have left, taking with them the sense of carnival and impending disaster that colored this summer...*
>
> Zelda Fitzgerald, 1925

Antibes has been a quieter place since the Fitzgeralds and their self-destructive high jinks set a precedent no alcoholic writer or artist has been able to match. The frolicking now takes place over at Juan-les-Pins, which took off as a resort shortly after F. Scott and Zelda's holiday, leaving Antibes to tend its rose nurseries. After the war, when developers cast an eye over to Antibes, there were enough building restrictions intact to keep out most of the concrete. Even so, inlanders regard the town with jaundiced eyes: instead of 'go to hell' they say '*Vai-t'en-à-n-Antibo!*'

A relic of Antibes' earlier incarnation as France's bulwark against Savoyard Nice are its sea-walls, especially the massive 16th century **Le Fort Carré**. Though it's recently been bought by the town of Antibes, it is not possible to visit. It provides a decorative backdrop for Antibes' pleasure port, big enough to moor even the 90m behemoths of the ridiculously rich. The handsome 17th- and 18th-century houses of Vieil Antibes look over their neighbours' shoulders towards the sea, obscuring it from **Cours Masséna**, the main street of Greek Antipolis. Here the morning **market** sells a cornucopia of local produce, from *fromage de chèvre aux olives* to a profusion of cut flowers that leave the paintings in Antibes' galleries pale by comparison. From the Cours, Rue Sade leads back to café-filled Place Nationale and the **Musée Peynet** (✆ *92 90 54 32; open summer 10–6pm, winter 10–12 pm and 2–6pm, closed Mon and November*), offering a queasy journey back to the 1960s paved with the love postcards drawn by Raymond Peynet, the father of the genre.

Back towards the sea, Tour Gilli houses the **Musée de la Tour**, ✆ 93 34 50 91, devoted to the costumes, furniture, household items and tools of Antibes' fisher-folk of yore (*open only Wed, Thurs and Sat afternoons*).The best sea views are monopolized by the **Château Grimaldi**—a seaside castle built by the same family who ran most of this coast at one time or another, and who had possession of Antibes from 1385 to 1608. It became a history museum in the 1920s, and for six months in 1946, the owner, Romuald Dor, let Picasso use the second floor as a studio. Picasso, glad to have space to work in, even if it was cold and damp, quickly filled it up in a few months, only later discovering to his annoyance that all along Dor had intended to make his efforts into the **Musée Picasso**, ✆ 92 90 54 20 (*open summer 10–6pm, winter 10–12pm and 2–6pm, closed Mon and Nov; adm*). As it is, and despite a post-war lack of canvases and oil paint (he used mostly fibro-cement and boat paint) you can't help but get the feeling that Picasso was exuberantly happy, inspired by the end of the war, his love of the time, Françoise Gillot, and the mythological roots of the Mediterranean, expressed in *La Joie de Vivre*, *Ulysse et ses Sirènes* and 220 other paintings, drawings, and ceramics (the plates are especially good); many of the paintings are reproduced on raised metal plaques for the blind. It's a deeply civilised space, with room for the imagination, without much effort, to dispense with the crowds and see how Antibes might have been not that long ago. Among the other artists represented, note the eight striking works that Nicolas de Staël painted in Antibes shortly before he committed suicide (or merely fell out of the upstairs window) in 1955. Outside, the garden is crammed with sculptures, while below, a speedboat crosses the sea like a slow rip in a blue canvas.

Just across the street is the **Church of the Immaculate Conception**, where a leaflet in your chosen language entreats you to 'Listen....listen to the silent echo of prayers down the ages...' but you'll have to listen hard for silence over the Almighty Muzak. Built over a Greek temple, it's a hotchpotch of art and idols, gawpers, hawkers, and rows of burning candles, dedicated to St Sebastian and St Roch. Further south, at the end of Promenade Amiral-de-Grasse, the Vauban-built Bastion St-André houses the **Musée d'Histoire et d'Archéologie**, ✆ 92 90 54 35 (*open Mon–Fri 9–12pm and 2–6pm*), where Greek and Etruscan amphorae, monies and jewels dredged up from the sea and soil trace the history of Antibes.

Cap d'Antibes

Further south along the peninsula (follow the scenic coastal D2559) the beautiful, free, sandy beach of **La Salis** marks the beginning of Cap d'Antibes, scented with roses, jasmine and the smell of money—there's more concentrated here than almost anywhere else in France. Jules Verne was among the first to retreat here, where he found the inspiration for *Twenty Thousand Leagues under the Sea*; nowadays, to maintain the kind of solitude and high-tech luxury enjoyed by Captain Nemo aboard the *Nautilus*, the owners of the Cap's villas need James Bond security systems and slavering Dobermanns. At 41 Boulevard du Cap is the lovely **Jardin Thuret**, © 93 67 88 00 (*with a villa which can't be visited, but the garden's free, Mon–Fri 8.30–5.30*), laid out in 1866 as an acclimatization station, where the first eucalyptus was transplanted to Europe (the park now contains over 100 varieties).

The **Plateau de la Garoupe** is the highest point of the headland, with a **lighthouse**, a grand view stretching from Bordighera to St-Tropez, and the ancient seamen's **Chapelle de la Garoupe**. Its two naves, one 13th-century and one 16th-century, hold a fascinating collection of ex-votos, the oldest one commemorating a surprise attack on Antibes by Saracen pirates. At the tip of the peninsula is **Villa Eden Roc**, © 93 67 74 33 (*open Wed pm only, closed July and Aug; adm free*), and further west, a 12th-century tower holds the **Musée Naval et Napoléonien**, Av. Kennedy, © 93 61 45 32 (*open 9.30am–12pm and 2.15–6pm, except Sat afternoons, Sun, and Oct*), with ships' models and items relating to Napoleon's connections with Antibes—he left Madame Mère and his sisters here during the siege of Toulon (they were so poor that the girls had to steal figs) and began 'The Hundred Days' at nearby Golfe-Juan.

The Makings of a Legend

The cape is practically synonymous with the first hotel in Antibes, the Grand Hotel du Cap, built in 1870—just in time for the Franco-Prussian War, driving its first owner into bankruptcy before he opened the doors. In 1889, an Italian named Antoine Sella bought the hotel and nearly went bankrupt himself, when in his first season he only attracted a pair of old English biddies. Sella's bacon was saved when James Gordon Bennett, owner of the *New York Herald*, found himself burdened with his widowed sister and rented a whole floor of the hotel to keep her out of his hair. In the next two decades Sella had an unusual feature: an outdoor swimming pool, which was a popular feature among the lucky American soldiers sent down there to recuperate in the First World War.

There had been talk as early as 1889 about a summer season on the Riviera, but the suggestions only began to become reality in 1922. Noel Coward came that summer and rented the Château de la Garoupe (with the motto over the door; 'Abandon Sorrow All Ye Who Enter Here') and invited his charming, gracious, hospitable old chums from Yale, Gerald and Sara Murphy, both of whom had sizeable family incomes to keep them from ever having to work for a living. Already a fixture of the social scene in Paris, the Murphys fell in love with the place, and discovered the hitherto unheralded joys of sunbathing on the beach, and they were back the next summer, staying in the Grand Hotel because Sella had decided to stay open to recoup losses from the bad season. They had the place to themselves, along with Picasso's family and an unknown Chinese couple. That same summer, the Côte d'Azur's top trend-setter Coco Chanel astonished everyone with her suntan. A fad was born. Within two years, Sella created Eden Roc, still rated as the most beautiful place for a swim and a tan on the whole Riviera.

In the Roaring 20s a dollar went a long way in France and Prohibition, the bugbear of America, was unknown. The Murphys, famous for holding the very best parties, bought a house on the beach and turned it into the 14-room Villa America where they created and lived the carefree but elegant sunny seaside existence that became the essential myth of the Riviera, sharing it with everyone who happened by, including Zelda and Scott Fitzgerald, the latter of whom based his characters Dick and Nicole Diver in *Tender is the Night* on the Murphys. But by the early 1930s it was all over: the Murphys sold their villa when their two sons became ill and afterwards wistfully recalled that their only real accomplishment in Antibes had been to enjoy themselves. Which isn't half bad.

Juan-les-Pins

When a good idea is in the air, it's not uncommon for different people to pick up on it. In 1924 Edouard Baudoin, a Nice restaurateur, saw a film about Miami Beach and was inspired to recreate it on the Côte. He found his location at Juan-les-Pins amongst the silver sands and pines of the best natural beach on the Riviera, and bought some land and opened a restaurant and a little casino. As it had suddenly become desirable to bake brown on the beach, Baudoin's inventment flourished, attracting the attention of the ever-acquisitive Frank Jay Gould, who bought Baudoin out, built roads and injected the essential money and publicity to help Juan-les-Pins really take off. By 1930 it was the most popular and scandal-ridden resort on the Riviera, where women first dared to bathe in skirtless suits. The presence of Edith Piaf and Sidney Bechet boosted its popularity in the 1950s; all the young come here from Antibes and further (the rich and posh go to Nice). It's still going strong, not a beauty but a brash and sassy tart of a resort, with nightclubs and a magnificent jazz festival in the last two weeks of July.

Golfe-Juan

Next up the coast is **Golfe-Juan**, with its pines, sandy beach and pleasure port, famous as the very spot where Napoleon disembarked from Elba on 1 March 1815, proclaiming that 'the eagle with his national colours will fly from bell tower to bell tower all the way to the towers of Notre-Dame'. An obelisk and a column commemorate the landing, which in fact was slightly less than momentous: the locals quickly arrested a few of his men, a cold reception that decided the eagle to sneak along the back roads to Paris. In one of many Napoleonic coincidences, Bonaparte, as he landed, met the Prince of Monaco, who informed him that he was on his way to reclaim his tiny realm after being removed during the Revolution. 'Then, Monsieur, we are in the same business,' Napoleon told him, and each continued on his way, the Prince to his orange groves, Napoleon to Waterloo.

Vallauris

Two km inland from Golfe-Juan, **Vallauris** has two things in common with Biot: it was given an injection of Genoese in the 1400s and was famous for its pottery, in this case useful household wares. Because of competition with aluminium, the industry was on its last legs in 1946 when Picasso rented a small villa in town and met Georges and Suzanne Ramié, owners of the Poterie Madoura. Playing with the clay in their shop, Picasso discovered a new passion, and spent the next few years working with the medium. He gave the Ramiés the exclusive right to sell copies of his ceramics, and you can still buy them at **Madoura**, just off Rue du 19 Mars 1962. Thanks to Picasso, 200 potters now work in Vallauris, some talented, others trying.

In 1951 the village asked Picasso if he would decorate a deconsecrated chapel next to the castle. The result is the famous plywood paintings of *La Guerre et la Paix*, said to have taken Picasso less time to do than if a house-painter had painted the wall. The work was as spontaneous as *Guernica* was planned, and every bit as sincere (it's known as the **Musée National Picasso**, Place de la Liberation, ✆ 93 64 16 05 (*open 10am–2pm, closed Tues*). The same ticket admits you to the **Musée Municipal** (*same details*) up in the castle, which used to have many of Picasso's original pieces until art thieves struck in 1989; now to be seen are the winners of the ceramic Biennale and paintings by Italian abstract master Alberto Magnelli. There's more Picasso in Place Paul-Isnard: a rather grumpy bronze man with a sheep.

Sophia-Antipolis

Meanwhile, as all this modern art appreciation and nightclubbing goes on around Antibes, 15,000 international business people are punching away on their new generation computers in 'France's Silicone Valley', the spooky new town complex of Sophia-Antipolis off D103, north of Vallauris, where cars are directed Scalextrix-style around endless bends and roundabouts. Created in 1969 and funded in part by Nice's chamber of commerce, it seems popular with executives: Air France's international reservations network is here, as well as Dow Corning, Toyota and others.

Where to Stay and Eating Out

Antibes (✉ 06600)

A short walk from central Antibes is ★★★**Mas Djoliba** (06600), 29 Av. de Provence, ✆ 93 34 02 48, ✆ 93 34 05 81, a serendipitous *mas* in a small park with a heated pool. You can combine pleasure with thalassotherapy and beauty treatments at ★★★**Thalazur**, 770 Chemin des Moyennes Breguières, ✆ 93 74 78 82, ✆ 93 65 74 78, with four heated pools, saunas, and a doctor on duty (*open all year*). ★**L'Auberge Provençale**, 61 Place Nationale, ✆ 93 34 13 24, ✆ 93 34 89 88, is a cosy house under the plane trees, with Provençal furniture and canopied beds. There are only 7 rooms, so reserve long in advance. Right in the middle of Antibes the ★★**Belle Epoque**, 10 Av. du 24-Août, ✆ 93 34 53 00, has rooms with or without bath, and a good restaurant downstairs (*menu 60F*). *Closed Jan.*

Cap d'Antibes' ★★★★**Hôtel du Cap Eden Roc**, Bd. Kennedy, ✆ 93 61 39 01, ✆ 93 67 76 04, is still very much there, set in an idyllic park overlooking the Iles de Lérins, where the rest of the world seems very far away. No hotel on the Riviera has hosted more celebrities, film stars or plutocrats; you could easily drop 1000F at the exalted restaurant, the Pavillon Eden Roc. *Closed Oct–April.* A more reasonable choice in Cap d'Antibes is ★★★**La Gardiole**, 74 Chemin de La Garoupe, ✆ 93 61 35 03, ✆ 93 67 61 87, with large, luminous rooms set in a pine wood and a magnificent wisteria over the terrace. Rooms vary greatly in price; half-board is obligatory in season. *Closed Nov–Mar.* If you're young and come outside July and August, you may find a room at the **Relais International de la Jeunesse**, Bd. de La Garoupe, ✆ 93 61 34 40, set in the pinewoods; 70F including breakfast (windsurf rental in summer). Near the bus station, ★**Le Nouvel Hôtel**, 1 Av. du 24-Août, ✆ 93 34 44 07, ✆ 93 34 06 66, has twenty rooms which fill up rapidly in summer.

In Roman times, Antibes was famous for its *garum*—a sauce made of salted tuna guts left to dry in the sun. You can eat nearly anything else that was once seaworthy at **Bacon**, in Cap d'Antibes, on Bd. de Bacon, © 93 61 50 02, as stylish and elegant as its perfectly prepared seafood and *bouillabaisse*, at classy prices: lunch menus at 260F. In the same price range, try some of the Côte's finest *nouvelle cuisine* at the renowned **La Bonne Auberge**, on the N7 near La Brague, © 93 33 36 65. Chef Jo Rostang's son Philippe has inherited the kitchen, and has already made a name for his *Saint-Pierre au pistou* and *soufflé glacé de lavande au miel de Provence*; the lunch menu is good value at 188F. More reasonable choices abound in Antibes: **Les Vieux Murs**, © 93 34 06 73, on the Promenade Amiral-de-Grasse (near the Picasso museum, looking out over the road to the sea) is cool and spacious, with wooden décor, and serves well-presented traditional food made modern. For good Provençal favourites there's **Chez Olive**, 2 Bd. Maréchal-Leclerc, © 93 34 42 32 (*closed Sun evenings, Mon and Dec*). Don't be tempted by the aroma of *bruschetta* next to the market on Cours Masséna; it's glorified cheese on toast. Instead, head for the **Comic Strip Café**, 4 Rue James-Close, © 93 34 91 40, for crammed-full just-baked baguettes, every sort of salad, and sticky but unpretentious cakes. It's informal and as jolly and bright as the comic library downstairs. *Open 12–10pm summer, 12–8pm winter*. The **Café Sans Rival**, 5 Av. du 24-Août, © 93 34 12 67, not far from the *gare routière* yet off the beaten tourist track, is a tiny wooden-floored shop fitted to the ceiling with coffee beans, teas, herb teas, rice cakes, rye breads, fat sultanas and all things wholesome and *complet*. You can perch outside, drink *real* cappuccino and eat cake. O*pen 8.30am–7pm*. **L'Oursin**, 16 Rue de la République, © 93 34 13 46, is famous for fresh fish (*menus begin at 95F*).

Juan-les-Pins (✉ 06160)

Juan isn't exactly made for sleeping, but it makes sense to stay if you want to join in the late-night revelry. Unlike Antibes, everything closes tight from November to Easter. There are two grand survivors from the 1920s: the beautiful Art Deco ★★★★**Juana**, not on the sea but in a lovely garden facing the pines on Av. Georges Gallice La Pinède, © 93 61 08 70, ✆ 93 61 76 60, with a private beach and heated pool, and the resort's top restaurant, the luxurious **La Terrasse**, © 93 61 20 37, with delicate dishes imbued with all the freshness and colour of Provence, and excellent wines to match from the region's best vineyards (lunch menus from 260–620F, or you can eat *à la carte*). The second palace, ★★★★**Belles Rives**, Bd. du Littoral, © 93 61 02 79, ✆ 93 67 43 51, offers de luxe rooms, vintage 1930, facing the sea. There's a private beach and jetty, and a good restaurant with a fine view over the gulf, or you can eat on the beach (*menus start at 180F and rise steeply*).

More reasonably priced beds may be found at ★★★**Hôtel des Mimosas**, in quiet Rue Pauline, 500m from the sea, © 93 61 04 16, ✆ 92 93 06 46, where the rooms have balconies overlooking the pool and garden; or at ★★ **Le Pré Catelan**, set among the palms at 22 Av. des Palmiers, © 93 61 05 11, ✆ 93 67 83 11, with a private beach only a short walk away. There are doubles at all prices in the charming ★★**Auberge de l'Esterel**, 21 Chemin des Iles, © 93 61 86 55, ✆ 93 61 08 67, tucked in a garden, where the hotel's restaurant (© 93 61 86 55) serves a very reasonable 120–180F menu with *aïoli* and other Provençal dishes. *Closed Nov, Sun eve, Mon.*

An excellent array of sea and land dishes fill the menu of **Le Bijou**, directly on the sea on Bd. Charles-Guillaumont, ✆ 93 61 39 07; during the Cannes festival it's a good place to find the stars tucking into a *bouillabaisse* (*300F*). Slightly cheaper is **La Rue**, 17 Av. Dr-Dautheville, for *bistrot* cuisine (*80–130F*), or **Le Capitole**, 26 Av. Amiral-Courbet, ✆ 93 61 22 44, with a charming welcome and generous menus (*at 95F and 120F; reduced menu price mid-week*). *Closed Tues, Dec.*

Entertainment and Nightlife

There's plenty to entertain, all along the Route de Biot. Be one of the 600,000 who visit **Marineland** each year; it's Europe's largest marine park, with sea-lions, sea-elephants, dolphins, seals and penguins (or *Manchots*, which means 'armless' in French). Get closer to the animals at **La Petite Ferme**, and a chance to wet yourself at **Aquasplash**, complete with a pool with waves. For the timid and the adventurous there's **Mini-Golf** and **Adventure-Golf**. **La Jungle des Papillons** is for butterfly fanciers and **Antibe Land, Luna Park** (*open June–Sept*) for whosoever chooses (same number for all ✆ 93 33 49 49).

If you've lost all your money at the gaming or dining tables, then **Parc Exflora** on the N7 at Antibes-les-Pins is a park full of flora, *adm free.*

Six boats a day sail to the **Iles de Lérins** between 9am and 4pm, from Ponton Courbet, Juan-les-Pins (✆ 92 93 02 36), or Quai Saint-Pierre, Porte de Golfe-Juan (✆ 93 63 45 94) for 60F.

But the best fun to be had is the **Vieille Ville** (of Antibes), full of *confiseries* and *pâtisseries*; a mêlée of locals, lubbers, sailors and who knows who; a mix reflected in the gamut of polyglot newspapers, even the British grubbies. At **Antibes Books** (formerly Heidi's English Bookshop), 24 Rue Aubernon, ✆ 93 34 74 11, Heidi's one word answer to why-did-you-come-to-the-South-of-France is 'hedonism'; yet she runs the local community centre, and a tiny **theatre** below the bookshop. If you're homesick, baked beans, Marmite, tea and crumpets can be got at the English supermarket in the **Galerie du Pont**.

For cinema there's **Cinéma Casino**, 17 Bd. du 24-Août, ✆ 93 34 04 37 (*adm 42F*), but mostly the nightlife keeps you moving: in Antibes, the famous **La Siesta**, on the road to Nice, ✆ 93 33 31 31, which operates as a beach concession by day, with activities for kids, and at night turns into an over-the-top nightclub where thousands of people flock every summer evening to seven dance-floors, fountains, and fiery torches.

The whole of Juan's swinging during the jazz festival, but otherwise there's jazz at **Le Madison**, Av. Louis-Gallet, ✆ 93 61 81 85 (*Thurs, Fri and Sat*); or a piano bar at **Captain's Club**, 15 Ave de la Libération, ✆ 93 65 92 40. In Juan, '*ça bouge,*' the young say; they move it at **Whisky à Gogo**, La Pinède, ✆ 93 61 26 40; older shakers and movers bop at **Voom Voom**, 1 Bd. de la Pinède, ✆ 93 61 18 71. If you can't get in, amongst others there's **Le Bureau**, Av. G.-Gallice, ✆ 93 67 22 74, or **Les Pêcheurs**, on Av. Baudoin, ✆ 93 61 82 58. For techno, get to **L'Institut**, Av. Georges, ✆ 93 67 22 74.

Grasse

It was Catherine de' Medici who introduced artichokes to the French and the scent trade to Grasse. Although it may seem obvious that a town set in the midst of France's natural floral hothouse should be a Mecca for perfume-making, Grasse's most important industry throughout the Middle Ages was tanning imported sheep-skins from the mountains of Provence and buffalo-hides from her Italian allies, Genoa and Tuscany. Part of the tanning process made use of the aromatic herbs that grew nearby, especially powdered myrtle which gave the leather a greenish lustre.

In Renaissance Italy, one of the most important status symbols an aristocrat could flaunt were fine, perfumed gloves. When Catherine asked Grasse, Tuscany's old trading partner, to start supplying them, the Grassois left the buffalo hides behind to become *gantiers parfumeurs*. When gloves fell out of fashion after the Revolution they became simply *parfumeurs*, and when Paris co-opted the business in the 1800s, the townspeople concentrated on what has been their speciality ever since—distilling the essences that go into that final costly tiny bottle. And in that, this picturesque but unglamorous hilltown, with approximately 30 *parfumeries*, leads the world, even though most of the flower fields that surrounded Grasse only 40 years ago have now been planted with poxy, boxy villas.

Getting There

There are no trains, but there are frequent buses from Cannes to Grasse. The **gare routière** (© 93 36 37 37), is on the north side of town, at the Parking Notre-Dame-des-Fleurs. Leave your car here or in one of the other places just outside the centre: Grasse's steep streets are narrow for motorists.

Tourist Information

Palais des Conarès, © 93 36 66 66, @ 93 36 86 36.

market days

Place aux Aires: daily except Monday; and Place aux Herbes: Wednesday morning fleamarket.

Vieille Ville

Grasse's name may sound like the French for 'fat', but it comes from *Grâce*—the state in which its original Jewish inhabitants found themselves once they converted to Christianity. In the Middle Ages it was an independent city-state on the Italian model, with close ties to the republics of Genoa and Pisa—a relationship witnessed these days by the austere Italian style of its architecture. During the 13th-century turmoil between the Guelphs and the Ghibellines, the town put itself under the protection of the Count of Provence. Today, a large percentage of the population hails from North Africa: the perfume magnates themselves live in Mougins and surrounding villages.

The one place where they often meet is at the morning food and flower market in arcaded **Place aux Aires** near the top of the town, where the handsome Hôtel Isnard (1781) with its wrought-iron balcony looks as if it escaped from New Orleans. From here Rue des Moulinets and Rue Mougins-Roquefort lead to the Romanesque **Cathédrale Notre-Dame-du-Puy**, its spartan façade similar to churches around Genoa, matched by its spartan nave. The art is to the right: the *Crown of Thorns* and *Crucifixion*, by Rubens at the age of 24, before he hit the big time; a rare religious subject by Fragonard, the *Washing of the Feet*; and, most sincere of all, a triptych by Ludovico Bréa. Across the Place du Petit-Puy, a plaque on the **Tour de Guet** (the former *évêché*) commemorates the Grassois poet Bellaud de la Bellaudière, whose songs of wine and women, the *Obras et Rimos Provençalos* (1585), are the high point in Provençal literature between the troubadours and Mistral. But then, as now, it's a rare poet who can live off his verse: Bellaud supplemented his income by joining a band of brigands and sang his swan-song on a scaffold.

Place du Cours and Four Museums

The Cannes road leads into Grasse's promenade, **Place du Cours**, with pretty views over the countryside. Close by at 23 Bd. Fragonard is the **Musée Villa Fragonard**, ✆ 93 40 32 64 (*open summer 10am–7pm, winter 10am–12pm and 2–5pm, closed Mon, Tues, and Nov*), in a 17th-century home belonging to a cousin of Grasse's most famous citizen, Jean-Honoré Fragonard (1732–1806). Son of a *gantier parfumeur*, Fragonard expressed the inherent family sweetness in chocolate-box pastel portraits and mildly erotic rococo scenes of French royals trying their best to look like well-groomed poodles. Some of these are on display, along with copies of *Le Progrès de l'Amour dans la Cœur d'une Jeune Fille*, which even his client, Mme du Barry, Louis XV's most beautiful mistress, rejected as too frivolous (the originals are in the Frick Collection in New York). Losing La Barry's favour was the beginning of the end for Fragonard; he lost most of his clients to the guillotine and in 1790 he washed up in Grasse feeling very out of sorts, until one very hot day in 1806 he died from a cerebral haemorrhage induced by eating an ice-cream.

Just north of the Cours, at 2 Rue Mirabeau, the **Musée d'Art et d'Histoire de Provence**, ✆ 93 36 01 61 (*same hours as Villa Fragonard*) has its home in the 1770 Italianate mansion built by the frisky sister of Count Mirabeau of Aix was married to one of several degenerate Marquis who pepper the history of Provence—this one, the Marquis de Cabris, is remembered in Grasse for having covered the walls of the city with obscene graffiti about the local women. Besides Gallo-Roman funerary objects, *santons* and furniture in all the Louis styles, there's Count Mirabeau's death mask, his sister's original *bidets*, an exceptional collection of faïence from Moustiers and Apt, and paintings by Granet. At 8 Cours Honoré-Cresp, the **Musée International de la Parfumerie**, 8✆ 93 36 80 20 (*open 10–12 and 2–5*), displays lots of precious little bottles from Roman times to the present, plus Bergamot boxes of the 1700s and Marie-Antoinette's travel case, while around the corner in Bd. du Jeu-de-Ballon, the **Musée de la Marine**, ✆ 93 09 10 71 (*open Mon–Sat 10am–12pm and 2–6pm*) is devoted to the career of the intrepid Admiral de Grasse, hero of the American War of Independence.

Parfumeries

It's hard to miss these in Grasse, and if you've read Patrick Süskind's novel *Perfume* the free tours may seem a bit bland. The alchemical processes of extracting essences from freshly cut mimosa, jasmine, roses, bitter orange etc. are explained—you learn that it takes 900,000 rose-buds to make a kilo of rose essence, which then goes to the *haute couture* perfume-bottlers and hype-merchants of Paris. Even more alarming are some of the other ingredients that arouse human hormones: the genital secretions of Ethiopian cats, whale vomit, and Tibetan goat musk.

Tours in English are offered by **Parfumerie Fragonard** at 20 Bd. Fragonard, ✆ 93 36 44 65, and at Les 4 Chemins, on the Route de Cannes; **Molinard**, 60 Bd. Victor-Hugo, ✆ 93 36 01 62 and **Gallimard**, 73 Rte de Cannes (N85), ✆ 93 09 20 00. The visits are free, and they don't seem to mind too much if you don't buy something at the end.

Up Your Nose

If nothing else, the Côte d'Azur makes you more aware of that sense we only remember when something stinks. Every *village perché* has shops overflowing with scented soaps, pot-pourris and bundles of *herbes de Provence*; every kitchen emits intoxicating scents of garlic and thyme; every cellar wants you to breathe in the bouquets of its wines; and the perfumeries of Grasse will correct this 'scentual' ignorance with a hundred different potions and essential oils. And when you begin to almost crave the more usual French smells of Gauloise butts, *pipi* and *pommes frites*, you discover that this nasal obsession is not only profitable to some, but healthy for all.

Aromathérapie, a name coined in the 1920s for the method of natural healing through fragrances, is taken very seriously in the land where one word, '*sentir*', does double duty for 'feel' and 'smell'. French medical students study it, and its prescriptions are covered by the national social security. For as an aromatherapist will tell you, smells play games with your psyche; the nose is hooked up not only to primitive drives like sex and hunger, but also to your emotions and memory. The consequences can be monumental. Just the scent of a madeleine cake dipped in tea was enough to set Proust off to write *Remembrance of Things Past*.

Aromatherapy is really just a fashionable name for old medicine. The Romans had a saying, '*Cur moriatur homo, cui salvia crescit in horto?*' ('Why should he die, who grows sage in his garden?') about a herb still heralded for its youth-giving properties. Essential oils distilled from plants were the secret of Egyptian healing and embalming, and were so powerful that there was a bullish market in 17th-century Europe for mummies, which were boiled down to make medicine.

Essential oils are created by the sun and the most useful aromatic plants grow in hot and dry climates—as in the south of France, the spiritual heartland of aromatherapy. Lavender, the totem plant of the Midi, has been in high demand for its mellow soothing qualities ever since the Romans used it to scent their baths (hence its name from the Latin *lavare*, to wash). Up until the 1900s, nearly every farm in Provence had a small lavender distillery, and you can still find a few kicking about today. Most precious of all is the oil of *lavande fine*, a species that grows only above 3000 feet on the sunny side of the Alps; 150 pounds of flowers are needed for every pound of oil.

For centuries in Provence, shepherds were regarded as magicians for their plant cures, involving considerable mumbo-jumbo about picking their herbs in certain places and at certain times—and indeed, modern analysis has shown that the chemical composition of a herb like thyme varies widely, depending on where it grows and when it's picked. When the sun is in Leo, shepherds make *millepertuis*, or red oil (a sovereign anaesthetic and remedy for burns and wounds) by soaking the flowers of St John's wort in a mixture of white wine and olive oil that has been exposed to the hottest sun. After three days, they boil the wine off, and let the flowers distil for another month; the oil is then sealed into tiny bottles, good for one dose each, to maintain the oil's healing properties.

Still awaiting a fashionable revival are other traditional Provençal cures: baked ground magpie brains for epilepsy, marmot fat for rheumatism, dried fox testicles rubbed on the chest for uterine disease, and mouse excrement for bedwetting.

Around Grasse: Dolmens and Musical Caves

The Route Napoléon (N 85), laid out in the 1930s to follow the little emperor's path to Paris, threads through miles of empty space on either side of medieval **St-Vallier-de-Thiey** (12km). Things were busier here around 800 BC, when the people built elliptical walls with stones as much as 2m high. An alignment of 12 small **dolmens**, most of them buried under stone tumuli, stands between St-Vallier and St-Cézaire-sur-Siagne; a balanced flat rock nearby is known as the *pierre druidique* (St-Vallier's tourist office in Place du Tour has a map). Just to the southwest, signposted on the D5, there's a subterranean lake in the **Grotte de la Baume Obscure**, © 93 42 61 63 (*open Easter–Oct daily 10am–6pm, weekends only the rest of the year; adm*). **Cabris**, 6km west of Grasse on the D4, a *village perché* once favoured by Camus, Sartre and Antoine de Saint-Exupéry, is now a town of artisans and perfume executives. The D11 and D13 to the west lead to more caves: the red **Grottes de St-Cézaire**, © 93 60 22 35; (*open 2.30–5pm, in summer 10.30am–12pm and 2.30–6pm, closed Nov–Feb except Sun 3–5pm; adm*), where the iron-rich stalactites, when struck by the guide, make uncanny music. **St-Cézaire-sur-Siagne** itself is an unspoiled medieval town; its white 13th-century cemetery-chapel built on pure, sober lines, is one of the best examples of Provençal Romanesque near the coast.

Where to Stay

Grasse (✉ 06130)

There is the **Grasse Country Club** at 1 Rte des 3 Ponts, © 93 60 55 44, ✆ 93 60 55 19, which is small, exclusive and expensive. **★★★Best Western Hôtel des Parfums**, Bd. Eugène-Charabot, © 93 36 10 10, ✆ 93 36 35 48, has pretty views, a pool and a jacuzzi, and offers a 1½hr 'Introduction to Perfume' that takes you into the secret heart of the smell biz, lending you a 'nose' to help create your own perfume. Modern **★★Hôtel du Patti**, overlooking the Monoprix supermarket in the centre of medieval Grasse on Place du Patti, © 93 36 01 00, has very comfortable rooms, all with air-conditioning and TV. Up the steps from the main street, at 6 Rue du Palais du Justice, **★Pension de Michèle**, © 93 36 06 37, has inexpensive, simple rooms in a quiet side street. *Closed Nov and Dec.*

St-Vallier-de-Thiey (✉ 06460)

Here there's a charming choice: **★★Le Préjoly**, Place Rouguière, ✆ 93 42 60 86, 🖅 93 42 67 80, with 17 rooms in a large garden, most with terraces, and an excellent restaurant frequented by film stars up from Cannes (*menus at 96F upwards*).

Cabris (✉ 06820)

The friendly **★★Hôtel l'Horizon**, ✆ 93 60 51 69, 🖅 93 60 56 29, is a well-situated Provençal-style hotel far from the crowds (*rooms 300–500F*).

Eating Out

Grasse (✉ 06130)

Grasse's culinary specialities are if anything, *grasse*, especially *sous fassoun* (cabbage stuffed with pig's liver, sausage, bacon, peas and rice and cooked with turnips, beef, carrots, etc.) or *tripes à la mode de Grasse*. Both dishes appear frequently on the menu at **Maître Boscq**, 13 Rue de la Fontette, ✆ 93 36 45 76, the local master of traditional cuisine, contempt, and object of *International Herald Tribune* acclaim, with a 180F menu. For lunch underneath the arches, head to **Les Arcades**, Place aux Aires, ✆ 93 36 00 95, with Provençal dishes and fishes (*menus from 80F*). Orange-blossom essence goes into the delicious sweet *fougassettes* sold at **Maison Venturini**, 1 Rue Marcel-Journet, ✆ 93 36 20 47.

Cabris (✉ 06820)

Le Petit Prince, 15 Rue F.-Mistral, ✆ 93 60 51 40, has a lovely terrace, with delicious *filets de bœuf aux morilles* and *rascasse* (*menus begin at 98F*).

Mougins

Cooking, that most ephemeral of arts, is the main reason most people make a pilgrimage to Mougins, a luxurious, fastidiously flawless village of *résidences secondaires*, with more gastronomy per square inch than any place in France, thanks to the magnetic presence of Roger Vergé (*see* below). But there are a few sights to whet your appetite before surrendering to the table: a **Musée de la Photographie**, at Porte Sarrasine, Place de l'Eglise, ✆ 93 75 85 67 (*open 1–11pm summer, 1–8pm winter, closed Tues and Nov*), with changing exhibitions, often featuring the work of Jacques Lartigue, who lived in nearby Opio. Other exhibitions take place in the old village **Lavoir** (wash-house) in the pretty Place de la Mairie. Two km southeast of Mougins, Picasso spent the last 12 years of his life in a villa next to the exquisite hilltop **Chapelle de Notre-Dame-de-Vie**, a 12th-century priory founded by monks from St-Honorat, and rebuilt in 1646. Until 1730, when the practice was banned, people would bring stillborn babies here to be brought back to life, just long enough for them to be baptized and avoid limbo.

Appropriately located just off the *autoroute* to Cannes, at the Aire des Breguières, the de luxe **Musée de l'Automobiliste**, ✆ 93 69 27 80 (*open 10am–6pm, 7pm summer; adm*), is a

MUSÉE DE L'AUTOMOBILISTE, MOUGINS

modernistic cathedral to the car (Alfa-Romeos to Zumdaps, from its first faltering steps as an 1882 Grand Bi, to Bugattis and Mercedes (with their perfectly reconstructed garages *c.* 1939), to recent winners of the murderous Paris-Dakar rally.

Mougins ✉ *06250*   **Where to Stay and Eating Out**

In 1969 chef Roger Vergé bought a 16th-century olive mill near Notre-Dame-de-Vie and made it into the internationally famous luxury ★★★★ **Le Moulin de Mougins**, Chemin du Moulin, ✆ 93 75 78 24, 📠 93 90 18 55. Of late, France's gourmet bibles have been sniffing that the mild-mannered celebrity chef, author of *The Cuisine of the Sun* (1979), has lost a bit of his touch—and little faults seem big when you shell out 1000F for a meal. But it's still a once-in-a-lifetime experience for most, in the most enchanting setting on the Côte. *Closed end of Jan–Mar; reserve now if you want a table in two or three months.* If you can't get a table, Vergé's shop in central Place du Com.-Lamy, with tableware and a selection of the master's sauces, may offer some consolation.

Another gourmet temple, **Le Relais à Mougins**, run by André Surmain at Pl. de la Mairie, ✆ 93 90 03 47, serves exquisite, classic French cuisine (*gelée de saumon fumé au caviar* etc.) on a delicious garden terrace (*menus 280F and 380F*). *Closed Sun eve, Mon; open all year.* The *nouvelle cuisine* and chocolate desserts at the hôtel-restaurant ★★★★**Les Muscadins**, at the village entrance, 18 Bd. Courteline, ✆ 93 90 00 43, 📠 92 92 88 23, have received excellent reviews (*menus 165F and up*), and the hotel has sumptuous bedrooms of charm and character. *Closed mid-Jan–mid-Mar.* Mougins even has affordable restaurants like **Feu Follet**, Place de la Mairie, ✆ 93 90 15 78, 📠 92 92 92 62, owned by André Surmain's daughter, offering excellent menus (*selle d'agneau en croûte*) for 128–158F. *Closed Sun eve, Mon; open all year.*

Cannes

In 1834, the 3000 fisherfolk and farmers of Cannes were going about their business when Lord Brougham, retired Lord Chancellor, and his ailing daughter checked into its one and only hotel, stuck in the village because a cholera epidemic in France had closed the border with Savoy. As they waited, Lord Brougham was so seduced by the climate and scenery that he built a villa, where he spent every winter. English milords and the Tsar's family played follow-my-leader, and flocked down to build their own villas nearby. 'Menton's dowdy. Monte's brass. Nice is rowdy. Cannes is class!' was the byword of the 1920s. Less enthusiastic commentators mention the dust, the bad roads, the uncontrolled building, and turds bobbing in the sea.

If nothing else, the French Riviera proper ends with a bang at Cannes. The spunky sister city of Beverly Hills, France's Hollywood, and a major year-round convention city (Cannes was the first place on the Côte d'Azur to note that business travellers spend over three times as much per head than tourists), Cannes offers a moveable feast of high fashion, showbiz trendiness, overripe boutiques, and glittering nightlife. Depending on your mood, and perhaps on the thickness of your wallet, you may find it appalling or amusing, or just plain dizzy. You can always catch the next boat to the offshore Iles de Lérins, some of the most serene antidotes to any city.

by train

The frequent *Métrazur* between St-Raphaël and Menton, and every other train whipping along the coast, calls into the station at Rue Jean-Jaurès. For information call ✆ 36 35 35 35, but have some extra French wits about you, as it's an unforgiving computerised system that flits you from place to place.

by bus

There is a multiplicity of private bus companies, all arriving and departing from different places; though there is one central number, ✆ 93 39 18 71, at Place de l'Hôtel de Ville.

by boat

Every hour in the summer, the glass-bottomed boat, *Nautilus*, at Jetée Albert-Edouard, departs for tours of the port and its sea creatures; tickets 70F.

Boat trips out to the Iles de Lérins, ✆ 93 39 11 82, depart from the *gare maritime*, Allées de la Liberté, approximately every hour, and much less frequently between October and June. The general tour is a whirlwind trip—you're no sooner there than it's time to go back; you're best off going to one island at a time.

by bike

You can rent bikes at the train station or at Location Mistral, Rue Georges-Clemenceau, ✆ 93 39 33 60.

Cannes ✉ *06400*   *Tourist Information*

Palais des Festivals, 1 La Croisette, ✆ 93 39 24 53, ✉ 93 99 84 23; another office is in the **Gare SNCF**, ✆ 93 99 19 77. **Cannes Information Jeunesse**, 5 Quai St-Pierre, ✆ 93 06 31 31, has listings of events, jobs, etc.

Post office: 22 Bivouac Napoléon, ✆ 93 06 26 50.

market days

Marché Forville: daily (*except Mon in summer, Mon–Tues in winter*); Saturday flea market in the Allées de la Liberté.

La Croisette

Besides ogling the shops, the shoppers and their dogs there isn't much to see in Cannes. Characterless luxury apartment buildings and boutiques have replaced the gaudy Belle Epoque confections along the fabled promenade **La Croisette**, its glitter now clogged by incessant traffic in the summer, its lovely sands covered by the sun-beds and parasols of the beach concessions. The shoreline is divided into 32 sections (you can get a map), as memorably named as 'Waikiki', 'Le Zénith' and 'Long Beach' (which is all of several metres long). One rare public beach is in front of the fan-shaped **Palais des Festivals**, a 1982 construction that may have been the prototype for one of Saddam Hussein's cosier bunkers. **Hand-prints** of film celebrities line the '*Allée des Etoiles*' by the '*Escalier d'Honneur*' where the limos pull up for the festival. Outside May, this orange monster engorges conventioneers attending events such as the Festival of Hairdressing or Dentistry.

Birth of a Festival

In 1938, Philippe Erlanger, the Popular Front's minister of tourism, was given the task of finding a suitable venue for a festival to rival Mussolini's new Venice film festival: the French were not about to let the Fascists have all the starlets to themselves. Erlanger went down to the Côte d'Azur, where his Villefranche friends, especially Jean Cocteau, took a close interest in his mission. Erlanger had a weakness for Cannes, but it lacked hotels, and he was about to choose Biarritz instead when Cocteau intervened, and insisted on Cannes: it would be more fun, he said. The first festival, slated to start 1 August 1939 was cancelled owing to a party-pooper named Hitler's spoiling a huge cardboard model of Notre Dame erected on the beach and forcing a liner full of movie stars sent over by MGM to sail home unrequited.

The second festival, in 1946, drew some fifty journalists who hobnobbed and drank complimentary rosé wine. The jury gave every film a prize, which set the tone from the start: the competition bit was only an excuse for a week of carousing and hanky panky; the real festival would always be outside the screenings. Cannes' historians cite 1954 as the year when everything coelesced, when the essential ingredients of sex and scandal were added to the glamour of film: the décolletage of newcomer Sophia Loren made a big impression, grabbing attention and headlines away from Gina Lollobrigida. Another well-endowed starlet (English this time) named Simone Silva went on to the Iles de Lérins for a photo session with Robert Mitchum and removed her brassiere. Two hours later she was told to leave Cannes and a few years later, no longer able to find work because of her precocious gesture, she committed suicide. Cannes should have made her an honorary citizen. Two years later, the new sensation was Brigitte Bardot, who coyly spun her skirts around to reveal her dainty *petites culottes*. The atmosphere was so ripe that even the straightest of arrows, Gary Cooper and Esther Williams, the MGM mermaid, had flings during the festival.

In the 1990s would-be starlets strip down completely and bump and grind on the Croisette hoping to attract attention, any kind of attention from the 6000 journalists. The directors and stars, all carefully groomed in the spirit of Riviera casual give the same careful interviews all day. Although the big American studios have traditionally shunned the festival—what's the point, they said, when their own Oscars mean more at the box office than a Cannes' *Palme d'Or*—the importance of the international entertainment market has brought a growing stream over from Hollywood. But the wheeling and dealing that goes on has not diminished expectations of fun and wild times, sometimes from unexpected quarters. In 1993, a ship full of raw Russian sailors caused a sensation by anchoring within spitting distance of the Palais des Festivals with a vast contraband cargo of vodka and smoked salmon. The next day, most of the jurors slept through the screening of the films in competition. Nor was it the first time.

For all the present emphasis on glitter, tourist Cannes still remembers its English roots. Behind the Carlton Hotel, at 2–4 Rue Général-Ferrié, the **Holy Trinity Church** was rebuilt in 1971 on the site of its 19th century predecessor, preserving some Victorian odds and bobs: a mosaic, glass medallions of the arms of the archbishop of Canterbury and the bishop of Gibraltar and other Anglican paraphernalia. But because it's built with ferro-concrete its glories are its stained glass and seventies style, enough to give points to your collars and make you reach for your wedges. The vicar willl be pleased to conduct a tour.

The Old Port and Le Suquet

The **Vieux Port**, with its bobbing fishing-boats and plush, luxury craft, is on the other side of the Palais des Festivals. Plane trees line the **Allées de la Liberté**, where the flower market and Saturday flea market takes place. Two streets further back, narrow pedestrian **Rue Meynadier** is the best place to buy cheese (Ferme Savoyarde), bread (Jacky Carletto), and fresh pasta (Aux Bons Raviolis), near the sumptuous **Forville** covered market.

Cannes' cramped old quarter, **Le Suquet**, rises up on the other side of the port, where the usual renovation and displacement of the not-so-rich is just beginning. At the city's highest point, the monks of St-Honorat built the square watchtower, the **Tour du Mont Chevalier** in 1088, and their priory is now the **Musée de la Castre**, ✆ 93 38 55 26 (*open 10am–12pm and 2–6pm, summer 3–7pm*), a little museum at a little price (10F), with an archaeological and ethnographic collection donated by a Dutch Baron in 1873, containing everything from Etruscan vases to pre-Columbian art and a 40-armed Buddha.

A good way to get Cannes into proportion is to see it by night. Climb up through **Le Suquet** (if you're out of season, restaurateurs stand outside their restaurants, as if by staring they could make you come in) to **La Tour**, and join the lovers to look beyond the white boats and lights.

The Iles de Lérins: Saint-Honorat and Sainte-Marguerite

When Babylon begins to pall, you can take refuge (and a picnic, for the island restaurants are dear) on a delightful pair of green, wooded, traffic-free islets just off the coast. Known in antiquity as Lero and Lerina, they are now named after two saints who founded religious houses on them at the end of the 4th century: little **Ile Saint-Honorat** and the larger **Ile Sainte-Marguerite**. According to legend, when St Honorat landed on the islet that bears his name in 375, he found it swarming with noxious snakes and prayed to be delivered of them. They immediately dropped dead but the stench of the cadavers was so hideous that Honorat climbed a palm tree and prayed again, asking for the bodies be washed away. God obliged again, and in memory the symbol of the island became two palm trees intertwined with a snake.

Saint Honorat shares with Jean Cassien of St-Victor in Marseille the distinction of introducing monasticism to France. The island became a beacon of light and learning in the Dark Ages; by the 7th century, St-Honorat had 4000 monks, and 100 priories and lordships on the mainland (including Cannes, which belonged to the monastery until 1788). Its alumni numbered 20 saints, including St Patrick, who, before going to Ireland, trained here and picked up some tips on dealing with pesky snakes.

The monastery was also a big boon to local sinners: a journey to St-Honorat could earn a pilgrim an indulgence equal to a journey to the Holy Land. Other visitors, especially Saracen pirates, were not as welcome. To protect themselves, the monks built a fortress, connected to the abbey by means of an underground tunnel. Although the abbey is long gone, the evocative, crenellated **donjon** remains strong, lapped by the wavelets on three sides, mellowed by sea and time; within there's a vaulted cloister and chapel, and a terrace with views that stretch to the Alps. In 1869 Cistercians from Sénanque purchased St-Honorat, rebuilt the abbey (men only are admitted on weekdays, but there's not much to see) and have done all they could to preserve the islet's natural beauty and serenity, so close to and yet so far from the sound and fury of Cannes.

Sainte Marguerite, and the Man in the Iron Mask

Legend has it that Marguerite, sister of St Honorat, founded a convent for holy Christian women on this island, but it broke her heart that her austere brother would only come to visit her when a certain almond tree blossomed. Marguerite asked God to make him come more often, a prayer answered when the almond tree miraculously began to bloom every month.

Ste-Marguerite has nicer beaches than St-Honorat, especially on the south end of Chemin de la Chasse. On the north end stands the gloomy **Fort Royal**, built by Richelieu as a defence against the Spaniards (who got it anyway) and improved by Vauban in 1712. By then the fortress mainly served as a prison, especially for the mysterious Man in the Iron Mask, who was transferred here from Pigneroles in 1687, and then ended up in the Bastille, in 1698. Speculation about the man's identity continues at least to amuse historians (who insist that the mask was actually leather): was he Louis XIV's twin, as Voltaire suggested, or, according to a more recent theory, the gossiping son-in-law of the doctor who performed the autopsy on Louis XIII and discovered that the king was incapable of producing children? Later prisoners included six Huguenot pastors who dared to return to France after Louis XIV's revocation of the Edict of Nantes, and were kept in solitary confinement until all but one of them went mad.

Cannes ✉ *06400*   ***Where to Stay***

expensive

Although there are sizeable discounts if you come to Flash City in the off-season, you can't book too early for the film festival or for July and August. Cannes' two tourist offices offer a free reservation service, but they won't be much help at that time of year if you want a room that costs less than a king's ransom; if, however, you possess one of those, you can drop a considerable lump of it at the ★★★★**Carlton**, 58 La Croisette, ☎ 93 68 91 68, ⊠ 93 38 20 90, one of the great landmarks of the Riviera, with its two black cupolas, said to be shaped like the breasts of the *grande horizontale* Belle Otero, the Andalusian flamenco dancer and courtesan of kings. Given a thorough renovation by its new Japanese owners, the seventh floor has been endowed with a pool, casino, beauty centre, and more. In the same category, the traditional ★★★★**Majestic**, Bd. de la Croisette, ☎ 92 98 77 00, ⊠ 93 38 97 90, is the movie stars' favourite with its classic French décor, heated pool, private beach etc. A third, the ★★★★**Martinez**, 73 Bd. de la Croisette, ☎ 92 98 73 00, ⊠ 93 39 67 82, has kept its Roaring Twenties character, but with all imaginable modern comforts, including tennis courts, a heated pool and, from the seventh floor, grand views over the city.

moderate–inexpensive

If you aren't in Cannes on an MGM expense account, there are other alternatives, such as the elegant, stuccoed ★★★**Bleu Rivage**, 61 Bd. de la Croisette, ☎ 93 94 24 25, ⊠ 93 43 74 92, a renovated older hotel amidst the big daddies on the beach where rooms overlook the sea, or the garden at the back. The modern, kosher ★★★ **King David**, 16 Bd. d'Alsace, ☎ 93 99 16 16, ⊠ 93 68 97 69, inspected by the regional rabbi, has a heated pool on the roof, a back terrace, and 60 comfortable rooms. The 19th-century ★★**Molière**, 5–7 Rue Molière, ☎ 93 38 16 16, ⊠ 93 68 29 57, sits in the midst of a garden, with bright rooms and terraces. Another quiet choice, the modern ****Sélect**, 16 Rue Hélène-Vagliano, © 93 99 51 00, ● 92 98 03 12, has air-conditioned rooms, all with bath, while **Le Chanteclair**, 12 Rue Forville, © 93 39 68 88, has decent doubles with showers. **Hôtel National**, 8 Rue Maréchal-Joffre, © 93 39 91 92, ● 92 98 44 06, is inexpensive, near the station, and popular with budget travellers.

Cannes ✉ *06400*   ***Eating Out***

expensive

Good food follows money, and Cannes is well-endowed with opportunities for gastro-nomic indulgence. Two of the top restaurants on the whole Riviera are here: **La Palme d'Or** in the Martinez hotel (*see* above), has a fabulous Art Deco dining room; the Alsacian cook, Christian Willer, prepares dishes including *salade de pigeonneau* or a succulent *agneau de Sisteron persillé*. *Closed mid-Nov–mid-Jan, Mon, Tues.* **La Belle Otero**, © 93 68 00 33, is on the 7th floor of the Carlton (*see* above)—and the seventh heaven of gastronomy. If *loup de Méditerranée en croustillant de parmesan poêlée de légumes niçois* doesn't make your mouth water, then be guided by numbers; it shares two Michelin stars with the Palme d'Or. *Closed 1st half Nov, and last 3 weeks of June.* **Le Royal Gray**, by the luxurious Lebanese hyper-mall at 6 Rue des Etats-Unis, © 93 99 79 79, ● 92 99 79 81, is a citadel where ingredients such as fresh shrimp from Tunisia and tiny morels from Canada to create the extraordinarily rare and delightful dishes, at rarefied prices—although there's a tempting 185F weekday lunch menu that definitely bears thinking about. *Open all year.*

moderate–inexpensive

For well-prepared versions of the French classics, try **Stop'in Rescator**, 7 Rue Maréchal-Joffre, © 93 39 44 57, a favourite with its generous menus from 90F. For affordable seafood and fine views of its original habitat, try *marmite du pêcheur* and a pretty good *aïoli* at the nautical **Lou Souléou**, 16 Bd. Jean-Hibert, © 93 39 85 55. *Closed Mon-Wed off-season, mid-Nov–mid-Dec.* There's only one 195F menu at **La Brouette de Grand-Mère**, 9 Rue d'Oran, © 93 39 12 10, and it's only served in the evenings, but it will fill you up, with everything that could possibly be crammed between an apéritif and coffee, with as much *vin du pays* as you want—but be sure to reserve. *Closed Sun, and end June–early July.* **Au Bec Fin**, 12 Rue du 24-Août, near the station, © 93 38 35 86, serves good food and plenty of it, with a wide selection of *plats du jour* for 85F. *Closed Sat eve, Sun, late Dec–late Jan.* Spread out along the Vieux Port, **La Pizza**, 3 Quai St-Pierre, © 93 39 22 56, has fine pizzas, *saltimbocca à la Romana*, a very passable *tarte tatin* and a congenial atmosphere. *Open until 2–5am in the summer.*

Cannes ✉ *06400*   ***Entertainment and Nightlife***

If you want your stars on celluloid, choose between **Les Arcades**, 77 Av. Félix-Faure, © 93 39 00 98; **Olympia**, 5 Rue d'Antibes, © 93 39 13 93; and **Star**, 98 Rue d'Antibes, © 93 68 18 08—all of which sometimes show VO films (*version originale*).

Otherwise, the fleshpot will keep you entertained if you have the wherewithal to afford it. Its casinos draw in some of the highest rollers on the Riviera, although the adjoining casino discos are fairly staid. There's **La Grande Aventure**, at 50 La Croisette, ✆ 93 68 43 43, where you can eat 'theme cuisine' while you gamble away the readies, or the **Casino Croisette**, in the Palais des Festivals, ✆ 93 38 12 11.

To get into the most fashionable clubs (those with no signs on the door) you need to look like you've just stepped off a 30m yacht to get past the sour-faced bouncers. **Jimmy'Z** at the Casino in the Palais des Festivals, ✆ 93 68 00 07, is a glitzy showcase billing itself '*La discothèque des stars*': it's certainly for those with stars in their eyes—gamblers, their ladies and mainstream music (*11pm–dawn*). There's usually live music to go with the food at **La Chunga**, 24 Rue Latour-Maubourg, ✆ 93 94 11 29 (*open 8pm–dawn; meals about 300F*). **Le Whisky à Gogo** has a well-heeled crowd grinding away to the top of the pops, at 115 Av. de Lérins, ✆ 93 43 20 63. **Velvet**, 22 Rue Macé, ✆ 93 39 31 31 (*open midnight–dawn*) attracts a young crowd of every possible sexual persuasion. Cannes also has two gay bars of long standing: **Le Bar Basque**, 14 Rue Macé, ✆ 93 39 35 61, (*open 7pm–6am*) and the noisier **Zanzi-Bar**, 85 Rue Félix-Faure, ✆ 93 39 30 75 (*6pm–6am*); newer on the scene, **Disco 7** at 7 Rue Rougière, ✆ 93 39 10 36, has dancing and a transvestite show (*open 11pm–dawn, 90F cover charge*).

Festivals

The **Festival International du Film** erupts for 12 days beginning around the second week of May with a hurricane of hype, *paparazzi*, journalists, movie stars, gawking fans and characters who come every year, like the trucker from Kansas who's a dead ringer for Liz Taylor and flounces up and down the Croisette signing autographs. There are some 350 screenings, but most of the tickets are reserved for the cinema people themselves, while 10 per cent go to the Cannois, who bestow the *prix populaire* on their favourite film. The few seats left over go on sale at the Palais' box-office a week before the festival. From 4–14 July, the **Festival Américain** brings in jazz and country music.

The Esterel to Bandol

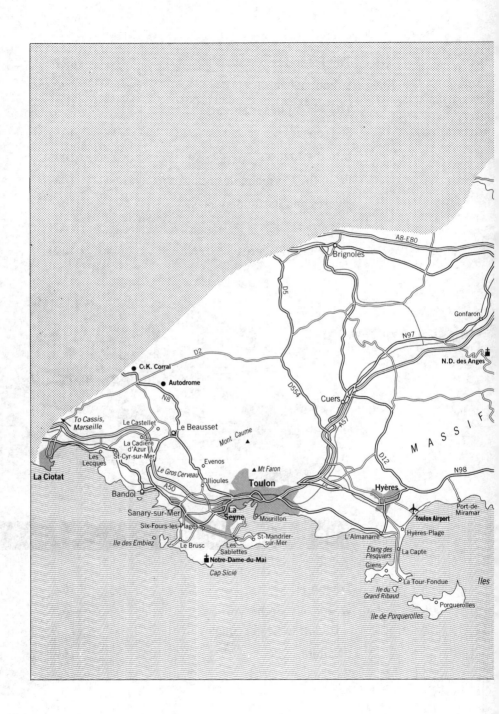

A8-E80

Brignoles

D5

Gonfaron

N97

D2

C.K. Corral

Autodrome

D554

N.D. des Anges

Cuers

N8

To Cassis,
Marseille

Le Castellet

Le Beausset

Mont Caume

A57

La Cadière
d'Azur
St-Cyr-sur-Mer

Evenos

Mt Faron

D12

Les
Lecques

Le Gros Cerveau

Ollioules

Toulon

Hyères

N98

MASSIF

La Ciotat

A50

Bandol

Sanary-sur-Mer

La
Seyne

Mourillon

Toulon Airport

Port-de-
Miramar

Six-Fours-les-Plages

St-Mandrier-
sur-Mer

L'Almanarre

Hyères-Plage

Ile des Embiez

Le Brusc

Les
Sablettes

Notre-Dame-du-Mai

Etang des
Pesquiers

La Capte

Giens

Cap Sicié

Ile du
Grand Ribaud

La Tour-Fondue

Iles

Porquerolles

Ile de Porquerolles

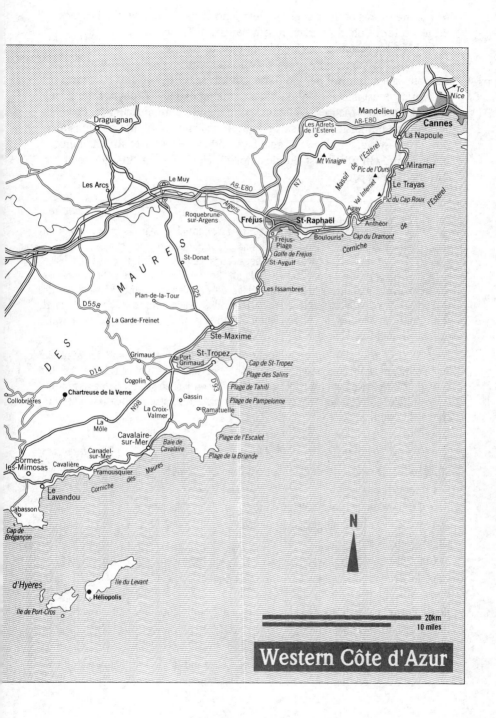

Draguignan

Les Adrets
de l'Esterel

A8-E80

Mandelieu

Cannes

La Napoule

Mt Vinaigre ▲

Pic de l'Ours ▲

Miramar

Massif   de   l'Esterel

N7

Val Internet ▲

Le Trayas

Les Arcs

Le Muy

A8 - E80

Argens

Roquebrune-
sur-Argens

Fréjus

St-Raphaël

Agay

Pic du Cap Roux ▲

l'Esterel

Anthéor

Boulouris

Cap du Dramont

de

Fréjus-
Plage

Golfe de Fréjus

Corniche

St-Donat

St-Aygulf

M   A   U   R   E   S

D25

Plan-de-la-Tour

Les Issambres

D558

La Garde-Freinet

D   E   S

Ste-Maxime

Grimaud

Port
Grimaud

St-Tropez

Cap de St-Tropez

Plage des Salins

D14

Cogolin

D93

Plage de Tahiti

Chartreuse de la Verne ●

Gassin

Plage de Pampelonne

Collobrières

N98

La Croix-
Valmer

Ramatuelle

La
Môle

Cavalaire-
sur-Mer

Plage de l'Escalet

Canadel-
sur-Mer

Baie de
Cavalaire

Plage de la Briande

**Bormes-
les-Mimosas**

Cavalière

Maures

Pramousquier

des

Corniche

des

Maures

Le
Lavandou

Cabasson

Cap de
Brégançon

d'Hyères

Île du Levant

Île de Port-Cros

● **Héliopolis**

N

20km

10 miles

Western Côte d'Azur

To
Nice

Where the shores of the eastern Riviera tend to be all shingle, the beaches of the western Côte d'Azur are mostly soft sand. The crowds, cars, art, yachts, boutiques and prices are less intense as well, with the outrageous exception of St-Tropez, the pretty playground of the jet set and dry-martini louts on yachts. But just behind these careless seaside pleasures bulge two of the world's most ancient chunks of land, the prodigious porphyry Esterel and the dark, forested Maures, while tucked in between are museums of Post-Impressionism, music boxes, ships' figureheads and booze; Roman ruins and a tortoise reserve; an island national park and the oldest baptistry in France; and to begin with, the most Gothic of follies, Henry Clews' little house of horrors in La Napoule.

Beaches

This region contains some of the most enticing beaches in France. From Cannes to St Tropez the dramatic *corniche* road offers glimpses down to small sandy coves hiding between jagged rocks. This is above all a place to take your time, stopping where fancy dictates. The beaches of St-Tropez are actually 5km south of the town—Plage de Tahiti is most infamous, Plage de Pampelonne the least spoiled. True aficionados head south to Plage de l'Escalet and round Cap Lardier to Gigaro. The footpath east of Gigaro takes you to a well-patronised nudist beach.

From St-Trop to Toulon the road climbs and falls along the Corniche des Maures. Some of the most revered beaches in Europe lie off this stretch of coastline—the Iles de Porquerolles have national park status and offer unrivalled sand (catch a ferry from Hyères). West of Toulon, Sanary and Bandol have thin strips, but these get very crowded in summer.

best beaches

St-Aygulf: long sand, lots of space, but crowded in summer.

Les Issambres: as above.

Port Grimaud: long beach backing on to Spoerry's *cité lacustre*.

St-Tropez: Plage de Tahiti, Plage de Pampelonne, Plage de l'Escalet.

Gigaro: long beach, favourite with families.

St-Clair: just outside Le Lavandou; views across to the islands.

Cap de Brégançon: wilder coves, off the beaten track. Cabasson is the French President's summer retreat.

Ile de Porquerolles: Plage de Notre Dame, or any of the northern coastal beaches.

Ile du Levant: Héliopolis, premier nudist beach.

Hyères: large town beach.

Bandol/Sanary/La Ciotat: thin beaches, crowded in summer, restful off-season.

The Esterel is supposed to receive its name from the fairy Esterelle,
who intoxicates and deceives her ardent lovers and thus fittingly makes
her home on the Coast of Illusion.

Douglas Goldring, *The South of France* (1952)

Between Cannes and St-Raphaël this fairy Coast of Illusion provides one of nature's strangest but most magnificent interludes: a wild *massif* of blood-red cliffs and promontories, with sandy or shingle beaches amid dishevelled porphyry boulders tumbling into the blue blue sea—the kind of romantic landscape where holy hermits like St Honorat and unholy brigands like Gaspard de Besse once felt equally at home. The handsome Gaspard, from a bourgeois family of Besse-sur-Issole, was himself the stuff of romance—a generous highwayman with knightly manners, a lover of good food and wine, a man able to entertain the jury at his trial in Aix by reciting long passages of Homer and Anacreon in Greek. When they hanged him anyway, many a woman wept bitter tears.

Unfortunately, the virgin cork forests that once hid Gaspard's band in the Esterel have been ravaged by fire—environmental tragedies with the side-effects of clearing sites for property brigands and their cement-mixers, who race neck-and-neck with the forestry service's gallant attempts to reforest the arid mountain with drought- and disease-resilient pines and ilexes. Come in the spring if you can, when wild flowers ignite this Fauvist volcanic fairyland; in the summer, to lower the risk of real fires, the internal roads are often closed to traffic.

Getting Around

The Corniche de l'Esterel is well served by 5 **trains** per day and **buses** (2 per hour from Cannes) between Cannes and St-Raphaël. From Mandelieu-La Napoule there are regular **boats** to the Iles de Lérins, from the harbour (*see* p.119), ✆ 93 49 15 88, 50F.

Tourist Information

Mandelieu-La Napoule (✉ 06210): Av. de Cannes, ✆ 93 49 14 39 and Bd. Henri Clews, ✆ 93 49 95 31.

Agay (✉ 83700): Bd. de la Mer, ✆ 94 82 01 85.

Mandelieu-La Napoule

Golf is what makes Mandelieu famous; there are nine- and eighteen-hole courses; the first laid out a hundred years ago by the nephew of the Tsar, the latest by an American. The brochures speak of 'panoramas to stop you from breathing'. If you recover your breath, down below on the coast its sister town, La Napoule, has the usual beaches and hotels and the nuttiest folly ever built by a foreigner on this shore, the **Fondation Henri Clews**, ✆ 93 49 95 05 (*open for tours Mon–Fri, 3pm and 4pm, closed Tues, closed to visitors from Nov 1st–March 1st*), a pseudo-medieval fantasy castle beautifully located on Pointe des Pendus (hanged men's point).

Clews or Clueless: One Man's Hideaway from Modern Times

Henry Clews, born in 1863 to a wealthy American banking family, was a sculptor and designer who fancied himself the Don Quixote of the 20th century. He began to re-invent his own life when he married the beautiful Elsie Whelen Goelet, whom he renamed Marie because she reminded him of the Madonna. They had a son and moved to Paris, only be chased out by the noise of the bombardments in 1917. The Clewses came down to the coast and bought the ruined fort first built by the Saracens known as the Château de la Napoule, and converted it into a crenellated fantasy castle that Henry called La Mancha, his refuge from the modern world, scientists, reformers, the middle class, democrats and everything else (although everyone noticed he didn't extend his hatred to telephones and the other mod cons of the day. Over the door he carved his life's motto: 'Once Upon a Time'.

Once installed, the Clews rarely left the fairytale world they created. Henry designed the costumes, not only for himself and Marie but for the maids and the Senegalese butler. They filled the château and garden with peacocks and flamingos and other exotic birds and loved to stage dramatic elaborate dinner parties that to the bewildered guests seemed to come straight out of a Hollywood movie. The most lasting of all is Henry's personal mythology, devoted to something he called Humormystics, amply illustrated in stone throughout the castle, cloister capitals, and gardens: weird monsters and grotesques, human figures and animals, many in egg and phallic shapes with cryptic inscriptions and most carved in stone out of his private quarry in the Esterel with the help of 12 stone-cutters. Here too is Clews' own self-designed tomb and epitaph ('Grand Knight of La Mancha Supreme Master Humormystic Castelan of Once upon a Time Chevalier de Marie') completed by Marie who survived until 1959 and made sure all was preserved intact by founding the charitable La Napoule Arts Foundation, where American and French artists and writers can work immersed in Clews' phantasmagoria.

Corniche de l'Esterel

Laid out by the French Touring Club way back in 1903, the Corniche (N98) is dotted with panoramic belvederes overlooking the extraordinary red, blue, and green seascapes below. The largest beaches of sand or shingle are served by snack wagons in the summer, and in between, with a bit of climbing, are rocky coves and nooks you can have all to yourself. Heading south from La Napoule, **Théoule-sur-Mer**, which claims to be only 10 minutes from Cannes' Croisette, has small beaches and an 18th-century seaside soap factory converted into a castle, which isn't bad compared to **La Galère** (the next town east on the same road), infected in the 1970s by a private housing estate which looks as if it were modelled on cancer cells. This is a suburb of fashionable **Miramar**, where the best thing to do is walk out along **Pointe de l'Esquillon** for the view of the sheer cliffs of **Cap Roux** plunging into the sea. The nearby slopes and jagged shore, pierced with inlets and secret coves, belong to the villas and hotel of **Le Trayas**.

Beyond Le Trayas, a road at **Pointe de l'Observatoire** ascends to the **Grotte de la Ste-Baume**, where St Honorat resided as a hermit when four-star views were free of charge. Meanwhile the Corniche road itself twists and turns towards **Anthéor** and the Esterel's biggest resort, **Agay**, a laid-back village dominated by porphyry cliffs, set around a perfect horseshoe bay rimmed with sand and pebble beaches. In 1944 the American 36th Division disembarked just to the west at the **Plage du Dramont**, where you can pick up the path to the **Sémaphore du Dramont**, with broad panoramas over the Gulf of Fréjus and the two porphyry sea rocks at its entrance called the *Le Lion de Mer* and *Le Lion de Terre*.

The Esterel: Inland Routes

From Cannes, the N7 follows the path of the Roman Via Aurelia, passing through the bulk of the Esterel's surviving cork forest. This is ravishing scenery, ravished by the world that wants to see it: it is possible to see it underneath all its tourists; at least at dawn, in sunny near-silence, when only a few sleepy campers are stirring. The high point of the trip, both literally and figuratively, is **Mont Vinaigre**, rising to 600m; from the road a short path leads to its summit and a fantastic viewing platform in an old watchtower. Other hairpinning roads begin in Agay and lead to within easy walking distance of the Esterel's most dramatic features: the hellish **Ravin du Mal-Infernet**, and the panoramic **Pic de l'Ours** and **Pic du Cap Roux**, where the Esterelle is at her most ravishing, and the Coast of Illusion a flaming vision of colour and light.

Where to Stay and Eating Out

Mandelieu-La Napoule (✉ 06210)

In Mandelieu, golf-enthusiasts can sleep near their favourite sport at the modern ★★★**Hostellerie du Golf**, 780 Av. de la Mer, 93 49 11 66, ✆ 92 97 04 01, equipped with a pool and spacious rooms with terraces. La Napoule's ★★★★**Ermitage du Riou**, Av. Henri Clews, ✆ 93 49 95 56, ✆ 92 97 69 05, is a luxurious refuge built like a Provençal *bastide*, with a garden and pool overlooking the sea. The much more affordable ★★**La Calanque**, Bd. Henri Clews, ✆ 93 49 95 11, has a shady terrace and views of the sea and Clews' folly. *Closed Nov–Mar.* For dinner, try the *soupe de poissons* or *plateaux de fruits de mer* at **Le Boucanier**, by the Port de Plaisance, ✆ 93 49 80 51 (*good 140F menu*). *Closed Sun eve, Mon.*

Le Trayas (✉ 83700)

The one hotel, ★★**Le Relais des Calanques**, Corniche de l'Esterel, ✆ 94 44 14 06, has 12 rooms plus a pool and a good fish restaurant (*menus from 140F*) with marine views. There's a superb **Auberge de Jeunesse** (Youth Hostel cards required), ✆ 93 75 40 23, but as usual it's hard to reach—a 2km march uphill from the station (last bus from the train station 7.30), so ring ahead; and in summer, book. *Closed Jan–mid-Feb.*

Anthéor (✉ 83700)

★★**Les Flots Bleus**, on the N 98, ✆ 94 44 80 21, is the best place to sleep and eat; the rooms have views of the sea and the seafood served on the terrace is fresh and copious (*menus from 98F*). *Closed mid-Oct–mid-Mar.*

Agay (✉ 83700)

There are mostly campsites here, and among the handful of hotels the most comfortable is the isolated ★★★**Sol e Mar**, at Plage Le Dramont, ✆ 94 95 25 60, ✆ 94 83 83

61, right on the sea, with two salt-water pools and a restaurant with adequate food but tremendous views. ★★★**France Soleil**, ✆ 94 82 01 93, ✉ 94 82 73 95, in Agay itself, is a reliable choice on the beach. *Open from Easter to October only.*

Along the N7, the ★**Auberge des Adrets**, ✆ 94 40 36 24, is a lonely inn (dating back to 1653), once notorious as a refuge for bandits. It now has simple but bandit-less rooms just beyond Mt Vinaigre.

St-Raphaël and Fréjus

Between the Esterel and the Massif des Maures, in the fertile little plain of the river Argens, St-Raphaël and Fréjus are the largest towns on the coast between Cannes and Hyères. After the fireworks of the Esterel, St-Raphaël is all too predictable: more beaches, blocks of holiday flats and yachts. It has swollen to merge with its venerable neighbour Fréjus (*Forum Julii*), a market town and naval port on the *Via Aurelia* founded by Julius Caesar himself to rival Greek Marseille. Octavian made it his chief arsenal, to build the ships that licked Cleopatra and Mark Antony at Actium. Even today, Fréjus is a garrison town, with France's largest naval air base.

Getting Around
by train

St-Raphaël is the terminus of the *Métrazur* trains that run along the coast to Menton. Other trains between Nice and Marseille call at both St-Raphaël and Fréjus stations, making it easy to hop between the two towns; St-Raphaël also has direct connections to Aix, Avignon, Nîmes, Montpellier and Carcassonne, and it's a mere 6hrs 15mins on the TGV direct from Paris (train information, ✆ 94 91 50 50, or 93 99 50 50).

by bus

Both towns have buses for Nice and Marseille (*gare routière* ✆ 94 95 24 82), more expensive ones for St-Tropez and Toulon (SODETRAV, ✆ 94 95 24 82) and buses inland for Bagnols, Fayence, and Les Adrets (Gagnard, ✆ 94 95 24 78).

by boat

Les Bateaux Bleus, ✆ 94 95 17 46, depart regularly from the Quai Albert 1er, to St-Tropez and St-Aygulf, and make day excursions to the Iles de Lérins and Ile de Port Cros, as well as jaunts around the Golfe de Fréjus and its *calanques* (creeks); be sure to reserve ahead in July and Aug. The *Capitaine Nemo* will submerge you in the murky depths.

bike hire

Jojo Bikes in Le Dramont, ✆ 94 95 20 59, **Holiday Bikes** in Agay ✆ 94 82 85 81, and **Cycles Michel**, ✆ 94 51 45 56, **Cycles Trevisan**, ✆ 94 51 74 02 can both be found in Fréjus. For mountain bike excursions into the Esterel, contact **Mountain Bike Grenouillet** in Agay ✆ 94 82 81 89 for bikes, also ✆ 94 82 75 28 for **horses**.

Tourist Information

St-Raphaël (✉ 83702): Place de la Gare, ✆ 94 19 52 52, ✉ 94 83 85 40.
Fréjus (✉ 83601): 325 Rue Jean-Jaurès, ✆ 94 17 19 19, ✉ 94 51 00 26.
Fréjus-Plage (✉ 83600): Bd. de la Libération, ✆ 94 51 48 42, summer only.

St-Raphaël

The fiefdom of the ambitious François Léotard, newly elected leader of the centre-right UDF party, St-Raphaël has money if not much heart. Its once glittering turn-of-the-century follies and medieval centre were bombed to smithereens in the war, sparing only the Victorian-Byzantine church of **Notre-Dame** in Bd. Felix-Martin, and the **Eglise des Templiers** (1150) intact, with its Templar watchtower, in Rue des Templiers (just north of the station). This is the third church to occupy the site, re-using the same old Roman stones—one in the choir vault is carved with something you won't often see in church: a flying phallus, an ancient charm for averting evil (Pompeii has lots of them). If the church is closed, pick up the key at the adjacent **Musée Archéologique**, ✆ 94 19 25 75 (*open mid-Sept–mid-June 10am–12pm and 2–5pm, closed Sun; June–Sept 10am–12pm and 3–6pm, closed Tues*). For centuries there were rumours of a sunken city off St-Raphaël, apparently confirmed by the bricks that divers brought to shore. Jacques Cousteau went down to see and found, not a new Atlantis, but a Roman shipwreck full of building materials. Some are displayed here along with a fine collection of amphorae.

Fréjus: the Roman Town

Founded in 49 BC, *Forum Julii* was the first Roman town of Gaul, but not the most successful; the site was malarial and hard to defend, and eventually the river Argens silted up, creating the vast sandy beach of **Fréjus-Plage** but leaving the Roman harbour, once famous for its enormous size, high and dry a mile from the sea. A path tracing the ruined quay begins at Butte St-Antoine, south of central Fréjus, but even then it's hard to picture a hundred Roman galleys anchored in the weeds. The one monument still standing, the **Lanterne d'Auguste** isn't even Roman, but a medieval harbourmaster's lodge built on a Roman base.

Other fragments of *Forum Julii* are a long hike away across the modern town—Fréjus is one place where those ubiquitous little tourist trains make sense. Best preserved is the ungainly, greenish **Amphithéâtre Romain**, Rue Henri-Vadon, ✆ 94 17 05 60 (*open summer, 9.30am–12pm, 2–6.30pm; and winter, 9am–12pm, 2–4.30pm; adm free*), flat on its back like a beached whale with the rib arches of its *vomitoria* (entrance) exposed to the sky. Arches from a 40km **aqueduct** still leapfrog alongside the road to Cannes; the **Théâtre Romain**, north on Av. du Théâtre Romain has had new seats installed for modern performances (*same ✆ and times as the amphithéâtre*).

The Oldest Baptistry in France

On a map marked with walls that once contained *Forum Julii*, modern Fréjus looks like the last lamb-chop on a platter. The Saracens had much of the rest in the 10th century, coming back seven times to pillage and destroy the bits they missed. When the coast was clear, the Fréjussiens rebuilt their **Cathédral Saint-Léonce** in Place Formigé, ✆ 94 51 57 81, and made it the centre of a small *cité épiscopale* with a crenellated defence tower, a chapterhouse and a bishop's palace. Built from the 12th to the 16th centuries, the cathedral has a superb pair of **Renaissance doors** carved with sacred scenes, a Saracen massacre, and portraits of aristocratic ladies and gents, including King François Ier. Inside, over the sacristy door, there's a *retable de Ste-Marguerite* (c. 1450) by Jacques Durandi, of the School of Nice.

The **Baptistry**, the one bit of Fréjus the Saracens missed, dates from the 4th or 5th century, and like most paleo-Christian baptistries it was built as an octagon, defined by eight black granite columns with white capitals borrowed from the Roman forum. Only adults were baptized in the early days, and they would enter the narrow door and have their feet washed at the terracotta basin; the bishop would then baptize them in the pool in the centre, and as new Christians, they would leave through the larger door to attend mass.

Fairest of all is the beguiling 12th-century **Cloître** (cloister), with slim marble columns and a 14th-century ceiling. This is coffered into 1200 little vignettes, of which a third still have curious paintings that comprise a whole catalogue of monkish fancies: grotesques, mermaids, animals, portraits, and debaucheries. Upstairs, the **Archaeology Museum** has a collection of finds from *Forum Julii*, among them a perfectly preserved mosaic, a fine head of Jupiter, and a copy of the superb two-faced bust of Hermes discovered in 1970.

DETAIL OF THE CATHEDRAL DOOR – FRÉJUS

Just off Place Formigé at 53 Rue Sieyes are two Atlantes, all that remains of the house of the Abbé Sieyes (1748–1836), pamphleteer of the Revolution, deputy at the Convention and mastermind of the 18th Brumaire coup that brought Napoleon to power. Later exiled as a regicide, he returned to Paris in 1830; and when asked to sum up his career in politics he gave the famous laconic reply: 'I survived.'

Around Fréjus

Just outside Fréjus stand a pair of remarkable monuments recalling the rotten days of the First World War, when states supplemented their manpower by importing men from the colonies to fight wars that weren't theirs. The Vietnamese built a colourful **Pagode IndoChinoise** as a memorial to their 5000 dead, 2km from the centre on the N7, © 94 53 25 29 (*open daily 9am–12pm, 3–7pm*), while the Sudanese sharpshooters at the local marine base built a **Mosquée Soudanaise 'Missiri'** (a concrete reproduction of the Missiri Mosque at Djenne, Mali) on Rte de Bagnols-en-Forêt, 5km from Fréjus by way of the N7 and D4 towards Fayence). Further along the D4, the modern **Musée des Troupes de Marine** covers the history of the marines from 1622 to the present (*open summer, 10am–12pm, 3–7pm, and afternoons only in winter*). Another mile further on at Le Capitou you can drive and walk through the **Parc Zoologique**, © 94 40 70 65 (*open daily, 10am–7.30pm*), where parrots and yaks don't look too out of place under the parasol pines.

Ten km up the River Argens from St-Aygulf (Fréjus' resort suburb to the west), the picturesque 16th-century village of **Roquebrune-sur-Argens** offers a break from coastal craziness with a wine and orchid centre that boasts the largest mulberry tree in France. Along the road to Le Muy the **Rochers de Roquebrune** form a peculiar red baby *massif* that toddled away from the Esterel.

Where to Stay and Eating Out

St Raphaël (✉ 83700)

This town is rich in pricey campsites, but few hotels stand out. Some of St-Raphaël's best choices are outside the centre, like ★★★**La Potinière**, in Boulouris, 5km east, ✆ 94 95 21 43, 🖷 94 95 29 10, a modern hotel dedicated to sports (pool, tennis, sailing) and R and R, set in a pretty park of mimosas and eucalyptus. In town, try the ★**Pyramides**, 77 Av. P.- Doumer, ✆ 94 95 05 95, with a little garden; or in the old town, ★**Templiers**, Place de la République, ✆ 94 95 38 95. There's a youth hostel, **Centre International du Manoir**, Chemin de l'Escale (near the Boulouris station), ✆ 94 95 20 58, 🖷 94 83 85 06, more expensive than most, but fancier as well and close to the beach.

Fish dishes like *mousseline de sole* are the fare at **L'Orangerie**, Promenade René Coty, ✆ 94 83 10 50, along with fresh pasta (*good value menus, during the week at 98F; rising at the weekends*). Otherwise go for the Friday special 155F *aïoli* menu at **Pastorel**, an excellent address with a pleasant-no-nonsense proprietress and a garden terrace at 54 Rue de la Liberté, ✆ 94 95 02 36.

Fréjus (✉ 83600)

★★★**Résidence du Colombier**, Rte de Bagnols, ✆ 94 51 45 92, 🖷 94 53 82 85, is perfect for families with modern rooms in bungalows, each with a private garden and terrace, spread out in a pine-wood, plus a heated pool, tennis, volley ball, etc. *Usually booked up by March until the end of November.* ★★**Il Etait une Fois**, 254 Rue F.-Mistral, ✆ 94 17 19 69, is a charming, reasonably priced Provençal-style hotel in a garden near the sea. *Closed mid-Dec–mid-Jan.* In Fréjus centre, the best of the cheapies is the quiet ★**Bellevue**, a minute from the cathedral in Place Paul-Vernet, ✆ 94 51 39 04. There's a pleasant but inconvenient **Auberge de Jeunesse** 2km from Fréjus' historic centre, in a large park east on the N7 (also a campsite), ✆ 94 53 18 75, 🖷 94 53 25 86. *Open all year.* For dinner, **La Romana**, 155 Bd. de la Libération at Fréjus-Plage, ✆ 94 51 53 36, offers a seaside setting and an honest *soupe de poisson*, along with Italian and Provençal favourites (*menu 95F*). *Open all year.* For more *nouvelle cuisine* try **Les Potiers** at 135 Rue des Potiers, in town near Place Agricola, ✆ 94 51 33 74, (*impressive 165F menu*). Or eat for less from the popular *crêperie* **Cadet Rousselle**, 25 Place Agricola, ✆ 94 53 36 92, or at its pizzeria neighbour **Lou Grilladou**, ✆ 94 53 48 27 (*both around 50F*).

Entertainment and Nightlife

Beer-lovers can chug down one of a hundred varieties at Fréjus-Plage's **Maison de la Bière**, 461 Bd. de la Libération, ✆ 94 51 21 86. For more strenuous entertainment, gamble and dance at the **Casino de St-Raphaël** and its **Madison Club**, Square de

Gand, ☎ 94 95 10 59, or maybe curiosity will take you to find out what's going on at **Le Kilt**, 130 Rue Jules-Barbier, ☎ 94 95 29 20; or make for the **Coco-Club** at the Nouveau Port, ☎ 94 95 95 56.

The Massif des Maures

Between Fréjus and Hyères, the coast bulges out and up again to form the steep rolling hills and arcadian natural amphitheatres of the ancient Massif des Maures. Although it lacks the high drama of the Esterel, this mountain range (760m at its highest point) is as much of a geological oddball, its granite, gneiss and schist completely unrelated to the limestone that dominates the rest of Provence. The name Maures is derived from *maouro*, Provençal for black, describing its dark, deep forests of umbrella and Aleppo pines, chestnuts and cork. For centuries the latter two trees provided the main source of income of the few inland villages.

Until the 19th century this was the most dangerous coast in France. The Saracens made it their chief stronghold in the area in 846, building forts (*fraxinets*) on each hill to watch for ships to plunder, and to defend themselves from the Franks. They were finally forced out in the campaign of 972, led by William of Provence, who was greatly assisted by a knight from Genoa named Grimaldi, the first of that family to appear in what is now France. But although the pirates had to abandon their *fraxinets*, they hardly abandoned the coast, and maintained a reign of terror that continued until 1830, when the French captured Algiers. A hundred years later, the fashion for seaside bathing spread west from the Riviera, giving every crowded beach a holiday town to call its own.

Ste-Maxime and Port Grimaud

In the seaside conurbation spread between Fréjus and St-Tropez, the only place that may tempt a detour is Ste-Maxime, a modern resort town with a beach of golden sand facing St-Tropez. It willingly takes the overflow of fashionable and bankable holidaymakers from the latter, an attractive proposition as it's easy to commute by frequent boat to the capital of see-and-be-seen; St-Tropez may not look far away but it's two hours' traffic jam in high season. If you do stay there's the **Musée des Traditions Locals**, ☎ 94 96 70 30, opposite the port. The remarkable **Musée du Phonographe et de la Musique Mécanique**, is in the unlikely setting of the wooded Parc de St-Donat, ☎ 94 96 50 52, 10km north towards Le Muy on the D25, or take the Le Muy bus from Ste-Maxime (*open Easter–Oct, 10am–12pm and 2–6pm, closed Mon, Tues; adm*). About half of the music boxes, barrel organs, automata and player pianos still work, as well as some of the rare prizes: one of Edison's original phonographs of 1878, an accordion-like 'Melophone' of 1780, a 1903 dictaphone, and an audio-visual '*pathé-graphe*' to teach foreign languages, built in 1913.

From Ste-Maxime the road passes through **Port Grimaud**, a posh private housing estate designed in 1968 by Alsatian architect François Spoerry, inspired by the lagoon pleasure complexes around St Petersburg, Florida, where wealthy home-owners, like Venetians, can park their boats by the front door. The traditionally styled, colourful houses themselves are a preview of the real McCoys in St-Tropez; the pseudo-Romanesque **church**, sitting on its own islet, has stained glass windows designed by Vasarely, the Hungarian master of op-art who spent much of his life in the south of France.

For all the usual 4-star comforts, including parking, pool, private beach and
gastronomic restaurant, ★★★★**La Belle Aurore** will oblige, at 4 Bd. Jean-
Moulin, ✆ 94 96 02 45, 🖂 94 96 63 87. *Open Mar–Oct, otherwise*
intermittently. ★★★**Le Petit Prince**, 11 Av. St-Exupéry, ✆ 94 96 44 47,
🖂 94 49 03 38, is a small, modern hotel with no-nonsense charm enough
to make you believe you might even be welcome. You can park right
outside, and although there is no hotel restaurant, they are in happy cahoots with the
owners of **Le Dauphin**, 10 Av. Charles de Gaulle, ✆ 94 96 31 56, which is where
you will be directed. Pretty but not elaborate good food fresh from the kitchen: the
rabbit in mustard is gourmet quality, and you don't have to decide on a dessert, simply
order a selection which come in miniature dishes—each so delicious one dithers over
which to eat first. The ★★**Le Revest**, 48 Av. Jean-Jaurès, ✆ 94 96 19 60, is moderate
in price, central (with parking) and has a restaurant.

There are over 80 restaurants in Ste-Maxime. Aside from Le Dauphin, try **Le Lotus
Bleu**, 30 Av. Gen. Leclerc, ✆ 94 49 28 00, for *cassolette de la mer*, and
Thai/Vietnamese specialities. Also Le Calidianus, Bd. Jean-Moulin,
✆ 94 96 23 21, who serve a *crème brulée à la lavande* that won't break
the bank (*100–160F*).

St-Tropez

It made the headlines in France when St-Tropez's mayor, Alain Spada, forced the discos to
close at 2am and declared the beaches off limits to dogs, inciting the fury of Brigitte Bardot,
that crusading Joan of Arc of animal rights and the town's most famous citizen. For ever since
BB came down here to star in Roger Vadim's *Et Dieu créa la femme* in 1956 the French have
kept close tabs on this former fishing village, regarding it as the official throbbing showcase of
the fun, sun and sex side of their national character, a showcase veneered with glamour and
fashion and tainted with the pouts of spoiled grown-ups. Everyone who wants to be associated
with fun and fashion tries to squeeze into St-Tropez in the summer, booking one of the few
hotel rooms nearly a year in advance, or just coming down for the day for a gawk at the yachts.

The French fondly call this St-Trop (St Too Much) and in the summer it really is: too many
people (100,000 on an average day) clogging the roads, lanes, and beaches; too much rubbish;
too many artists hawking paintings around the port; too many crowded cafés and restaurants
charging unholy prices. At other times of the year it's easier to understand what started all the
commotion in the first place—although beware that in winter St-Tropez, the only town on the
Côte d'Azur to face north, can be extremely blustery.

History

One of the strangest but somehow most fitting legends along the coast has it that St-Tropez's
first incarnation, the Greek colony Athenopolis, was founded by Praxiteles' famous model
Phryne, who had a face like a toad but the body of a goddess. Put on trial in Athens for
unseemly behaviour, she lifted up her skirt, astonishing the jury with her charms, and was
acquitted on condition that she leave Athens. She ended up here, wedded to a Ligurian chief-

tain. Together they founded Athenopolis, although Phryne was later sacrificed to the Ligurian gods with the request that they please keep outsiders away in the future.

In 68 AD, Torpes, an officer of Nero, was beheaded in Pisa for his Christian beliefs. As anyone who knows the *Lives of the Saints* knows, the Romans had no lack of ingenuity in dealing with martyrs; in this case, they buried Torpes' head in Pisa, and put his body in a boat with a dog and a cock, who were to slowly devour it. But the animals had no appetite, and their boat floated safely to Athenopolis (the Roman *Heraclea Cacabria*) which eventually adopted St Torpes' name. The saintly body was hidden and lost during the Saracen attacks, one of which destroyed St-Tropez in 739.

St-Tropez was repopulated in 1470 with settlers imported from Genoa. Good King René of Provence exempted them from taxes in return for defending the coast, and until the 1600s the Tropéziens enjoyed a special autonomous status under their *Capitaines de Ville*. Their most glorious moment came on 15 June 1637, when they courageously defended St-Tropez from an attack by 22 Spanish galleons, an event annually celebrated in the *Bravade des Espagnols*. Later invaders were more successful. The first famous visitor from the outside world, Guy de Maupassant, drifted into the port in 1880s and in his pre-syphilitic madness was a preview of the 1960s. In 1892, the Post-Impressionist painter Paul Signac was sailing his yacht along the coast and was forced by the weather to call in at St-Tropez; enchanted, he bought a villa called La Hune and invited his friends down to paint. St-Tropez was a revelation to many: Matisse, who had previously painted in a rather dark style, came down in 1904 and produced his key, incandescent picture of nudes on a St-Tropez beach, *Luxe, calme, et volupté*, thereby joining the Fauvist revolution begun by Signac's friends Derain, Vlaminck, Van Dongen, and Dufy; today their hot-coloured scenes of St-Tropez illuminate the town's museum.

Writers, most famously Colette, joined the artists' 'Montparnasse on the Mediterranean' in the 1920s, but even then thoughts of making a franc out of fashion and beauty were in the air; Colette herself had a shop in the port selling Colette-brand cosmetics in the 1930s. The third wave of even more conspicuous invaders, Parisian existentialists and glitterati, began in earnest in the 1950s, when Françoise *Bonjour Tristesse* Sagan and Bardot made it the pinnacle of *chic*. Back then Sartre could sit in the Café Sénéquier and write *Les Chemins de la liberté* in peace, but these days he'd be hard put to it to even think, with all the showbusiness people who come to show themselves and the paparazzi who still come to snap them. Joan Collins has a house here, so has George Michael, and Elton John's manager paid £7m in 1995 to join the set. Guest appearances are made by Prince Albert, Clint Eastwood, Naomi Campbell, Robert De Niro, Jack Nicholson, Rupert Everett and even a cavorting once-royal duchess (for an oral pedicure).

Getting Around

On its peninsula, St-Tropez is a dead end; the one road leading into it (D98A), and the lanes leading off to the beaches, are packed solid with vehicles from June to August.

by bus

Besides the St-Raphaël–Hyères coastal bus (for info contact SODETRAV Hyères 47, Av. Alphonse-Denis, © 94 12 55 12, or the *gare routière* at St-Tropez © 94 97 88 51), there's a regular bus in season linking Toulon to St-Tropez (contact SODETRAV Toulon © 94 93 11 39). Note that there's no place at all to leave your luggage if you want to stop off en route.

You may be better off catching a boat from St-Raphaël (*gare maritime* © 94 95 17 46) or Ste-Maxime (MMG © 94 96 51 00).

The ghastly traffic makes bike and moped hire an attractive alternative (**M.A.S**, 5 Rue Quaranta, near Place Carnot, © 94 97 00 60; open daily, closed October).

Should you need a **horse**, contact © 94 56 16 55, and for a **helicopter**, **RCE Helistation Za**, © 94 43 39 30, @ 94 43 39 60.

The **Maison du Tourisme du Golfe de St-Tropez/Pays des Maures**, © 94 43 42 10, @ 94 43 32 78, at the N98/D559 junction before the long traffic jam into St-Tropez, is a touristic godsend. Cool, calm and collected, with fountains and sculptured pools, this is the Var tourist board's *pièce de résistance*. The helpful staff will call ahead to St-Tropez to book hotels, offer advice on restaurants, excursions both coastal and inland, wine tours, and generally provide a thoroughly pleasant introduction to the area.

If for some reason you miss the Maison du Tourisme, head into St-Tropez, and the two offices at Quai Jean-Jaurès, © 94 97 45 21, @ 94 97 82 66, and 23 Av. du Général-Leclerc, © 94 97 41 21, @ 94 97 79 08 (fax no. from May–Sept only).

Tuesday and Saturday.

Musée de l'Annonciade

© 94 97 04 01; open Oct–May 10am–12pm and 2–6pm, June–Sept 10am–12pm and 3–7pm, closed Tues, Nov.

If nearly everything about St Tropez in the summer fills you with gridlock and dismay, let this alone be your reason to visit. This 17th-century chapel next to the port houses a collection of works mostly by the painters in Paul Signac's St-Tropez circle, Post-Impressionists and Fauves who began where Van Gogh and Gauguin left off and blazed the trail for Cubism and abstract art—and blaze they do, saturated with colour that takes on a life of its own with Vlaminck (*Le Pont de Chatou*) and Derain (*Westminster Palace* and *Waterloo Bridge*). Seurat's small but fascinating *Canal des Gravelines* (1890) gives an idea of his mathematical, optical treatment of Impressionism, a style his disciple, Signac, moved away from while painting in St-Tropez. Other highlights include Braque's *Paysage de l'Estaque*, painted in homage to Cézanne; Matisse's *La Gitane* (1906); Vuillard's *Deux Femmes sous la Lampe*, Bonnard's *Nue devant la Cheminée*) and key paintings by Van Dongen, Friesz, Dufy, Marquet, and Cross.

From the Port to the Citadelle

Just outside the museum, the **port** is edged with the colourful pastel houses that inspired the Fauves, a scene that regains much of its original charm if you can get up before the trippers and the scores of hack painters who block the quay. The view is especially good from the

Môle Jean Réveille. In the street above, the church of **St-Torpes** contains the gilt bust of St Torpes and a sculpture of his little boat, carried in the *bravades*. Seek out Place de l'Ormeau, Rue de la Ponche and Place aux Herbes, poetic corners of old St-Tropez that have refused to shift into top gear. You can look down on the shiny roof tiles from the 16th- to 18th-century citadelle at the top of town (or visit its little **Musée de la Citadelle**, ✆ 94 97 06 53 (*open 10am–6pm, closed Tues, Thurs*). Another essential ingredient of St-Tropez is the charming **Place Carnot**, better known by its old name of Place des Lices, an archetypal slice of Provence with its plane trees, its Tuesday and Saturday market, its cafés and never-ending games of *pétanque*.

Beaches, and St-Tropez's Peninsula

Although the beaches begin even before you enter St-Tropez, those famous sandy strands where girls first dared to bathe topless (circumventing local indecency laws by placing Coke bottle tops over their nipples), skirt the outer rim of the peninsula. In the summer minibuses link them with Place Carnot, a good idea as beach parking is as expensive as the beaches themselves. **Plage des Graniers** is within easy walking distance, but it's the most crowded. A path from here skirts Cap de St-Tropez and, in 12km, passes **Plage des Salins** (4km direct from St-Tropez), the gay beach **Neptune**, and ends up at the notoriously decadent **Plage de Tahiti**, the movie stars' favourite. Tahiti occupies the north end of the 5km **Plage de Pampelonne**, lined with cafés, restaurants, and luxury concessions where any swimming-costumes at all are optional. On the other side of Cap Camarat, **Plage de l'Escalet** is hard to reach, but much less crowded and free (take the narrow road down from the D93); from L'Escalet you can pick up the coastal path and walk in an hour and a half to the best and most tranquil beach of all, **Plage de la Briande**.

The centre of the peninsula, swathed with Côtes de Provence vineyards, is dominated by two villages of sinuous vaulted lanes and medieval houses: **Gassin**, up a dizzy series of hairpin turns, and below it the larger **Ramatuelle**. Both were Saracen *fraxinets*, and both have caught a hefty dose of fashion and artsy boutiques from St-Trop, but they still make refreshing escapes from the anarchy down below. In Ramatuelle's cemetery you can see the romantic tomb of actor Gérard Philipe (*Le Diable au Corps* and *Fanfan la Tulipe*), who was only 37 when he died in 1959.

Where to Stay

St-Tropez (✉ 83990)

If you haven't already booked a hotel long ago, forget about arriving in St-Tropez on the off-chance between June and September. There are acres of campsites in the area, although in the summer they are about as relaxing as refugee camps; the tourist offices keep tabs on which ones have a few inches to spare. As for prices, expect them to be about 20 per cent higher per category than anywhere else on the coast. And if you want to come in the off season, beware that most hotels close in the winter.

If money's no object, you can sleep in one of the most fashionable hotels on the entire Côte d'Azur, ★★★★**Le Byblos**, Av. Paul Signac, ✆ 94 56 68 00, ✉ 94 56 68 01, built by a Lebanese millionaire, designed like a *village perché*, with rambling corridors, patios, and opulent rooms furnished with Middle Eastern arts. In the middle there's a magnificent pool, and the nightclub is one of most desirable to be seen in. *Closed mid-Nov–mid-Mar.* More discreet swells check in at the Relais et Châteaux ★★★★**Résidence la Pinède**, Plage de la Bouillabaisse, ☎ 94 97 04 21, 🖷 94 97 73 64, or at the ★★★**Hermitage**, Av. Paul-Signac, ☎ 94 97 52 33, 🖷 94 97 10 43, a charming hotel set in a garden at the foot of the *citadelle* and 5mins from Place Carnot, and (by St-Tropez standards) reasonably priced for its category. As is Picasso's old watering hole, ★★★**La Ponche**, 3 Rue des Remparts, ☎ 94 97 02 53, 🖷 94 97 78 61, located in a group of old fishermen's cottages—a romantic nook to entice your special darling. *Closed 30 Oct–1 April.* Or you can sleep in the port overlooking the yachts at ★★★**Le Sube**,☎ 94 97 30 04, 🖷 94 54 89 08, the oldest hotel in town and an historic monument to boot. *Open all year.* Budget specials that must be reserved a light year in advance: the sweet and intimate garden-hotel ★**La Romana**, Chemin des Conquêtes, ☎ 94 97 15 50, with a good Italian restaurant (*hotel open April–Oct; restaurant open summer only*), and at the entrance of town ★**Les Chimères**, Port du Pilon, ☎ 94 97 02 90. *Closed 15 Dec–30 Jan: ask for a room on the garden, since road-side can be noisy.*

Ramatuelle (✉ 83350)

This includes all the hotels along Tahiti and Pampelonne beaches, nearly all of which sport three stars and close mid-Oct–Easter. As does ★★★**La Figuière**, Rte de Tahiti, ☎ 94 97 18 21, 🖷 94 97 68 48, an old farmhouse in the middle of a vineyard, with a relaxed atmosphere, tennis, and a pool, and the less expensive ★★★**La Ferme d'Augustin**, Plage de Tahiti, ☎ 94 97 23 83, 🖷 94 97 40 30, set in a garden a stone's throw from the sea. The views are enchanting further up among the vineyard terraces at ★★★**Le Baou**, Rue Gustave-Etienne, ☎ 94 79 20 48, 🖷 94 79 28 36, which also has a heated pool and a good restaurant (*see* below).

Gassin (✉ 83580)

★★**Bello Visto**, Place de Barri, ☎ 94 56 17 30, offers simple, inexpensive rooms next to Gassin's magnificent belvedere, but again, book early for a chance of staying in one. The restaurant (*menu 120F*) has a pleasant terrace. *Open April–Oct.*

Eating Out

St-Tropez (✉ 83990)

Top of the Trop(s) at the moment, without doubt, is the Michelin-starred **L'Olivier**, Route des Carles, ☎ 94 97 58 16. In a garden of oleander, figs, palms, eucalyptus and parasol pines, the food is flamboyant, generous, and unexceptionaly delicious; *fricassée de légumes verts et rôti de jeune lapin à la marjolaine* or *pigeon fermier doré au miel et au gros sel*, will set you back between 230–500F. Gourmets also flock to the tables of Hervé Quesnel at **La Pinède**, Plage de la Bouillabaisse, ☎ 94 97 04 21, where eating *à la carte* costs approximately 500F. **Le Café des Arts**, Place des Lices, ☎ 94 97 02 25, is a Tropezian institution, making all the flavoursome staples of traditional Provençal cuisine up-to-date (courgette, aubergine, lamb, rabbit with mustard, and *macaronis au pistou*), with menus starting at 199F. For steak tartare with fine fat chips fried in goose fat, glorified pies and the like at glorified prices (*300F plus*) go to **La Table du Marché**, 38 Rue Clemenceau, ✆ 94 97 85 20. Part of the price is for being seen in the right place.

If you want to be seen with the likes of George Michael, Claudia Schiffer or Carla Bruni, you'll be haunting **Yvan**, Place de la Garonne, ✆ 94 97 89 65, or **Nano**, Place de l'Hôtel-de-Ville, ✆ 94 97 01 66, which are both open until late, though the food is nothing particular to speak of.

Café Sud, 12 Rue Etienne-Berny, ✆ 94 97 42 52, has a terrace. Try the *tarte fine chaude aux sardines de pays* (*65F*), or *gnocchis au pistou* (*menus start at 175F*). At **L'Echalotte**, 35 Rue du Général-Allard, ✆ 94 54 83 26, you can beef up on your *chanutenes*, black puddingss, and all things meaty (*menus from 150F*). **Le Petit Tante Marie**, 2 Rue de la Miséricorde, ✆ 94 97 23 16, is open all year, and the menu begins at a modest 140F, even since Brigitte Bardot had her birthday party there.

Ramatuelle (✉ 83350)

Ramatuelle has two excellent restaurants: **La Terrasse du Baou** (*see* above) with delicious sunny Provençal treats like *daube de Saint-Pierre* and pasta with truffles from the Haut Var (*menus 180–300F*). Amid the vines at Quartier La Rouillère, **La Ferme Ladouceur**, ✆ 94 79 24 95, will fill you up with solid home cooking and the family's home-brew wine (*155F menu*). *Open eves only except Tues, closed Nov–mid-Mar.*

Gassin (✉ 83580)

On the outskirts of Gassin, **La Verdoyante**, 866 Av. de Coste-Bugade, ✆ 94 56 16 23, seems lost in the countryside, an old Provençal manor with a fine view, serving old Provençal dishes (*menus from 155F, reservations advised*). *Closed Wed and Nov–Easter.*

Shopping

Although many of the once trendsetting boutiques are now owned by big designer chains, a few exclusive shops remain for die-hard St-Trop fans: **Vilebrequin**, Bd. Louis-Blanc, for 99 colours of ballet slippers; **Gas**, Place Sibilli, specializing in costume jewellery made of coral and turquoise; **Rondini**, 16 Rue Clemenceau, for the famous *sandales tropéziennes*, invented in 1927 on the Roman gladiator model; **Sugar**, Rue Victor-Laugier, for cotton tops and shorts, and **Galeries Tropéziennes** for fabrics, espadrilles, garden furniture and just about everything else.

Entertainment and Nightlife

The bars in Place Carnot provide an entertaining sideshow in which to pass the average evening, especially the resolutely old-fashioned **Café des Arts**, ✆ 94 97 02 25, with its zinc bar and crowd of St-Germain-des-Prés habitués (closes after the Nioulargue). By the port, **Sénéquier**, ✆ 94 97 08 98, is still *the* bar in which to order a coffee, but note that all the Joe Cools sit in the back. Younger bars include **La Bodega**, on Quai d'Epi, ✆ 94 97 07 56, nearby **Hysteria** at Résidence du Port, ✆ 94 97 07 56, and **Le Barocco** on Quai Jean-Jaurès, ✆ 94 97 00 63. Dancing and much besides goes on until dawn at St-Trop's clubs. Try **Le Bal** by the new port, ✆ 94 97 14 70, **Les Caves du Roy** at Hotel le Byblos, ✆ 94 56 68 00, or **Le Papagayo** across from the Annonciade, ✆ 94 97 07 56. Don't take it too personally if you have trouble getting in: St-Tropez's bouncers have a reputation to uphold.

Festivals

Not to miss if you're anywhere in the vicinity, the *Bravade des Espagnols* (15 June) sees St-Tropez's finest lads and lasses in 18th-century uniforms and Provençal costumes for a morning procession of the relics of St Torpes. At every square the bands stops playing as the 'soldiers' fire an earsplitting fusillade from their blunderbusses straight into the stone pavement, while clouds of acrid smoke choke bystanders. St Torpes himself is honoured with an even more important two-day shooting-spree *bravade* in the middle of May.

Besides the *Bravades*, the most exciting annual event in St-Tropez is the **Nioulargue**, the last French yacht race, *pour fêter la fin de la saison et de l'été* (last week of September and the first week of October). The oldest and most beautiful yachts in the world take on the autumn billows, accompanied by a predictable parade of Rolex watches, blond but balding British sailors, and Germans with an air of practised hauteur. There are two crowds: them and us (lubbers and sailors). This being St-Tropez, you can also follow the course by sea in special boats, or by helicopter.

Into the Maures

Beckoning just a short drive from the coastal pandemonium are the quiet chestnut woodlands of the Massif des Maures, or at least what's left of them after a quarter of the forest burned in 1990; note that some of the few roads that penetrate the mountain may be closed in dry summers. The main walking path through the hills, the GR9, begins at Port Grimaud and passes through La Garde-Freinet on its way west to Notre-Dame-des-Anges; if you're going by road, the most rewarding route is the D14, beginning at Grimaud.

Getting Around

Grimaud and Cogolin are stops on the St-Raphaël-Hyères **bus** routes. Other villages are much harder to reach by public transport: two buses a day go from Le Lavandou to La Garde-Freinet, and there's but one linking La Garde-Freinet and Grimaud to Toulon.

Tourist Information

Cogolin (✉ 83310): Place de la République, ✆ 94 54 63 17, ✉ 94 54 10 20.
Grimaud (✉ 83310): Place des Ecoles, ✆ 94 43 26 98, ✉ 94 43 32 40.
La Garde-Freinet (✉ 83680): Place Neuve, ✆ 94 43 67 41, ✉ 94 43 08 69.

market days

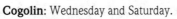

Cogolin: Wednesday and Saturday.
Grimaud: Thursday.
La Garde-Freinet: Wednesday and Sunday.
Collobrières: Thursday and Sunday.

Cogolin and Grimaud

Perhaps by now you've noticed signs advertising pipes from **Cogolin** (6km inland from Port Grimaud), not an especially pretty town but a busy one. For once the craftsmen are not just loose ends from Paris and Picardy selling artsy gimcracks to tourists; for over a century the famous pipes of Cogolin have been carved from the thick roots of the briars (*erica arbores*) that grow up to 6m high in the Maures. A second craft was started up in Cogolin in the 1920s by Armenian immigrants, who introduced their ancestral art of hand-knotted wool rugs, the origin of a local industry that now sells its *tapis de Cogolin* to the best addresses in Paris and the Arab emirates (watch the carpets being woven Mon–Fri at **La Manufacture de Tapis de Cogolin**, Bd. Louis-Blanc, ✆ 94 54 66 17). Another important industry harvests an ancient swamp to produce top-quality reeds for saxophones and clarinets. And Provence's only bamboo forest provides the raw material for Cogolin's cane furniture.

Unlike Cogolin, **Grimaud** is all aesthetics and boutiques. A former Saracen and Templar stronghold, it can hold its own among the most perfect *villages perchés* on the coast, crowned by the ruined castle of the Grimaldis, after whom the village is named. The Romanesque church of **St-Michel** is in surprisingly good nick; from here, Rue des Templiers (formerly Rue des Juifs), lined with arcades of 1555, passes the **House of the Templars**. This is one of the few surviving structures in Provence built by that religious and military order of knights founded in Jerusalem during the First Crusade in 1118. Before their wealth, influence and secret rites incited the deadly envy of King Philip the Fair of France and Pope Clement V, the Templars acquired extensive properties in exchange for their military services. They often built their castles and churches in Jewish or Saracen quarters, both to learn from their ancient wisdom and to protect them from the Christians—hence the damning charge of heresy raised against them by Pope and King, who conspired together to dissolve the order in 1307.

La Garde-Freinet

When Charles Martel defeated the Moorish invaders at Poitiers in 732 and pushed them back to Spain, a few managed to give the Franks the slip and escape into Provence, where they generally made a nuisance of themselves (but are also credited with introducing the tambourine, medicine, and flat roof tiles). Their strongholds, or *fraxinets*, gave their name to La Garde-Freinet, a large village full of medieval charm and British ex-pats. A path, past chestnuts said to be 1000 years old, ascends to the site of the Saracen fortress (the standing walls are from the 15th century); from here look-outs would signal the approach of fat merchant ships down to the pirates' cove of St-Tropez.

One of the arts brought to Provence by the Saracens was working in cork, which involves stripping the tree of its outer layer of bark during certain years when the tree can survive the loss; the bark is then boiled, cut into strips, boiled again, and set to dry and season for six months before being carved into bottle stoppers. This was the chief industry in the 19th century, and in 1851 the cork workers of La Garde-Freinet, men and women, formed a co-operative that stood up to the bosses, beginning an experiment in socialism in the same dark year as Louis Napoleon declared himself emperor; you don't have to be a historian to guess what happened. Things are quieter now in La Garde-Freinet. Below the village on the D558, Europe's first **Musée Pigeon**, ✆ 94 43 65 32, (*open 10am–12.00pm and 3–6pm, closed Tues and Sun*) is a haven for *colombophiles*, with hundreds of the flying doo-droppers on display, plus videos of great moments in pigeon history. The only other thing to do in La Garde-Freinet, according to the tourist office, is walk.

Collobrières and Around

Six km off the D 14 from Grimaud to Collobrières stands the moody, ruined **Chartreuse de la Verne**, © 94 43 45 41 (*open 11–6pm, closed Tues and whole of Nov; adm*), founded in 1170 in one of the most desolate corners of France. Rebuilt several times before it was abandoned and burned in the Revolution, the vast Carthusian complex (great and small cloisters, guest house, church, and porch) is mostly of interest for its use of local stone—a combination of reddish schist and hard greenish serpentine. Since 1983, restoration work has been carried out by the brothers of Bethlehem. Near the crossroads for the Chartreuse, a minor road leads to the *maison forestière* Ferme Lambert, where you can ask permission to see the two largest **menhirs** in Provence (3.5m and 3m high) and the largest chestnut tree, the **Châtaignier de Madame** (10m in circumference).

The air is sweet in the biggest settlement of the western Maures, **Collobrières**, an attractive old village scented with chestnuts being ground into paste and purée or undergoing their apotheosis into delectable *marrons glacés*. The village's name comes from *couleuvre* (grass snake), due to the snake-like patterns in the prevalent serpentine stone. But the thick forests all around are known for other natural delights: boar and deer (and their hunters), not to mention a fabulous array of mushrooms.

Due north of Collobrières, narrow roads squiggle up through the forests to **Notre-Dame-des-Anges**, a sanctuary sitting on top of the highest point in the Var, with brave views over the Maures. Further squiggles north, just east of **Gonfaron** (on the N97) will bring you to the **Village des Tortues**, (© 94 78 26 41 (*open daily 9am–7pm, closed Nov–Mar, when a notice on the gates explains that 'the tortoises are sleeping'*), devoted to saving France's last native land tortoise, the yellow and black Hermann's tortoise of the Maures. Some 1200 tortoises live at this non-profit-making centre until they reach the age of three, when they are released into the Maures where the lucky ones will live to be 80. The best months to visit the centre are April and May when the tortoises mate, June when they lay their eggs, and September, when they hatch.

Where to Stay and Eating Out

Grimaud (✉ 83310)

★★★**Le Côteau Fleuri**, Place des Pénitents, © 94 43 20 17, 🖂 94 43 33 42, is a comfortable inn built in the 1930s on the quiet western outskirts of town, with grand views over the Massif des Maures; its restaurant serves reliably good Provençal dishes (*filet de rouget au pistou* and *carré d'agneau*); the lunch menu at 145F is good value. For more great views and silence, but with a pool and tennis and a video library to boot, try the intimate ★★★**La Boulangerie**, Rte de Collobrières, © 94 43 23 16, 🖂 94 43 38 27. In dining rooms full of *santons*, indulge in a gourmet spread of lobster salad, seafood, or thyme-scented *selle d'agneau* at **Les Santons**, Rte Nationale, © 94 43 21 02 (*menus 260F and up*). Pennywise, the best bet for food is the **Café de France**, Place Neuve, © 94 43 20 05, an old stone house with a summer terrace and an average 125F menu.

La Garde-Freinet (✉ 83680)

In the centre, there's ***La Sarrazine**, ✆ 94 43 67 16, with simple, inexpensive rooms and a good restaurant with very filling menus (*60, 105 and 115F for seafood*).

Collobrières (✉ 83610)

Collobrières has just two hotels, ***Notre-Dame**, 15 Av. de la Libération, ✆ 94 48 07 13, with adequate rooms and a garden; and **Auberge des Maures**, 19 Bd. Lazare Carnot, ✆ 94 48 07 10; both have restaurants and are *open all year*. Ring ahead to make sure there's a table at **La Petite Fontaine**, Place de la République, ✆ 94 48 00 12, where you can dine on ribsticking polenta, rabbit in wine, mushrooms in season and the local wine, amid quirky curios and antique tools (*menus 105F and 145F*).

From the Corniche des Maures to Hyères

Apart from fashionable pockets like Bandol and Cassis, the Corniche des Maures is the last glamorous hurrah of the Côte d'Azur, where celebrities and other big money types have villas among the pines and flowers by the silver sand. No railways come between the towns and the sea, but the main road in season is a slow purgatory of fed-up motorists and bus passengers.

Getting Around

Besides the slow and expensive **buses**, there are summer **boat connections** from Cavalaire-sur-Mer and year-round services from Le Lavandou to the Iles d'Or. To explore the hinterlands, you can **rent bicycles** at **Neway Waikiki Bike Shop**, 15 Ave des Ilaires, ✆ 94 71 16 50, or scooters at **Moto Start**, Av. Maréchal-Juin, ✆ 94 71 25 38.

Tourist Information

Cavalaire-sur-Mer (✉ 83240): Square de Lattre de Tassigny, ✆ 94 64 08 28, ✍ 94 05 49 89.
Le Lavandou (✉ 83980): Quai Gabriél-Péri, ✆ 94 71 00 61, ✍ 94 64 73 79.
Bormes-les-Mimosas (✉ 83230): Place Gambetta, ✆ 94 71 15 17.

market days

Bormes-les-Mimosas: Wednesdays.
Le Lavandou: Thursdays.

Baie de Cavalaire

The bay on the underside of the St-Tropez peninsula, with its clear coves and large beaches of silken sand, has been given lock, stock and barrel to the property promoters. **La Croix-Valmer** is all new although the story of its name dates back to Emperor Constantine who, as mere co-emperor of Gaul, was on his way to Rome when he saw a cross lit against the sky here, telling of his future destiny as the victor at the Milvian bridge in Rome—where he would see another cross—and his role as the first Christian emperor. The longest beach in the bay is at **Cavalaire-sur-Mer** which, like La Croix-Valmer, is more popular with families than movie stars. Between Cavalaire-sur-Mer and Le Rayou Canadel, the **Domaine du Rayol**, Av. des Belges, ✆ 94 05 32

50, 🕿 94 05 32 51 (*open April–Jul and Sept–Nov, 9.30am–12.30pm and 2.30–6.30pm; Jul–Sept 9.30am–12.30pm and 4.30–8pm*) is well worth a stop for its Mediterranean gardens with global flora: South African, New Zealand, Mexican and Californian species thrive and abound among avenues and steps, a chance to glut your eyes on greenery after the Côte de Cement. For a quiet detour inland, take the narrow D27 from Canadel-sur-Mer west of Cavalaire to **La Môle**, a tiny village with a two-towered château, where Antoine de Saint-Exupéry (pilot and author of *The Little Prince*) spent much of his youth.

Le Lavandou and Bormes-les-Mimosas

Persevering west past Cap Nègre and the exclusive villages of **Pramousquier** and **Cavalière** you find the big boys on the Corniche-des-Maures, the fishing port and resort of **Le Lavandou** and **Bormes-les-Mimosas**, a cute hyper-restored medieval enclave that added the mimosas to tart up its name in 1968, although the honour of first planting and commercializing these little yellow Mexican ball blooms goes to Cannes, where in 1880 a gardener carelessly tossed a branch someone had given him into a pile of manure and *voilà*, the next morning he had the lovely flowers that are now the totem of the Côte d'Azur. Bormes' outskirts, **La Favière**, was once the favourite resort of the White Russian community in Paris, because the steep hills descending towards Cap Benet reminded the founder—the daughter of Chekhov's daughter—of the Crimea. All this has since been spoiled by Bormes' hyper-hideous pleasure port, the building of which was challenged by a group of residents and was declared completely illegal in French courts. Typical of the corruption that plagues the coast, the marina blithely continues to exist as a legal fiction.

Le Lavandou, where Bertolt Brecht and Kurt Weill composed *The Threepenny Opera* in 1928, is a good place in which to empty your wallet on seafood, watersports, boutiques and nightclubs; for glossy brochures ask at the tourist office. For a freebie, take the walk out along the coast to Cap Bénat. If you have a car or bike, don't miss the little coastal wine road, beginning at **Port-de-Miramar**, west of Le Lavandou (take D42 off the N98); it passes Cap de Brégançon and its fortified château (the late President Mitterrand's private retreat) and leads southeast to the delicious beach at **Cabasson**, with a campsite and hotel. Although the beach is crowded in the summer, it stands out as the one corner of the Côte d'Azur free from the scourge of cement.

Where to Stay and Eating Out

Bormes-les-Mimosas (✉ 83230)

The best hotel in the commune, ★★★**Les Palmiers**, 240, Chemin du Petit Fort, ✆ 94 64 81 94, 🕿 94 64 93 61, is a steep drive south along the D41 to Cabasson, and is only a few minutes from the sea; its restaurant serves solid classic food which is a good thing because board is obligatory in the summer (*menus from 140/160F*). In Bormes itself the ★★★**Grand Hôtel**, 167 Route de Baguier, ✆ 94 71 23 72, 🕿 94 71 51 20, is splendidly located and very reasonably priced for its category. In the centre of the medieval town, the ★**Provençal**, at 37 Rue Plaine des Anes, ✆ 94 71 15 25, 🕿 94 64 71 45, has pretty white-painted rooms, a pool and a restaurant with a 95/145F menu and good views. *Closed Dec.* ★**Le Bellevue**, 12 Place Gambetta, ✆ 94 71 15 15, has rooms with views over palm trees and a nest of red roofs, and a terrace restaurant serving simple but scenic food (*menus at 80F and 125F*).

The finest *nouvelle cuisine* in the area is found at **La Tonnelle des Délices**, Place Gambetta, ✆ 94 71 34 84, where tables are set under a gallery of vines, and the food is made entirely from local ingredients with the finesse of a master and perfectionist. The prices are very reasonable by Côte standards (*menus from 95 to 130F, à la carte up to 300F*). Exquisite Provençal fare is served by Guy Gedda at his **Jardin de Perlefleurs**, 100 Chemin de l'Orangerie, ✆/✉ 94 64 99 23, overlooking the village and the sea. The *langoustines, moules* and *daube au vin rosé de Provence* are mouthwatering. **L'Olivier**, 5 Rue Gabriél-Péri, ✆ 94 71 18 92, has Provençal dishes, not too big, with a terrace (*85F upwards*).

Le Lavandou (✉ 83980)

For luxury and style, the new and extragavant ★★★★**Les Roches**, 1 Av. des Trois-Dauphins, ✆ 94 71 05 07, ✉ 94 71 08 40, set magnificently over the *calanques* 4km east of Le Lavandou at Aiguebelle, has lovely, bright rooms furnished with antiques, marble bathrooms, a private beach and pool, tennis plus a golf course a mile away. The restaurant, ✆ 94 71 05 05, is just as palatial, and presided over by an extremely talented young chef, who waves a magic spoon over the typical ingredients of Provence, followed by heavenly desserts (*menus from 320F*). *Closed Jan–Mar*. The less extravagant but charming ★★★**Belle Vue**, at St-Clair on Chemin du Four des Maures, ✆ 94 71 01 06, ✉ 94 71 64 72, is as good as its name, with views over the coast. The good value ★★**L'Escapade**, 1 Chemin du Vannier, ✆ 94 71 11 52, ✉ 94 71 22 14, is a small but very cosy hotel in a quiet lane, with air-conditioning and TVs. At No.26 Av. Gén.-de-Gaulle, ★**Le Neptune**, ✆ 94 71 01 01, ✉ 94 64 91 61 provides a pleasant stay, only a hundred metres from the beach. *Closed Nov–Feb*.

For imaginative versions of the day's catch, try **Au Vieux Port**, Quai G.-Péri, ✆ 94 71 00 21 (*menus from 98F*). On the beach at St Clair, the summery **Le Tamaris**, ✆ 94 71 07 22, offers fresh grilled fish and *langoustines* that will warm the cockles of your heart (*à la carte only–200–300F depending very much on what you choose*).

Hyères and its Golden Isles

Known as *Olbia* by the Greeks from Marseille, who founded it in 350 BC, as *Pomponiana* by the Romans, and as *Castrum Arearum* ('town of threshing floors') during the Middle Ages, Hyères claims to be the original resort of the Côte d'Azur, with a pedigree that goes back to Charles IX and Catherine de' Medici, who wintered here in 1564. It knew its greatest fame in the early 19th century, when people like Empress Josephine, Pauline Borghese, Victor Hugo, Tolstoy and Robert Louis Stevenson built villas here and invited one another to teas and soirées, before it faded genteelly from fashion in the 1880s. For despite its mild climate and lush gardens, Hyères was, unforgivably, three miles from the newly popular seaside. But the town had more than one egg in its basket, and has since made the most of its salt pans on the peninsula, exploited since ancient times, and its nurseries of date palms (developed from a Californian species adaptable to sand and salinity) most of which are exported to Saudi Arabia and the Arab emirates. Now it's glorified itself into a triple-barrelled 'Hyères-les-Palmiers'.

Hyères' Aéroport du Palyvestre is served mainly by Air Inter from Paris (for information, call ℂ 94 22 81 60, Air Inter reservations ℂ 94 89 83 83).

by train

Hyères is a dead end, linked to Toulon but nowhere else; the railway station is 1.5km south of town (*Gare SNCF* ℂ 36 35 35 35).

by bus

Buses are tricky. Telephone first: SODETRAV, 47 Av. Alphonse Denis, ℂ 94 65 21 00, serves west to Toulon and east to Le Lavandou. City buses link Hyères to Hyères-Plage and the Giens peninsula.

by boat

Boats for all three of Hyères islands—Porquerolles, Port-Cros and Le Levant—depart at least twice a day, year-round, from **Port d'Hyères** (ℂ 94 12 54 40) and **Le Lavandou** (ℂ 94 71 01 02) with additional sailings in the summer. There are more frequent connections from **La Tour-Fondue**, at the tip of the Giens peninsula, to Porquerolles (ℂ 94 58 21 81, ▨ 94 58 91 73) and in summer, boats also sail from Toulon to Porquerolles. But note that inter-island connections are more rare; check the schedules before setting out.

by bike

Hire bicycles from **Holiday Bikes** on Av. Palyvestre near the port, ℂ 94 38 79 45.

Tourist Information

Hyères: Rotonde Jean-Salusse, Av. de Belgique, ℂ 94 65 18 55, ▨ 94 35 85 05.

market days

Hyères: Place de la République, Tuesday; Place de la Vicomtesse, Thursday; Av. Gambetta, Saturday.

Hyères

Mit Palmen und mit Ice-cream, ganz gewöhnlich, ganz gewöhnlich... (With palms and ice-cream, quite common, quite common...) so Bertolt Brecht, and so Hyères. There isn't much to do but take a brief wander into the Vieille Ville, beyond **Place Massillon**. Here stands the **Tour St-Blaise**, a remnant from a Templar's lodge, and on top of a monumental stair, the collegiate church of **St-Paul** (1599) (*open Wed–Sat inclusive, 10.30–6pm, afternoons only in winter*) with 400 ex-votos dating back to the 1600s. The Renaissance house next to St-Paul doubles as a city gate, through which you can walk up to **Parc St-Bernard** with Mediterranean plants and flowers. At the upper part of the park, the so-called Château St-Bernard or **Villa de Noailles** was designed as a *château cubiste* by Robert Mallet-Stevens in 1924 for art patron Vicomte Charles de Noailles, the financier of the first film by Cocteau, *Blood of the Poet* (1930) and Salvador Dali and Luis Buñuel's *L'Age d'Or*—which nearly got

Noailles excommunicated, not to mention thrown out of the Jockey Club. Austere cement on the outside, furnished with pieces commissioned from Eileen Gray and designers from the Bauhaus, this vast villa with 15 guest rooms and a covered pool was a busy hive of creativity between the wars—it even stars in Man Ray's murky 1929 film *Le Mystère du Château de Dé*. You can visit during exhibitions (© 94 65 22 72), or the garden (*any day*) for free. There are plans are to link the Noailles' garden to that of Edith Wharton, author of *The Age of Innocence*, who lived on the same slope in a former convent of Ste-Claire; also here is the little house where Robert Louis Stevenson stayed. Further up the hill are the hollow walls and towers of the **Vieux Château** with an overview of Hyères' peninsula and jumble of hills.

In 1254, when Louis IX returned to France from the Crusades, he disembarked at Hyères and went to pray in the 13th-century Franciscan church in Place de la République, now named **St Louis** in his honour. Inside, the main thing to see is a set of *santons* too large to move (*open 2.30–5pm*). Below, in Place Th.-Lefebvre, the heart of 19th-century Hyères, a **Musée Municipal**, © 94 65 39 67 (*open Mon–Fri 10am–12pm and 3–6pm, closed Sat, Sun and Tues*) houses the the fragmentary remains of Hyères' Greek and Roman seaside predecessors, as well as two engraved menhirs and a Celto-Iberian figure holding two heads, similar to the statues at Roquepertuse in Aix. Further south, on Av. Gambetta, you can relax in the **Jardin Olbius-Riquier** amongst the palms and rare tropical and semi-trop-ical trees, cacti, a lake, and a small zoo for the kids, with birds, ponies etc (*open 9–6pm; adm free*). Two neo-Moorish villas from the 1880s remain in this part of town: the **Villa Tunisienne** in Av. Beauregard and the **Villa Mauresque** in Av. Jean-Natte.

MARESQUE, HYÈRES

The Giens Peninsula

Over the centuries the island that was Giens has been anchored to the continent by two sand-bars whose arms embrace a salt marsh, the **Etang des Pesquiers**. Although the link has historically been dodgy—Giens became an island again in the storms of 1811—it hasn't stopped people from building villas and hotels, especially on the isthmus at **La Capte**. The barren west arm, dotted by shimmering white piles of salt, is traversed by the narrow *route du sel* beginning at **Plage de l'Almanarre**. In 1843, the archaeologist king, Frederick VII of Denmark, excavated the ruins of the Greek-Roman town at **Almanarre**, but most of it has since been reclaimed by the sand; there are curious Merovingian tombs in the village's 12th-century **Chapelle St-Pierre**. The salt road ends in **Giens**, a quiet little hamlet under a ruined castle that was the last home of the 1961 Nobel-prize-winning poet St-John Perse, who is buried in the cemetery; further up are extensive views from the ruined castle. To the south,

La Tour-Fondue is the principal port for Porquerolles, although beware that the often violent seas around the peninsula have caused scores of shipwrecks. In 1967, an intact cargo ship dating from the Roman republic was found in the Golfe de Giens, with sealed amphorae containing a clear liquid with reddish mud on the bottom—the ultimate fate of red wine aged too long.

The Iles d'Hyères

Known as the *Stroechades* or 'chaplet' by the ancient Greeks, and in the Renaissance as the *Iles d'Or*, owing to the shiny yellow colour of their rock, Hyères' three islands are voluptuous little greenhouses that have seen more than their share of trouble. In the Middle Ages they belonged to the monastery of St-Honorat, and attracted pirates like moths to a flame; in 1160, after the Saracens carried off the entire population, the monks gave up and just let the pirates have the islands. The expansion of the Turkish Empire throughout the Mediterranean in the 16th century made the kings of France sit up and notice the Saracens, and in 1515 an attempt was made to preach a crusade against the Hyères pirates, but the crusading spirit was long past. François Ier had a golden opportunity to install the then homeless Knights of St John on Porquerolles, but the two parties couldn't agree on terms, and the Knights settled for Malta, then belonging to Spain, paying their famous rent of one golden falcon. François had to build his own forts and send settlers to man them against Charles V and every other sea predator, but again the pirates carried everyone off.

Henri II, son of François, thought he had a good idea in populating the islands with criminals and malcontents. By this time, however, France had found the solution to her piracy problem: becoming allies with them and the Turks. On one memorable occasion in 1558, the French navy had a big party on Porquerolles to help the notorious Barbarossa and his cut-throats celebrate the end of Ramadan. Then the inhabitants of the islands spoiled Henri's plans by following their instincts and becoming pirates themselves, capturing numerous French ships and once even pillaging the naval base in Toulon. It took another century to eradicate them.

Later rulers rebuilt the island's forts. In the late 19th century, they were variously used to quarantine veterans of the colonial wars and as sanctuaries for homeless children: Levant and Porquerolles became Dickensian orphanages and juvenile penal colonies. In both cases the young inmates rebelled, and many were killed. Industrialists opened sulphur plants on the islands that no other place in France would have tolerated, and the navy bought Le Levant in 1892 and blew it to pieces as a firing range. In the 1890s fires burned most of the forests on Porquerolles and Port-Cros. Fortunately, in this century, the French government has moved decisively to protect the islands; strict laws protect them from the risks of fire and developers.

Porquerolles

Largest of the three, Porquerolles stretches 7km by 3km and has the largest permanent population, which in the summer explodes to 10,000. Its main village, also called Porquerolles, was founded in 1820 as a retirement village for Napoleon's finest soldiers and invalids. It still has a colonial air, especially around the central pine-planted **Place d'Armes**, the address of most of Porquerolles' restaurants, bars, hotels and bicycle hire shops. Even the village church was built by orders of the Ministry of War, and has military symbols on the altar. Although the cliffs to the south are steep and dangerous for swimming, there are gentle beaches on either side of the village, especially **Plage Notre-Dame** to the east and **Plage d'Argent** to the west. The previous owner (an eccentric Belgian, who discovered Mexico's largest silver lode) of the island took a special interest in acclimatizing flora, such as the *bellombra*, a Mexican tree with huge roots and bark-like elephant-skin, but today green thumbs concentrate on vines, producing exquisite but rare AOC Côte des Iles. You can try some at **Domaine de la Courtade**, at La Courtade, ℭ 94 58 31 44 (*open for visits by appointment*).

Between Porquerolles and Giens the now deserted little islet of **Grand Ribaud** was used in the early 1900s for 'spiritualist experiments' and other research by one Dr Richet, who also imported kangaroos. The kangaroos liked the islet, we are told, but banged themselves to untimely deaths by jumping too exuberantly on the sharp rocks.

Port-Cros

Although barely measuring a square mile, Port-Cros rising to 195m is the most mountainous of the three islands. Since 1963 it has been a national park, preserving not only its forests of pines and ilexes, recovered from a devastating fire in 1892, but nearly a hundred species of birds; brochures will help you identify them as you walk along the mandatory trails. There are a selection of these: the **sentier botanique** is for visitors pressed for time, while at the other end of the scale there's a 10km *circuit historique* for the lucky ones who have a packed lunch and all day. Two curiosities of the island are its abundant native catnip and its *euphorbe arborescente*, which loses all its leaves in the summer and grows new ones in the autumn.

Like the national park in the Florida Keys, Port-Cros also protects its surrounding waters, rich in colourful fish and plant life. There's even a 300-metre 'path' which divers can follow from Plage de la Palud to Rascas islet, clutching a plastic guide sheet that identifies the underwater flora. Of late some of the more fragile plants around the island have suffered as a result of Port-Cros' extraordinary popularity—from the emissions and anchors of the thousands of pleasure craft that call here each year.

Ile du Levant

The French navy still hogs almost all this flowering island, but they no longer use it for target practice. Nowadays, they test aircraft engines and rockets, which are marginally quieter. The island's remaining quarter is occupied by **Héliopolis**, France's first nudist colony (1931). Anyone who's been to St-Tropez and other fashionable Côte beaches will find the ideal of a specially reserved nudist area quaint by now, but Héliopolis still has its determined Adams and Eves, especially because it's so warm: 60 members of the colony stick it out here all year.

Hyères ✉ *83400*   **Where to Stay and Eating Out**

Hyères Town

The newly opened **★★Le Relais**, 45 Av. Victoria, ℭ 94 35 42 22, ✆ 94 35 51 98, is the most comfortable in town, with TVs and air-conditioning. Up in the Vieille Ville, **★★Soleil**, 2 Rue du Rempart, ℭ 94 65 16 26, ✆ 94 35 46 00, is a pleasant quiet choice near Parc St-Bernard. In the centre, the immaculate **★Hôtel de la Poste**, Av. du Maréchal-Lyautey, ℭ 94 65 02 00, is the best of the cheapies. *Open all year.* Or if you'd rather be near the sea, try little **★La Reine Jane**, by the sea at Ayguade, ℭ 94 66 32 64, with good rooms and food at bargain prices. For a more elaborate dinner, try the delicious *soupe de poissons* at the dove-decorated **La Colombe**, at La Bayorre, ✆ 94 65 02 15 (*menu 140F*).

Ile de Porquerolles

There are five hotels on the island, all priced a bit above the odds and all booked months in advance in the summer. All close in the winter. The most elegant, ★★★**Mas du Langoustier**, ✆ 94 58 30 09, ✉ 94 58 36 02, is a romantic old inn between the woods and a long sandy beach, with lovely rooms and a superb restaurant, where the chef imaginatively combines the best ingredients of Provence with a touch of the Far East—*lotte* in coconut sauce and *langouste* with black mushrooms. The wine list includes Porquerolles' famous rosé (*menu 270F*).

Of the other hotels, ★★**Le Relais de la Poste**, Place d'Armes, ✆ 94 58 30 26, ✉ 94 58 33 57, is the only one not requiring half-board. ★★**Sainte-Anne**, ✆ 94 58 30 04, ✉ 94 58 32 26, is a bit dilapidated but stays open longer than the rest. *Closed from mid-November to mid-February only.*

Il Pescatore, ✆ 94 58 30 13, for all things fish: not just the predictable *bouillabaisse* but *carpaccio* and sushi. Eat on the terrace overlooking the boats bobbing in the port. **L'Oustau de la Mer**, ✆ 94 58 30 13, ✉ 94 58 34 93, is a hotel with a good fish restaurant, with fresh dishes using only local market produce (*menus 60–200F*).

Port-Cros

There are only a couple of choices on paradise, and they need to be booked long in advance: the pricey but tranquil and casual ★★★**Le Manoir**, ✆ 94 05 90 52, ✉ 94 05 90 89, among the eucalyptus groves, has a fine little restaurant (*menus from 210F*). *Closed Nov–May.* The second choice, **Hostellerie Provençale** overlooks the port, ✆ 94 05 90 43, ✉ 94 05 92 90 (*menus from 165F*). *Hotel open Easter–Oct.*

Ile du Levant

If you can bare it, Ile du Levant with a greater selection of hotels makes a good base for visiting Port-Cros. The best is ★★★**Héliotel**, ✆ 94 05 90 63, ✉ 94 05 90 20, set in the mimosas and greenery, boasting a pool, a piano bar, a little beach down below and a restaurant with pretty views over the other islands. *Open Easter–Sept.* In Place du Village, ★**La Brise Marine**, ✆ 94 05 91 15, ✉ 94 05 93 21, is at the summit of the islet, with pretty rooms situated around a patio with a pool. *Closed Nov–May.*

Entertainment and Nightlife

With bar-life in Toulon restricted to seedy sailors' bars and nefarious goings-on in the old town, most Toulonnais head to Hyères for a night out, crowding the bars and clubs. The liveliest bar in Hyères is **L'Estaminet**, ✆ 94 65 06 52, at 14 Rue de Limas, with **L'Arlequin** coming a close second at Port La Gavine, ✆ 94 38 87 26, and **Le Blue Bell** to the south of Route de Giens, ✆ 94 58 92 99, which is very much a bar, with no disco. Favourites with the locals include **Le Louis XIII** at 13 Rue Garrel, ✆ 94 65 41 58, and **New Reve Nightclub**, Rue de la Badine, ✆ 94 58 00 07.

Lauso la mar e ten-ten terro.
(*Praise the sea but stick to the land*).

Provençal proverb

If Provençal traditionalists (and they are landlubbers all) look upon the cosmopolitan Côte d'Azur as an alien presence, they feel equally ill-at-ease in the south's two great ports, Toulon and Marseille: to the Provençal they are dangerous, salty cities, populated by untrustworthy strangers and prostitutes. But while Marseille is essentially a city of merchants and trade, Toulon has always been the creature of the French navy, and whatever piquant charms its old port and quarter once had were bombed into oblivion in the Second World War. The brash new Toulon that rose from the ashes, with nearly 200,000 people, is still more concerned with entertaining sailors on shore-leave than with entertaining you—both the tourist offices have recently shut—but it's a lively inexpensive place to go to, and a welcome one, after the sallow temperaments of the Côte.

History

For some reason the deepest, most majestic natural harbour in the Mediterranean tempted neither the Greeks nor the Romans. Instead Toulon (originally *Telo Martius*) was from Phoenican times a centre for dyeing cloth, thanks to its abundant murex shells (the source of royal purple) and the dried red corpses (*kermès*) of the *coccus illicis*, an insect that lived in the surrounding forests of oaks. Toulon's destiny began to change when Provence was annexed to France in 1481. The first towers and walls went up under Louis XII in 1514; Henri IV created the arsenal, but it was Louis XIV who changed Toulon forever, making it the chief port of France's Mediterranean fleet, greatly expanding the arsenal and assigning Vauban the task of protecting it with his star-shaped forts, built by forced labour. It was during this period that Toulon became the most popular tourist destination in Provence, when well-heeled visitors came to see not the new navy installations, but the miserable galley slaves—Turkish prisoners, African slaves, criminals and later, Protestants—chained four to an oar, where they worked, ate and slept in appalling conditions. The 17th century was such a rotten time that there were even volunteers for the galleys, distinguished by their moustaches and less likely to feel the cat o' nine tails.

Toulon's history is marked by three disasters. In 1720, nature's neutron bomb, the plague, killed 15,000 out of 26,000 inhabitants. The second disaster began after the execution of

Louis XVI, when Toulon's royalists had confided the city to the English and their Spanish and Sardinian allies. In 1793, a ragamuffin Revolutionary army of volunteers and ruffians under the painter Carteaux, fresh from massacring 6000 people in Lyon, arrived at the gate of Toulon and began an ineffectual siege of two months. A young Napoleon Bonaparte came on the scene, and convinced the commissioners to put him in charge of the artillery. Bonaparte turned his guns to the west side of the harbour, on the English redoubt of Mulgrave, so well fortified that it was nicknamed 'Little Gibraltar' (now Fort Caire), and captured it by 19 December. In spite of the opposition of the English commander Samuel Hood, the allies decided to abandon Toulon to its fate. The thousands who couldn't escape were mercilessly slaughtered by the Jacobins. The hitherto unknown Bonaparte, promoted to brigadier-general, became the darling of the Convention. Although the Revolutionaries hailed the galley slaves as 'the only decent men of the infamous city', convicts (like Jean Valjean in *Les Misérables*) continued to be sentenced to the *bagnes* (penal camps) in Toulon until the 1850s. Chained in pairs, with rats for pets, the cons envied the lucky few who made a fortune as executioners: 20 *livres* for breaking a nobleman (crushing all his bones, but not shedding a drop of his noble blood), 15 for a hanging or burning alive, down to 2 for cutting off a nose. In 1860 the convicts were packed off out of sight to Devil's Island in French Guyana.

The city's most recent sufferings began in 1942, when the Germans took the city by surprise, and the Vichy Admiral Laborde blocked up the harbour by scuttling the entire Mediterranean fleet to keep it from falling into the hands of the enemy. On 15 August 1944, after flattening the picturesque old port with aerial bombing raids, the Allies landed and the French army, under General De Lattre de Tassigny, recaptured Toulon, but not before the entrenched Germans blew up the citadel, the harbour and the dockyards. Toulon was rebuilt quickly, although without a great sense of design or beauty. Recently dark clouds have threatened Toulon's horizon: the principal shipbuilding yards in La Seyne have been under continuous threat of closure, and the ugly forces of reaction succeeded in electing France's first *Front National* deputy. Yet Toulon is a survivor. New developments include a rock concert venue, an international dance festival, and plans to redevelop La Seyne, creating a vast '*Marepolis*' around a central '*aquasphere*'—a museum/research centre which will continue La Seyne's lifelong love affair with the sea.

Getting Around

Toulon is the major transport hub of the region, and anyone dependent on public transport will find it hard to avoid.

by air

Toulon's airport is out near Hyères (for information, call ✆ 94 22 81 60, for Air Inter's reservations, ✆ 94 89 83 83).

by train

The train station is on the northern side of Toulon in Place Albert Ier, ✆ 94 09 51 20, with four daily TGVs to Nice and Marseille, four also direct to Paris (taking just over 5hrs), and frequent connections up and down the coast and to Hyères.

by bus

For St-Tropez and the coast between Hyères and St-Raphaël, catch a SODETRAV bus in the adjacent *gare routière*, ✆ 94 93 11 39. Other buses will take you frequently to

Hyères, Bandol, La Seyne, Six-Fours, and Sanary, and to inland towns like Brignoles, Draguignan, Aix, and St-Maximin. From Quai Cronstadt, sea-buses go to La Seyne, Les Sablettes and St-Mandrier.

by boat

From May to September there are daily sailings to Corsica and weekly sailings to Sardinia, (SNCM, Av. de l'Infanterie-de-Marine, ℂ 94 16 66 66). Companies departing from Quai Cronstadt offer tours of Toulon's anchorages, the *grande rade* and *petite rade*, and the surrounding coasts and islands: **Les Bateliers de la Rade**, ℂ 94 46 24 65, (year-round tours of the *rades* and all three Iles d'Hyères); **Transport Maritime Toulonnais**, ℂ 94 23 25 36, (tours of the *rades*); **Catarmaran Alain III**, ℂ 94 46 29 89 (tours of the *rades* and their battleships); **SNRTM**, ℂ 94 62 41 14 (tours of the *rades* and mini-cruises, and from 15 June–15 Sept a regular service to the Iles d'Hyères).

Tourist Information

The arrivals hall in the Toulon/Hyéres airport, ℂ 94 57 45 72. Due to a shortage of money, there is only a phone number.

The main **post office** is at Rue Jean-Bartolini, ℂ 94 16 66 20.

market days

Every morning except Monday on Cours Lafayette; don't miss it.

Central Toulon

From the train station, Av. Vauban descends to Av. Général-Leclerc; on the left at No. 113 are the **Muséum d'Histoire Naturelle**, ℂ 94 93 15 54, with stuffed birds and beasts (*open daily, 9.30am–12pm and 2–6pm; adm free*) and **Musée d'Art**, ℂ 94 93 15 54 (*open daily, 1–7pm; adm free*), containing an above-average collection of paintings and sculptures, although there's only room to display a fraction of the works by Breughel, Annibale Carracci, Fragonard, Vernet and Pierre Puget; there's also an especially strong contemporary collection (Bacon, Arman, Yves Klein, Christo, etc.). Avenue Vauban continues down to the large formal gardens of **Place d'Armes**, decorated with ordnance from the adjacent arsenal, one of the biggest single employers in southeast France with some 10,000 workers. Alongside the arsenal in Place Monsenergue are miniature versions of the ships that it once made, displayed in the **Musée de la Marine**, ℂ 94 02 02 01 (*open 10am–12pm and 1.30–6pm, 2.30–7pm in summer, closed Tues, and holidays; adm*). France's great Baroque sculptor and architect Puget started out in Toulon carving and painting figureheads for the ships, and the museum has works by his followers. The grand Baroque entrance to the building itself is the original Louis XIV arsenal gate of 1738.

The best surviving works of Puget in Toulon are the two **Atlantes** (1657) on Quai Cronstadt, *Force* and *Fatigue*, whose woe and exhaustion may well have been modelled on the galley slaves. They once supported the balcony of the old Hôtel de Ville, and were packed off to safety just before the bombings in the last war. Off the Quai, **Rue d'Alger**, now a popular evening promenade, used to be the most notorious street in Toulon's **Vieille Ville**, the pungent pocket of the pre-war town. Now blocked off from the sea by rows of new buildings, the Vieille Ville's narrow, dirty streets are still lit by the neon signs of bars, flophouses, greasy-spoons, sex shops, cheap clothes shops, etc., that belong after dark to the sailors, prostitutes and pick-pockets. Unfortunately, the city and the landlords of the Vieille Ville have little sense of historic preservation, and are content not only to let its old buildings fall down, but even push them over in an attempt to destroy the last bit of genuine sleaze on the coast.

Come in the morning to take in the colourful fruit and vegetable market in Cours Lafayette, and the fish market in Place de la Poissonerie. At 69 Cours Lafayette there's the dingy **Musée Historique du Vieux-Toulon**, ✆ 94 62 11 07 (*open 2–6pm daily, closed Sun*) with sketches by Puget and historical odds and ends. Around the corner is the **cathedral**, 17th-century on the outside and Romanesque-Gothic within, although its features are barely discernible in the gloomiest interior in the south of France; during the Revolution an attempt to convert it into a stable failed when the horses threw their riders rather than enter it. At the top of the adjacent pedestrian quarter is Toulon's prettiest fountain, the 18th-century **Fontaine des Trois Dauphins**. North of the three dolphins is Toulon's main street, Boulevard de Strasbourg, site of the **Opéra**, ✆ 94 92 70 78, the biggest opera-house in Provence, noted for its acoustics, with an interior inspired by Charles Garnier.

Mont Faron

Toulon looks better when seen from a distance. Bus 40 will take you to Boulevard Amiral-Vence in Super-Toulon, site of the terminus of the little red *téléphérique* (funicular) that runs 9am–5.30pm (later in summer), to the top of 535m Mont Faron (there's a narrow hairpin road circuit as well, beginning in Av. E.-Fabre). Besides a tremendous view over the city and its harbours, there's the **Musée du Mémorial du Débarquement**, ✆ 94 88 08 09 (*open daily, 9.30am–12.30pm and 2.30–6pm, except Mon; adm*), devoted to the August 1944 Allied landing in Provence, with models, uniforms and 1944 newsreels. It shares the summit with a large wooded park, two restaurants, and a **zoo**, ✆ 94 88 07 89 (*open daily 10am–7pm May–Sept, closed mornings in winter; adm*) that specializes in breeding jaguars, tigers, lions and monkeys.

Around the Harbour

Bus 3 from in front of the station or on Av. Général-Leclerc will take you to the **Plage du Mourillon**, Toulon's largest beach and site of the city's oldest fort, Louis XII's 1514 **Grosse Tour** or Tour Royale that once guarded the eastern approaches to Toulon with its rounded walls, some 5–7m thick. In later years the lower part, excavated in the rock, was used as a prison and now contains an annexe of the Musée Naval, with more figureheads in a baleful setting. The west shore of the *Petite Rade* is Toulon's business end, especially the yards and industry at **La Seyne**. To the south, at L'Aiguillette, stood 'Little Gibraltar' near **Fort Balaguier**, another English stronghold that fell to Bonaparte; this now contains the **Musée Naval du Fort Balaguier** of Napoleana, ✆ 94 94 84 72 (*open Wed–Sun 10am–12pm and 2–6pm; adm*). Further south is the residential suburb of **Tamaris**, once the home of officers and their families, and where George Sand wrote her novel *Tamaris* in 1861. In the 1880s, the mayor of nearby Sanary purchased much of Tamaris in the hopes of turning it into a resort. This mayor had a more exciting career than most: born Michel Marius in Sanary in 1819, he was employed by the Ottoman Empire as a builder of lighthouses, a job he performed so well that the Sultan made him a pasha before sending him home in 1860 with a fat pension.

Inspired by what he had seen in Turkey, Michel Pasha commissioned a number of fantasy neo-Moorish buildings in the area, especially Tamaris' **Institute of Marine Biology**. The resort was a flop, but a fad for neo-Moorish confections swept across the Riviera at the turn of the century. Beyond the fine sands of **Les Sablettes** beach, the hilly **St-Mandrier peninsula** closes off the west end of the *Grande Rade*, and includes a naval airbase, and the fishing village and pleasure port of **St-Mandrier-sur-Mer**, with wide views from the cemetery.

Toulon ✉ 83000	*Where to Stay*

Prices are about a third less than on the fashionable Côte, and fall even lower in the off-season. The most elegant place to sleep and eat in Toulon is ★★★**La Corniche**, 17 Littoral F.-Mistral, at Mourillon, ✆ 94 41 35 12, 📠 94 41 24 58, a cleverly designed modern Provençal hotel, air-conditioned and near the beach. The resturant, **Le Bistrot**, built around the massive trunks of three maritime pines, not only serves refined seafood and dishes such as *selle d'agneau en rognonnade* but also has one of the best wine cellars for miles around (*menus from 120–198F*). In the pedestrian zone, not far from the opera, ★★**Du Dauphiné**, 10 Rue Berthelot, ✆ 94 92 20 28, 📠 94 62 16 69, is a comfortable older hotel, no restaurant, but friendly. The new ★★**St-Nicolas**, in the centre at 49 Rue Jean-Jaurès, ✆ 94 91 02 28, 📠 94 62 29 08, has 39 soundproof rooms with colour TV, mini-bars etc. Nearby, the friendly ★**Le Jaurès**, 11 Rue Jean-Jaurès, ✆ 94 92 83 04, 📠 94 62 16 74, is the top bargain choice; the rooms all have baths. If that's full, try ★**Molière**, near the opera at 12 Rue Molière, ✆ 94 92 78 35, 📠 94 62 85 82.

Toulon ✉ 83000	*Eating Out*

If they don't go to the aforementioned Bistrot at La Corniche, the Toulonnais in search of a special meal drive 20km northeast to Cuers to eat at **Le Lingousto**, Rte de Pierrefeu, ✆ 94 28 69 10, 📠 94 48 63 79, located in an old *bastide*, where the freshest of fresh local ingredients are transformed into imaginative works of art—langoustines with fresh pasta, omelettes with *oursins* (sea urchins), cheeses that have 'worked' to perfection and divine chocolate desserts (*menus from 230F, closed Jan–Feb*). **Le Lido**, Av. Frédéric Mistral, ✆ 94 03 38 18, has nice, nautical décor, and a window on to the kitchen where you can watch your fresh fish being prepared (*menus 90, 135 and 195F*). **Le Jardin du Sommelier**, 20 Allée Amiral-Courbet, ✆ 94 62 03 27, provides gastronomic Provençal cuisine with wines to match in its small, intimate dining-room, perfect for *'un tête à tête en amoureux'* (*200F upwards*). For *moules* and good home-made *frites* try **La Frégate**, 237 Av. de la République for a thrifty 40F. Pizzas come at about the same price, and it's one of the few places in Toulon to eat late. The jovial and friendly **Le Cellier**, 52 Rue Jean-Jaurès, ✆ 94 92 29 78, has a good little 95F menu, including wine.

Entertainment and Nightlife

Pick up a copy of *Le Petit Bavard* or a similar booklet to tell you what's really going on—Toulon has some good local theatre, dance and jazz—but it's harder now the tourist offices are shut (try the Mairie, or a bookshop). Northwest of Toulon (Ollioules), a 17th-century tower was converted in 1966 into a handsome **Théâtre**

National de la Danse et de l'Image, ℰ 94 24 11 76, to host cultural events, especially the July Festival de la Danse et de l'Image. From the end of May to mid-July, the **Festival International de Musique** puts on a wide range of classical and non-classical music, ℰ 94 93 52 84. There's opera and theatre in the winter at the **Opéra Municipal**, Bd. de Strasbourg, ℰ 94 92 70 78. The likes of Elton John and Lenny Kravitz play at Toulon's **Zenith-Oméga** concert hall, on Bd. Commandant-Nicolas, ℰ 94 22 66 66, which is rapidly becoming the number one rock venue in the south of France. Slap bang in the centre is the **Pathé Liberté**, 4 Place de la Liberté, ℰ 36 68 20 22, with six screens and comfortable seats. The same cinema has a big brother— **Pathé Grand Ciel**, opposite the university at La Garde (same ℰ as Pathé Liberté); 12 screens and VO (*versione originale*) films (*48F, or less if you're under-age or over 65*). For **Café Theatre**, at Porte d'Italie, Place Armand Vallé, call ℰ 94 222 99 75. There's no lack of bars, both straight and gay, especially around Rue Pierre-Sémard, but they're not places where you'll feel comfortable alone. Smart Toulon society prefers the bars and restaurants along Littoral Frédéric-Mistral on Mourillon beach, or the **Piano Crêperie**, 45 Rue V.-Clappier, ℰ 94 91 93 04, which has jazz on Friday, 'polymusique' on Saturday, and videos to accompany your crêpes on other nights. Otherwise head to Hyères or Le Lavandou.

West Coast of the Var: Toulon to Les Lecques

West of Toulon, the coast tosses out the curious peninsula of Cap Sicié with the old town of Six-Fours before ending in a string of small towns with sandy beaches: Sanary, fashionable Bandol, one of the coast's great wine towns, and Les Lecques. Offshore you can be entertained on Paul Ricard's two little islets, or amuse yourself exploring the hills, woods, vineyards and gorges around Ollioules, La Cadière-d'Azur and Le Castellet.

Getting Around

Six-Fours and Sanary are easiest reached by **bus** from Toulon. The **train station** of Ollioules is halfway between the town and Sanary, with bus connections to both. Bandol is a stop on the Toulon–Marseille TGV, ℰ 36 35 35 35; for **bus** information ℰ 94 74 01 35.

In Bandol, you can **hire a bike** to explore the beautiful hinterlands at **Holiday Bikes** 127 Route de Marseille, ℰ 94 32 21 89, closed Oct–Mar, or **Hookipa**, Rue P.-Toesca, ℰ 94 29 53 15. Catch some waves by hiring **windsurfers and surf boards** from the **Société Nautique de Bandol**, ℰ 94 29 42 26.

Tourist Information

Ollioules (✉ 83190): 16 Rue Nationale, ℰ 94 63 11 74 (mornings only).
Bandol (✉ 83150): Allée Vivien, ℰ 94 29 41 35, 🖷 94 32 50 39.
Six-Fours: ℰ 94 07 02 21.

market days

Sanary: Wednesday.
Bandol: daily, with a big market on Tuesdays.

Around Cap Sicié: Six-Fours

Cap Sicié, like a clenched fist punching the sea, takes the brunt of the wind and rough swells from the west. If you can, avoid the depressing main roads and urban sprawl that cut across the peninsula from Les Sablettes to Sanary, and take the **Corniche Varoise**, a minor road that circles the cliffs of the Cap (not recommended on windy days, however). The cliffs tower up to 335m over the sea at **Notre-Dame-du-Mai**, named after a sanctuary much esteemed by sailors, who always approached it barefoot. On the west side of the peninsula, the little port of **Le Brusc**, set amid cliffs and pines, has two or three departures every hour for **Ile des Embiez**, owned by Paul Ricard, the *pastis* baron. Ricard has left the seaward side of the island alone, but facing the mainland he is busy developing what he calls 'the leisure centre of the future', a vast pleasure port and the **Fondation Océanographique Ricard**, © 94 34 02 49; (*open daily 10am–12.30pm and 1.30–6.45pm, open from 2pm Sat*), with 100 different species from the Mediterranean.

The rough winds and waves off Cap Sicié's west coast offer an exciting challenge to surfers and windsurfers who get their kicks at **Brutal Beach** and **Plage de Bonnegrâce**, part of the commune of **Six-Fours-les Plages** (from the Latin *sex furni*). The village once stood on the isolated mountain nearby, but was destroyed in the 19th century to build the **fort** (no entry, but you can drive up to the barbed wire outside for the view). Two churches were spared: a 10th-century **oratory** on the road to Le Brusc, commemorating a victory over Saracen pirates, and the 12th-century Collegiate church of **St-Pierre-aux-Liens** (*open every day, 2.30–6pm*), built in pure Provençal Romanesque over a 5th-century baptistry; Palaeo-Christian coins and gems found here are displayed in a case. The church has a number of medieval works of art, including a polyptych of Provence's favourite saints by Jean de Troyes (1520). The niche behind the altar, built to hold the Eucharist, was until 1914 (when the practice was banned) used by the faithful to deposit scraps of cloth taken from the clothes of dead relatives for whom they prayed. North of here, off the D63, is the stone-built **Chapelle Notre-Dame-de-Pépiole** (*usually open after 3pm*), with its three little barrel-vaulted naves modelled after the earliest Syrian churches. It goes back to at least the 8th century, the date of fragments of Islamic ceramics found inside, and may even be Carolingian.

Sanary-Sur-Mer, Ollioules and the Big Brain

Provençal for St Nazaire, Sanary is a little resort of pink and white houses and a sandy beach, one picked out by the Kislings and Aldous Huxley as good places to live, far from the Babylon further east. After 1933, Huxley was joined by the cream of anti-Nazi German intelligentsia, led by Thomas and Heinrich Mann and Bertolt Brecht. But Sanary was not far enough away, and under the Vichy régime many Germans were rounded up and imprisoned in an internment camp near Aix. On Sanary's promontory, the chapel **Notre-Dame-de-Pitié** has a delightful collection of naïve ex-votos.

Ollioules' funny name comes from olives, although these days it's better known for its wholesale Mediterranean flower market. The town itself has all the typical Provençal charms—arcaded lanes, a medieval castle and a Romanesque church—and numerous artisans who make barrels, bird-cages, nougat, olive woodwork, goats' cheese and the like, a welcome respite from trinkets and *objets d'art*. A kilometre north of town, just past the romantic ruins of an 18th-century oratory, is the Celto-Ligurian Iron Age *oppidum* of **La Courtine**, built on a basalt rock and covered with wild roses planted by two frustrated amateur archaeologists when they got tired of digging. You can still make out the dry-stone walls and wells. Over 300 Greek coins engraved with the features of Hercules and Hecate were discovered here, donated to a sanctuary destroyed by Romans in 123 BC.

Around **Evenos**, a restored *village perché* just to the north off the N8, the romantic scenery makes for good walks, especially in the fantastical yellow-tinted **Gorges d'Ollioules**, a natural Gothic landscape much admired by Victor Hugo. The D220 from Ollioules leads on to the wooded mountain ridge of **Le Gros Cerveau** or 'Big Brain', a curious name of uncertain derivation and site of another *oppidum*. It, too, has strange rock formations and is pitted with caves, where 'witches' hid in the time of Louis XIII—in 1616 three were sentenced to be strangled, hanged, and then burned.

Bandol

Sheltered from the ravages of the mistral, travellers will find Bandol either a preview or a *déjà vu* of the typical Côte d'Azur town: pretty houses and lanes festooned with flowers, palm trees, boutiques, a casino, the morning market in Place de la Liberté, and an over-saturation of villas on the outskirts. But Bandol has something most of the Riviera hotspots lack—its own excellent wine and a little island, **Ile de Bendor**. A barren 6-hectare rock when Paul Ricard bought it with his *pastis* fortune in 1953, it is now a little adult playground, a masterpiece of architectural dissonance from the 1950s and 60s—Ricard himself hopes that it will some day fall in ruins and become 'a 20th-century Delos'! There's a diving and windsurfing school, a nautical club that organizes yacht races, an art school and gallery, a business centre, hotels, and the **Exposition Universelle des Vins et Spiritueux**, ✆ 94 29 44 34 (*open Easter–Sept 10.15am–12pm and 2.15–6pm, closed Wed; adm free*). The building is decorated with frescoes by art students and the displays of 7000 bottles and glasses from around the world will whet your thirst for some Bandol AOC.

Bandol

When a courtier asked Louis XV the secret of his eternal youth, the king replied 'the wines of Rouve (in Bandol), which give me their vigour and spirit'. They had to have a certain vigour to survive the journey to Versailles, sloshing about in barrels in slow boats from the Mediterranean to the Atlantic and up the Seine. Today Bandol still flexes its charming muscle; at 40 to 80F a bottle, it gets top marks in Provence in value for money. The arid, wine-coloured *restanques* (or terraces) cut into the mountain flanks in the eight communes around Bandol have produced wines since 600 BC. Dominated by small, dense *mourvèdre* grapes mixed with *cinsault* and *grenache*, the reds are sombre of tone, but require patience to reach their peak. The excellent 89 or 90 are starting to drink well; 1991 and 1992 were more difficult, but the 93 and 94 are more promising. Bandol also comes in pale salmon-hued rosés, known for their delightful perfume, and dense whites that are to the taste what wild roses are to the nose, and make the ideal accompaniment to grilled fish—1990 was a great year for both. Some Bandols have extraordinary pedigrees: **Domaine des Salettes**, at La Cadière-d'Azur (✆ 94 90 06 06, ✉ 94 90 04 29), has been in the same family since 1602. Other estates to visit are the organic **Domaine de la Tour du Bon**, at Le Brulat du Castellet, ✆ 94 32 61 62, the rising superstar estate run by the charming Agnès Henry and her highly competent wine maker Thierry Puzelat, and **Domaine Ray-Jane**, at Le-Plan-du-Castellet, ✆ 94 98 64 08, ✉ 94 98 64 08, where besides wine, visitors can examine France's largest collection of cooper's tools. The Comte de Saint-Victor's estate of **Château de Pibarnon**, at La Cadière-d'Azur, ✆ 94 90 12 73, ✉ 94 90 12 98, is sculpted into rugged limestone flanks geologically millions of years older than their neighbours, which give its spicy reds, charming rosés and fruity whites a personality all their own. **Domaine de la Laidière**, at Sainte-Anne d'Evenos, ✆ 94 90 37 07, ✉ 94 90 38 05, is one of the most quality-conscious estates of the area, producing red, white and rosé, but it is the red wine that is the finest. Next to Bandol's tourist office, the **Maison des Vins du Bandol** sells most of the labels and has a list of all the other estates open for visits, ✆ 94 29 45 03.

Around Bandol

Besides wine, Bandol offers its visitors pink flamingos, toucans, cockatoos, and disgusting Vietnamese pigs in a lovely exotic garden of tropical flora at the **Jardin Exotique et Zoo de Sanary-Bandol**, Route du Beausset, 3km east on the D559, ✆ 94 29 40 38 (*open 8am–12pm and 2–7pm, closed Sun am*). This is near the *Moulin de St-Côme*, where you can tour the most important olive press in the Var (or in December and January, watch it at work) and buy a bottle of *huile d'olive vierge extra* to take home.

North of Bandol are a pair of medieval wine-producing *villages perchés*, both restored, both lovely nonetheless, and neither as virgin as their olive oil. **La Cadière-d'Azur** sits on a hill with cliffs sliced sheer on the north side, with views out to the Massif de Ste-Baume. **Le Castellet** is perched even more precariously over its sea of vines. Much refurbished, it looks like a film set, and indeed has often been used as such (the pioneering Provençal director Marcel Pagnol got here first, for his *Femme du Boulanger*); its 12th-century church is attractively austere, although the same cannot be said of the streets full of pseudo-arty shops. East of here (follow D26 towards the N8), the 16th-century agricultural villlage of **Le Beausset** sits on a plain 2.5 km from the 12th-century **Chapelle Notre-Dame-du-Beausset-Vieux** (*open daily July–Sept, Sat and Sun only other times*), with a basalt altar that once served as a millstone in an olive press, *santons* from the 16th century, and ex votos. North, on N8, is another Ricard installation, this time a race track and aerodrome. If all the above seems too staid, you can watch a cowboy and Indian shoot-out, have your face covered with war-paint, and ride the carousel at the **O.K. Corral**, a Wild West fantasyland owned by a Dutchman (*on N8, towards Cuges-les-Pins;* ✆ *42 73 80 05, open daily 10am to sundown, Wed, Sat and Sun out of season, every day June–Sept*).

Les Lecques and St-Cyr-sur-Mer

West of Bandol, **Les Lecques** is an unpresuming family resort with a sandy beach, set in front of the old Bandol AOC town of **St-Cyr-sur-Mer**. It also offers the cool, wet delights of **Aqualand**, ✆ 94 32 09 09, where you can dump the kids—or yourself—down the slides (*open June–Sept*). Les Lecques itself is one of several places that claim to be ancient *Tauroentum*, a colony of Greek Marseille where Caesar defeated Pompey in a famous naval battle and gained control of Marseille. But most of the finds in Les Lecques so far have been Roman, as displayed in the **Musée de Tauroentum** on the road to La Madrague, ✆ 94 26 30

46 (*open June–Sept 4–7pm, closed Tues; other times weekends only 2–5pm*). The museum protects the remains of two Roman villas built around the year 1, with mosaics and bits of fresco, vases and jewellery, and outside, an unusual two-storey tomb of a child. Ancient Tauroentum is supposed to be somewhere just off shore, lost under the sea. You can look for traces of it along a lonely coastal path (marked with yellow signs) that begins near the museum and continues to Bandol; along the way are little *calanques* for quiet swims.

Where to Stay and Eating Out

Le Brusc

Le Saint-Pierre, 47 Rue de la Citadelle, ✆ 94 34 02 52, will fill you to the brim with the offerings on its delicious menus, mostly fish (*from 138F to 170F, with a well-priced bouillabaisse at under 200F*).

Bandol (✉ 83150)

The delightful pink ★★★**Master Hotel**, Rue Raimu, ✆ 94 29 46 53, ✆ 94 32 53 54, once belonged to the Toulon-born actor Raimu, who starred in several Pagnol films. It has a seaside garden and private beach, and offers facilities for water sports. **La Ker-Mocotte**, the hotel's restaurant, offers a summer grill in gardens above the Mediterranean, and as much as you can eat for 130F. On Ile de Bendor there's Ricard's ★★★**Delos Palais**, ✆ 94 32 22 23, ✆ 94 32 41 44, with big, comfortable rooms decorated in extravagant bad taste—but the views of the sea below and the many watersports make up for it.

Of the budget hotels, the villa ★★**Coin d'Azur**, Rue Raimu, ✆ 94 29 40 93, ✆ 94 32 51 93, has the added plus of its location directly over the beach, west of the port, while the exceptionally pleasant ★★**L'Oasis**, 15 Rue des Ecoles, ✆ 94 29 41 69, has a cool, shady garden, a short walk from the beach. *Open all year.*

L'Auberge du Port, 9 Allée J.-Moulin, ✆ 94 29 42 63, is Bandol's gourmet rendezvous, specializing in seafood, where you can go the whole hog on a 250F *menu dégustation* or try the 80F platter of *aïoli*. **Au Fin Gourmet**, 16 Rue de la République ✆ 94 29 41 80, is a local favourite for simple filling dishes, both meat and fish based (*menus 79F, 135F and 165F*)

Le Castellet (✉ 83330)

Next to the medieval gate, ★**Le Castel Lumière**, ✆ 94 32 62 20, ✆ 94 32 70 33, has six rooms and a good restaurant with panoramic views, partially funished with antiques.

La Cadière-d'Azur (✉ 83740)

The one hotel in the village, ★★★**Hostellerie Bérard**, Rue Gabriel-Péri, ✆ 94 90 11 43, ✆ 94 90 01 94, is a charming and luxurious place to stay, in an old convent building with a shady terrace, a heated pool, gardens, and a good restaurant with panoramic views, serving delicately perfumed dishes (*try the* carré d'agneau *with basil, menus from 160F*).

abbaye	abbey
auberge	inn
bastide	a taller, more elaborate version of a *mas*, with balconies, wrought-iron work, reliefs, etc; also a medieval new town, fortified and laid out in a grid
calanque	a narrow coastal creek, like a miniature fjord
cave	cellar
château	mansion, manor house or castle
chemin	path
chevet	eastern end of a church, including the apse
cloître	cloister
col	mountain pass
côte	coast; on wine labels, *côtes, coteaux* and *costières* mean 'hills' or 'slopes'
cours	wide main street, like an elongated main square
couvent	convent or monastery
donjon	castle keep
église	church
gare	train station (SNCF)
gare routière	coach station
gisant	a sculpted prone effigy on a tomb
gîte	shelter
gîte d'étape	basic shelter for walkers
Grande Randonnée **(GR)**	long-distance hiking path
halles	covered market
hôtel	any large building or palace; a Hôtel de Ville is the city hall
mairie	town hall

Geographical and Architectural Terms

Maquis	Mediterranean scrub. Also used as a term for the French Resistance during the Second World War
marché	market
mas	a farmhouse and its outbuildings
pays	region
pont	bridge

porte	gateway
predella	small paintings beneath the main subject of a retable
presqu'île	peninsula
retable	a carved or painted altarpiece, often consisting of a number of scenes
rez-de-chaussée (RC)	ground floor
santon	a figure in a Christmas nativity scene, usually made of terracotta and dressed in 18th-century Provençal costume
source	spring
tour	tower
tympanum	sculpted semicircular panel over a church door
vieille ville	historic, old quarter of town
village perché	hilltop village

A working knowledge of French will make your holiday more enjoyable, but is hardly essential on the Côte d'Azur, where you can always find someone working in travel offices, banks, shops, hotels, and restaurants who speaks at least rudimentary English. Venturing into the less-travelled hinterlands may well require an effort to recall your school French; a small travel phrase book and English-French dictionary can come in handy.

Even if your French is brilliant, the soupy southern twang may throw you a curve. Any word with a nasal *in* or *en* becomes something like *aing* (*vaing* for *vin*). The last vowel on many words that are silent in the north get to express themselves in the south as well (*encore* becomes something like *engcora*). What stays the same is the level of politeness: use *monsieur*, *madame* or *mademoiselle* when speaking to anyone, from your first *bonjour* to your last *au revoir*.

Many of the restaurants in this book don't translate their menus, so we've included the decoder below; try the section on regional specialities (*see* pp.15–17) if an item isn't listed below.

Deciphering French Menus

Hors-d'oeuvre et Soupes

assiette assortie	mixed cold hors-d'œuvre
bisque	shellfish soup
bouchées	mini vol-au-vents
bouillon	broth
consommé	clear soup
crudités	raw vegetable platter
potage	thick vegetable soup
velouté	thick smooth soup, often fish or chicken
vol-au-vent	puff pastry case with savoury filling

Starters and Soups (column heading)

Poissons et Coquillages (Crustacés)

aiglefin	little haddock
anchois	anchovies
anguille	eel
barbue	brill

Fish and Shellfish (column heading)

Language

baudroie	anglerfish
belons	rock oysters
bigourneau	winkle
blanchaille	whitebait
brème	bream

brochet	pike
bulot	whelk
cabillaud	fresh cod
calmar	squid
carrelet	plaice
colin	hake
congre	conger eel
coques	cockles
Coquilles St-Jacques	scallops
crabe	crab
crevettes grises	shrimps
crevettes roses	prawns
cuisses de grenouilles	frogs' legs
darne	thin slice of fish
daurade	sea bream
écrevisse	freshwater crayfish
éperlan	smelt
escabèche	fish fried, marinated, and served cold
escargots	snails
espadon	swordfish
flétan	halibut
friture	deep fried fish
fruits de mer	seafood
gambas	giant prawns
gigot de mer	a large fish cooked whole
grondin	red gurnard
hareng	herring
homard	lobster
huîtres	oysters
langouste	spiny Mediterranean lobster
langoustines	Dublin Bay prawns
limande	lemon sole
lotte	monkfish
loup (de mer)	sea bass
maquereau	mackerel
merlan	whiting
morue	salt cod
moules	mussels
oursin	sea urchin
pageot	sea bream
palourdes	clams
poulpe	octopus
praires	small clams

raie	skate
rascasse	scorpion fish
rouget	red mullet
saumon	salmon
Saint-Pierre	John Dory
sole (à la meunière)	sole (with butter, lemon and parsley)
stockfisch	stockfish (wind-dried cod)
telline	tiny clams
thon	tuna
truite	trout
truite saumonée	salmon trout

Viandes et Volaille — Meat and Poultry

agneau (de pré salé)	lamb (grazed in fields by the sea)
ailerons	chicken wings
andouillette	chitterling (tripe) sausage
biftek	beefsteak
blanc	breast or white meat
blanquette	stew of white meat, thickened with egg yolk
bœuf	beef
boudin blanc	sausage of white meat
boudin noir	black pudding
brochette	meat (or fish) on a skewer
caille	quail
canard, caneton	duck, duckling
carré	the best end of a cutlet or chop
cervelle	brains
Châteaubriand	Porterhouse steak
cheval	horsemeat
chevreau	kid
civet	stew of rabbit (usually), marinated in wine
confit	meat cooked and preserved in its own fat
contre-filet	sirloin steak
côte, côtelette	chop, cutlet
cuisse	thigh or leg
dinde, dindon	turkey
entrecôte	ribsteak
épaule	shoulder
estouffade	a meat stew marinated, fried, and then braised
faisan	pheasant
faux filet	sirloin
foie	Liver

foie gras	goose liver
frais de veau	veal testicles
fricadelle	meatball
gésier	gizzard
gibier	game
gigot	leg of lamb
graisse	fat
grillade	grilled meat
grive	thrush
jambon	ham
jarret	knuckle
langue	tongue
lapereau	young rabbit
lapin	rabbit
lard (lardons)	bacon (diced bacon)
lièvre	hare
magret (de canard)	breast (of duck)
marcassin	young wild boar
Merguez	spicy red sausage
museau	muzzle
navarin	lamb stew with root vegetables
noix de veau	topside of veal
oie	goose
os	bone
perdreau (perdrix)	partridge
petit salé	salt pork
pieds (de porc)	trotters
pintade	guinea fowl
porc	pork
poularde	capon
poulet	chicken
poussin	baby chicken
queue de boeuf	oxtail
ris (de veau)	sweetbreads (veal)
rognons	kidneys
rôti	roast
sanglier	wild boar
saucisses	sausages
saucisson	dry sausage, like salami
selle (d'agneau)	saddle (of lamb)
steak tartare	raw minced beef, often topped with a raw egg yolk
suprême de volaille	fillet of chicken breast and wing
tête (de veau)	head (calf's)

taureau	bull's meat		
tortue	turtle		
tournedos	thick round slices of beef fillet		
travers de porc	spare ribs		
tripes	tripe		
veau	veal		
venaison	venison		

Légumes, Herbes, etc. Vegetables, Herbs, etc.

ail	garlic	*fleurs de courgette*	courgette blossoms
algue	seaweed	*frites*	chips (french fries)
aneth	dill	*genièvre*	Juniper
artichaut	artichoke	*gingembre*	ginger
asperges	asparagus	*girofle*	clove
aubergine	aubergine (eggplant)	*haricots*	beans
avocat	avocado	*(rouges, blancs)*	(kidney, white)
basilic	basil	*haricots verts*	green (french) beans
betterave	beetroot	*jardinière*	with diced garden vegetables
cannelle	cinnamon		
céleri (rave)	celery (celeriac)	*laitue*	lettuce
cèpes	wild dark brown mushrooms	*laurier*	bay leaf
		lentilles	lentils
champignons	mushrooms	*maïs (épi de)*	sweetcorn (on the cob)
chanterelles	wild yellow mushrooms	*marjolaine*	marjoram
chicorée	curly endive	*menthe*	mint
chou	cabbage	*mesclun*	salad of various leaves
chou-fleur	cauliflower	*morilles*	morel mushrooms
choucroute	sauerkraut	*moutarde*	mustard
ciboulette	chives	*navet*	turnip
citrouille	pumpkin	*oignons*	onions
cœur de palmier	heart of palm	*oseille*	sorrel
concombre	cucumber	*panais*	parsnip
cornichons	gherkins	*persil*	parsley
courgettes	courgettes (zucchini)	*petits pois*	peas
cresson	watercress	*piment*	pimento
échalote	shallot	*pissenlits*	dandelion greens
endive	chicory	*poireaux*	leeks
épinards	spinach	*pois chiches*	chick-peas
estragon	tarragon	*pois mange-tout*	sugar-peas
fenouil	fennel	*poivron*	bell pepper
fèves	broad beans	*pomme de terre*	potato
flageolets	white beans	*primeurs*	young vegetables

radis	radishes	*salé*	salted
raifort	horseradish	*sarrasin*	buckwheat
riz	rice	*sauge*	sage
romarin	rosemary	*seigle*	rye
safran	saffron	*serpolet*	wild thyme
salade verte	green salad	*thym*	thyme
salsifis (with *ess*)	salsify	*truffes*	truffles

Fruits, Desserts, Noix   Fruits, Desserts, Nuts

abricot	apricot	*fraises (de bois)*	strawberries (wild)
amandes	almonds	*framboises*	raspberries
ananas	pineapple	*fromage (plateau de)*	cheese (board)
banane	banana	*fromage blanc*	yoghurty cream cheese
bavarois	mousse or custard in a mould	*fromage frais*	similar to sour cream
		fruit de la passion	passion fruit
biscuit	cake	*gâteau*	cake
bombe	ice-cream dessert in round mould	*génoise*	rich sponge cake
		glace	ice cream
bonbons	sweets, candy	*grenade*	pomegranate
brebis	sheep cheese	*groseilles*	redcurrants, gooseberries
brioche	light sweet yeast bread		
brugnon	nectarine	*lavande*	lavender
cacahouète	peanut	*macarons*	macaroons
cajou (noix de)	cashew	*madeleines*	small sponge cakes
cassis	blackcurrant	*mandarine*	tangerine
cerise	cherry	*mangue*	mango
charlotte	custard and fruit in almond biscuits	*marrons*	chestnuts
		merise	wild cherry
chausson	turnover	*miel*	honey
chèvre	goat cheese	*mirabelle*	mirabelle plum
citron	lemon	*mûres*	mulberry, blackberry
citron vert	lime	*myrtilles*	bilberries
clafoutis	berry tart	*noisette*	hazelnut
coing	quince	*noix*	walnuts
compote	stewed fruit	*œufs à la neige*	meringue
corbeille de fruits	basket of fruit	*pamplemousse*	grapefruit
coupe	ice cream	*parfait*	frozen mousse
crème anglaise	custard	*pastèque*	watermelon
crème chantilly	sweet whipped cream	*pêche (blanche)*	peach (white)
crème fraîche	sour cream	*petits fours*	tiny cakes and pastries
crème pâtissière	thick cream pastry filling made with eggs	*pignons*	pine-nuts
		pistache	pistachio
dattes	dates	*poire*	pear
figues (de barbarie)	figs (prickly pear)		

pomme	apple	savarin	a filled cake, shaped like a ring
prune	plum	tarte, tartelette	tart, little tart
pruneau	prune	tarte tropézienne	sponge cake filled with custard and topped with nuts
raisins (sec)	grapes (raisins)		
reine-claude	greengage		
sablé	shortbread	truffes	chocolate truffles

Cooking Terms, Miscellaneous, Snacks

l'addition	the bill	confiture	Jam
aigre-doux	sweet and sour	coulis	strong clear broth
aiguillette	thin slice	couteau	knife
à l'anglaise	boiled	crème	cream
à l'arlésienne	with aubergines, potatoes, tomatoes, onions, rice	crêpe	thin pancake
		croque-monsieur	toasted ham and cheese sandwich
à la châtelaine	with chestnut purée and artichoke hearts	croustade	small savoury pastry
		cru	raw
à la grecque	cooked in olive oil and lemon	cuillère	spoon
		cuit	cooked
à la périgourdine	In a truffle and foie gras sauce	diable	spicy mustard sauce
		émincé	thinly sliced
à la provençale	cooked with tomatoes, garlic, olive oil	en croûte	cooked in a pastry crust
allumettes	strips of puff pastry		
à point	medium steak	en papillote	baked in buttered paper
au feu de bois	cooked over a wood fire		
au four	baked	épices	spices
auvergnat	with sausage, bacon, and cabbage	farci	stuffed
		feuilleté	flaky pastry
baguette	long loaf of bread	flambé	set aflame with alcohol
barquette	pastry boat	forestière	with bacon and mushrooms
beignets	fritters		
béarnaise	sauce of egg yolks, shallots and white wine	fourchette	fork
		fourré	stuffed
beurre	butter	frais, fraîche	fresh/cold (boissons)
bien cuit	well done steak	frappé	with crushed ice
bleu	very rare steak	frit	fried
bordelaise	red wine, bone marrow and shallot sauce	froid	cold
		fromage	cheese
broche	roast on a spit	fumé	smoked
chasseur	mushrooms and shallots in white wine	galantine	cooked food served in cold jelly
chaud	hot	galette	flaky pastry case or pancake
chou	puff pastry		

garni	with vegetables	piquante	Vinegar sauce with shallots and capers
(au) gratin	topped with crisp browned cheese and breadcrumbs	pissaladière	a kind of pizza with onions, anchovies, etc.
grillé	grilled	poché	poached
hachis	minced	poivre	pepper
hollandaise	a sauce of butter and vinegar	quenelles	dumplings of fish or poultry
huile (d'olive)	oil (olive)	raclette	toasted cheese with potatoes, onions and pickles
marmite	casserole		
médaillon	round piece	salé	salted, spicy
mijoté	simmered	sanglant	rare steak
Mornay	cheese sauce	sel	salt
nouilles	noodles	sucré	sweet
œufs	eggs	timbale	pie cooked in a dome-shaped mould
pain	bread		
pané	breaded	tranche	slice
Parmentier	with potatoes	vapeur (à la)	steamed
pâte	pastry, pasta	Véronique	green grapes, wine, and cream sauce
paupiette	rolled and filled thin slices of fish or meat		
		vinaigre	Vinegar
pavé	slab	vinaigrette	Oil and vinegar dressing

Boissons — Drinks

bière (pression)	beer (draught)	lait	milk
bouteille (demi)	bottle (half)	moelleux	semi-dry
café	coffee	pichet	pitcher
chocolat (chaud)	chocolate (hot)	pressé	fresh fruit juice
demi	a third of a litre	pression	draft
doux	sweet (wine)	sec	dry
eau (minérale)	water (mineral, spring)	sirop d'orange/ de citron	Orange/ lemon squash
eau de vie	brandy	thé	tea
gazeuse	sparkling	verre	glass
glaçons	Ice cubes	vin blanc/rosé/rouge	wine white/rosé/red
infusion (or tisane)	herbal tea		

Ardagh, John, *France Today* (Penguin, 1982, revised 3rd ed. 1995). One of Penguin's informative paperback series on contemporary Europe.

Barr, Alfred, *Henri Matisse: His Art and His Public* (Museum of Modern Art, NY, 1951).

Blume, Mary, *Côte d'Azur: Inventing the French Riviera* (Thames and Hudson, 1992) Delightful anecdotal account of the creation of the myth.

Cameron, Roderick, *The Golden Riviera* (Weidenfeld & Nicholson, 1975). One of the best travelogues of the region.

Colette, *Letters from Colette*, (Farrar, Straus & Giroux, 1980). Follow the progress of St-Tropez from idyll to mass tourism.

Donnelly, Honoria, *Sara and Gerald* (Holt, Rinehart & Winston, out of print). Biography of the Murphys.

Fitzgerald, F. Scott, *Tender is the Night*, many editions. 1920s Riviera decadence based on personal research.

Fortescue, Winifred, *Perfume from Provence* (1935, but recently reprinted). Poor, intolerable Lady Fortescue's misadventures with the garlicky peasants near Nice.

Greene, Graham, *J'Accuse: The Dark Side of Nice* (The Bodley Head, 1982). The late Graham Greene, resident of Antibes, discovers the mafia connections and graft in the government of discredited mayor Jacques Médecin.

Haedrich, Marcel, *Coco Chanel: Her Life, Her Secrets* (Little, Brown, 1972). All about the queen of fashion, who helped create the Côte d'Azur.

Hugo, Victor, *Les Misérables*, many editions. Injustice among the galley-slaves and basis for the hit musical.

Lyall, Archibald, *Companion Guide to the South of France* (Collins, 1978). Personal, well-written but dated guide of the entire Mediterranean coast.

Morris, Edwin T., *Fragrance: The Story of Perfume from Cleopatra to Chanel* (Charles Scribner & Sons, 1984).

Raison, Laura, compiler, *The South of France: An Anthology* (Cadogan, 1985).

Smollett, Tobias, *Travels through France and Italy* (Penguin, 1979). The irrepressible, grouchy Tobias 'Smelfungus' makes modern travel writing look like advertising copy.

Süskind, Patrick, *Perfume* (Penguin, 1989). Thrilling and fragrant murder in the 18th-century perfume industry in Grasse.

Vergé, Roger, *Cuisine of the Sun*, (London, 1979). The owner of the Moulin de Mougins tells some of his secrets of nouvelle Provençal cooking.

Whitfield, Sarah, *Fauvism* (Thames and Hudson, 1991). A good introduction to the movement that changed art history.

Further Reading

Worwood, Valerie, *Aromantics* (Pan, 1987). An amusing look at aromatherapy.

Page numbers in **bold** indicate main references to subject. Page numbers in *italics* indicate maps.

Index

'Cadogan Guides have a reputation as the outstanding series for the independent traveller who doesn't want to follow the crowd...'

Daily Telegraph

'The quality of writing in this British series is exceptional... The Cadogan Guides can be counted on for interesting detail and informed recommendations.'

Going Places

'The characteristic of all these guides is a heady mix of the eminently practical, a stimulating description of the potentially already familiar, and an astonishing quantity of things we'd never thought of, let alone seen.'

The Art Quarterly

'Cadogan Guides are entertaining... They go a little deeper than most guides, and the balance of infectious enthusiasm and solid practicality should appeal to first-timers and experienced travellers alike.'

Michael Palin

'Dana Facaros and Michael Pauls...give eminently knowledgeable advice...and are not afraid...to give due warning as well as recommendations.'

The Good Book Guide

'...proper companions...amusingly written with fascinating snippets on history and culture.'

Woman magazine

'What a pleasure it is to find an intelligent guide book that is actually fun to read. The writers obviously have a sense of humour, a love of history and a liking for food and drink. Accurate guide books that are also entertaining are rare, but this is one of them.'

Author Peter Mayle

'Acceptably enthusiastic, never gushing, firmly factual yet as absorbing as a really good novel.'

The Art Quarterly

The Cadogan Guides Series: Other Titles

Country Guides

THE CARIBBEAN & THE BAHAMAS
CENTRAL ASIA
EGYPT
FRANCE: SOUTHWEST FRANCE;
Dordogne, Lot & Bordeaux
FRANCE: SOUTHWEST FRANCE;
Gascony & the Pyrenees
FRANCE: PROVENCE
GERMANY
GERMANY: BAVARIA
GREEK ISLANDS
GUATEMALA & BELIZE
INDIA
INDIA: SOUTH INDIA
INDIA: GOA
IRELAND
IRELAND: SOUTHWEST IRELAND
IRELAND; NORTHERN IRELAND
ITALY
ITALY: THE BAY OF NAPLES &
THE AMALFI COAST
ITALY: LOMBARDY, Milan & Italian Lakes
ITALY: TUSCANY
JAPAN
MEXICO

MOROCCO
PORTUGAL
PORTUGAL: THE ALGARVE
SCOTLAND
SCOTLAND'S HIGHLANDS & ISLANDS
SOUTH AFRICA
SPAIN
SPAIN: SOUTHERN SPAIN
SPAIN: NORTHERN SPAIN
SYRIA & LEBANON
TUNISIA
TURKEY: WESTERN TURKEY

Also Available

HEALTHY TRAVEL: BUGS BITES &
BOWELS
TRAVEL BY CARGO SHIP
FIVE MINUTES OFF THE MOTORWAY
HENRY KELLY IN THE WEST OF IRELAND
LAZY DAYS OUT ACROSS THE CHANNEL
LAZY DAYS OUT IN TUSCANY
LAZY DAYS OUT IN ANDALUCIA
LAZY DAYS OUT IN THE DORDOGNE
& LOT
LONDON MARKETS

City Guides

AMSTERDAM
BRUSSELS, BRUGES, GHENT & ANTWERP
FLORENCE, SIENA, PISA & LUCCA
LONDON
MOSCOW & ST PETERSBURG

NEW YORK
PARIS
PRAGUE
ROME
VENICE & THE VENETO

Island Guides

BALI
THE CARIBBEAN: N. E. CARIBBEAN The
Leeward Islands
THE CARIBBEAN: S. E. CARIBBEAN
The Windward Islands
CYPRUS
GREECE: THE CYCLADES

GREECE: THE DODECANESE
GREECE: THE IONIAN ISLANDS
GREECE: CRETE
MADEIRA & PORTO SANTO
MALTA, COMINO & GOZO
SICILY